"This challenging book pushes us to think more deeply about God's great overarching purpose for our lives: transformation into the likeness of Christ. As the writers examine this great subject from different perspectives, shafts of light break through like rays reflected in the facets of a diamond, at times piercing in their illumination."

— MIKE TRENEER, international president, The Navigators

"What a wonderful resource for those seriously interested in personal or community spiritual formation. This diverse team of experts who lived in spiritual community with each other as a preface for writing this book provides a unique and meaningful integration of the practical and theoretical foundation for spiritual formation."

— G. CRAIG WILLIFORD, PhD, president, Trinity International University

"Christian discipleship in the American church is in crisis. The church is ready for a sober reevaluation. This is why I am thankful for *The Kingdom Life*. It is not another book on how to do discipleship as a program; rather, it reexamines the theology and practice of discipleship in light of the lordship of Christ and the life we have in His kingdom. In putting forth this project, Alan Andrews has assembled an extraordinary team of thinkers and practitioners to address an extraordinary need for these most critical of times."

— DAVID FITCH, Lindner chair of evangelical theology, Northern Seminary

THE
KINGDOM
LIFE

A Practical Theology of
Discipleship and Spiritual Formation

ALAN ANDREWS General Editor

NAVPRESS

NAVPRESS ⦿

NavPress is the publishing ministry of The Navigators, an international Christian organization and leader in personal spiritual development. NavPress is committed to helping people grow spiritually and enjoy lives of meaning and hope through personal and group resources that are biblically rooted, culturally relevant, and highly practical.

For a free catalog go to www.NavPress.com
or call 1.800.366.7788 in the United States or 1.800.839.4769 in Canada.

© 2010 by The Navigators

All rights reserved. No part of this publication may be reproduced in any form without written permission from NavPress, P.O. Box 35001, Colorado Springs, CO 80935. www.navpress.com

NAVPRESS and the NAVPRESS logo are registered trademarks of NavPress. Absence of * in connection with marks of NavPress or other parties does not indicate an absence of registration of those marks.

ISBN-13: 978-1-60006-280-3

Cover design by Arvid Wallen
Watercolor painting by Gary Bradley, Via Affirmativa

Some of the anecdotal illustrations in this book are true to life and are included with the permission of the persons involved. All other illustrations are composites of real situations, and any resemblance to people living or dead is coincidental.

Unless otherwise identified, all Scripture quotations in this publication are taken from the *Holy Bible, New International Version* (NIV). Copyright © 1973, 1978, 1984 by International Bible Society. Used by permission. All rights reserved. Other versions used include: the New American Standard Bible (NASB), Copyright © 1960, 1962, 1963, 1968, 1971, 1972, 1973, 1975, 1977, 1995 by The Lockman Foundation. Used by permission; the New Revised Standard Version (NRSV), copyright © 1989, by the Division of Christian Education of the National Council of the Churches of Christ in the USA, used by permission, all rights reserved; the *Holy Bible*, New Living Translation (NLT), copyright © 1996, 2004. Used by permission of Tyndale House Publishers, Inc., Wheaton, Illinois 60189. All rights reserved; the *Revised Standard Version Bible* (RSV), copyright 1946, 1952, 1971, by the Division of Christian Education of the National Council of the Churches of Christ in the USA, used by permission, all rights reserved; the New King James Version (NKJV). Copyright © 1982 by Thomas Nelson, Inc. Used by permission. All rights reserved; *THE MESSAGE* (MSG). Copyright © 1993, 1994, 1995, 1996, 2000, 2001, 2002. Used by permission of NavPress Publishing Group; the Holy Bible, *Today's New International Version* (TNIV). Copyright © 2001, 2005 by International Bible Society. Used by permission of International Bible Society. All rights reserved worldwide; the *Amplified Bible* (AMP), © The Lockman Foundation 1954, 1958, 1962, 1964, 1965, 1987; the King James Version (KJV); and author's paraphrase (PAR).

Library of Congress Cataloging-in-Publication Data
The kingdom life : a practical theology of discipleship and spiritual
formation / Alan Andrews, general editor.
    p. cm.
Includes bibliographical references.
ISBN 978-1-60006-280-3
1. Spiritual formation. 2. Discipling (Christianity) I. Andrews,
Alan (Alan K.)
BV4511.K47 2010
253.5--dc22
                                    2009033370

Printed in the United States of America

1 2 3 4 5 6 7 8 / 14 13 12 11 10

Contents

THE JOURNEY OF TACT

Alan Andrews with Christopher Morton

Spiritual formation creates music in the ears of a growing number of people in the body of Christ. For others, it is a topic of concern. Donald Bloesch's book *Spirituality Old and New*[1] emphasizes some of the blessings of the spiritual-formation movement as well as some of Dr. Bloesch's cautions. He specifically warned that classical Christian mysticism and new forms of spirituality may find their way into solid and traditional forms of maturing in Christ.

James Wilhoit, in his book *Spiritual Formation as if the Church Mattered*,[2] affirmed the spiritual-formation movement but emphasized the important place of community in the lives of those who are being formed. While few who have taught spiritual formation would object to Wilhoit's emphasis, it is clear that he would give community a very high priority in pursuit of spiritual formation.

For many, the term "spiritual formation" simply means we must give more attention to how people are formed in Christ. But for others, the topic conjures up multiple models of legalistic approaches to becoming more spiritual. Some see the subject as an attack on the fundamental tenet of the Reformation: justification by faith. Others even see spiritual formation as a backdoor code word for New Age infiltration into the church. Finally, many feel that the current interest in spiritual formation is merely a new and unnecessary term for what we have traditionally called "discipleship." As someone who has spent a lifetime working with a parachurch organization that takes both orthodoxy and discipleship very seriously, I understand these concerns and have had them myself from time to time.

Several years ago, a group of men and women, not preoccupied with many of the above concerns but deeply grieved by the spiritual condition of the church in America, came together and opened a dialogue concerning American culture, the church, and spiritual formation. Our hearts were drawn to the need for churches to focus on helping people in their congregations be formed in Christ. The feeling of the group was that the church in the United States has focused on a consumer mentality more than on the spiritual formation of its people. Programs and techniques have overwhelmed the natural processes that people need in order to be healthily formed in Christ.

We all recognized that programs are necessary and that relevance to the culture is very important. Some in the group have given their lives to trying to figure out how to get the gospel of the kingdom into American culture in sensitive and appropriate ways. However, we also realized that programs and relevance may come at the expense of people being carefully nurtured in Christ.

Our group is made up of theologians, cultural thinkers, and spiritual-formation practitioners. We have been careful to ensure that pastors or former pastors make up a healthy percentage of the group. Men, women, ethnic communities, and generations are all represented in the hope that we might receive a cross section of broad and diverse input.

One of our primary goals is to help churches that are reaching their spheres of influence in mission become spiritual-formation churches. With the full recognition and understanding that it is God alone who saves through the Word made flesh in Jesus Christ, we believe that spiritual formation is an outcome of three vital factors: sound personal spiritual growth, healthy formation of community, and participation in strong mission. We will explain this in greater detail in the epilogue to give clarification of these three factors.

But the point I want to address right now is that the key to these three factors is a vital and dynamic understanding of the gospel of Jesus and His kingdom. Our first priority must be entrance into the kingdom of God by the power of the Holy Spirit so that we may vitally follow Jesus into this kingdom that gives fire and energy to our personal walks, our communities, and the mission God has given.

Jesus told us that the kingdom of heaven is at hand. He then called us to repent, believe His good news, and follow Him. The gospel of the kingdom is both complex and amazingly simple. The complexity is found in the mysteries of the kingdom of God with all of its glory and beauty. The simplicity is found in the way we discover the kingdom — by putting our hand in Jesus' hand and following Him. We are formed in Christ as we become His faithful apprentices.

THE SIMPLICITY AND COMPLEXITY OF WALKING WITH JESUS

I have a little eight-year-old grandson with special needs. All of the complexities of the kingdom of God will probably be hard for him to grasp; however, following Jesus is something that he already understands more clearly than most of us do. His simple childlike faith is a remarkable witness to the simplicity of the gospel. The depth of his prayer around the dinner table amazes us.

We all begin this process like my grandson. I remember being a young man at Marshall University in the sixties and wanting to grow in Christ. I was confused and conflicted in many ways, not knowing where I was headed. Who was I and what was my purpose in life? Did the gospel have answers to these questions? How could I find my way in a world where professing to be a Christian and truly following Jesus were not necessarily the same? I yearned for direction and guidance.

I cannot help but wonder where I would be today if a young pastor had not befriended me during my college days. His friendship and personal commitment to me kept me journeying with Jesus, even through some pretty low days. Similarly, a banker with a deep walk with God made the choice to travel sixty miles between Charleston, South Carolina, and Huntington, West Virginia, each week to help me get more firmly grounded in my walk with God. Two men, both with deep personal walks with God, chose to personally invest their lives in me. And in so doing, they showed me that, yes, the gospel of Jesus Christ did indeed have real answers to what life was meant to be.

The legacy of these men has lived on through me for the past forty years as I have invested my life in helping people become disciples of Jesus Christ. The journey has been fascinating and fulfilling. It has also held its surprises with incredible highs and some very painful lows. One thing is certain: If not for these men long ago, I would certainly not have been able to journey in God's calling. I stand on their shoulders, and I am so humbled and grateful for every moment of love and sacrifice they chose to show me so many years ago.

My story is not unique. Many similar stories of investing in lives and seeing the love of Jesus Christ lived out are the backdrop of those people who make up what is known as the Theological and Cultural Thinkers (TACT) group. This common thread draws us together despite our varied life experiences, different cultural backgrounds, and unique callings. The commonality of deep relationships in Christ is what has led us to devote our lives to helping people not only come to know Christ but also to grow into His likeness. So in that same spirit of passing Christ's love along to the next generation, the question comes: How can we help people in the twenty-first century put their hand in Jesus' hand and follow Him as His apprentices?

SEEING PROBLEMS, MOVING FORWARD

From the time of TACT's earliest meetings, we looked at data coming in from Gallup, Barna, and other researchers that confirmed what many Christian leaders and committed followers of Jesus had felt for some time. Despite great efforts and countless amazing programs of the American church, transformed and changed lives were not the norm. We began to feel strongly that we in the American church have developed a reduced gospel that falls far short of Jesus' gospel of the kingdom. Instead we have focused on a "repent and receive" gospel that may give people a ticket to heaven, but it merely helps them manage their own sin until they see Jesus. As we studied the Scriptures, we all felt that the gospel of the kingdom calls us to far more than that.

Our hearts hungered for a more complete expression of the good news of Jesus. While we knew we would not develop a complete understanding of all the dimensions of spiritual transformation, we were aware that we had to go deeper into the greatness and depth of our formation in Christ. We wanted to determine the crucial elements—the key concepts—that have to be present in our personal lives, our communities, and our God-given mission if real transformation is going to take place.

TACT was officially formed in September 2002. We knew our common concerns, but we could never have dreamed where God was leading us. This was not a gathering, a movement, or any such grand idea. We were simply men and women who were passionate about growing in Christ.

Prior to attending the first TACT meeting, each participant was asked to write an introductory paper outlining what he or she felt was involved in being formed in Christ. Everyone submitted a paper for review. Upon arriving at the meeting, our first activity was sharing our personal stories of being helped to grow in Christ. What became immediately apparent to us was that our personal spiritual journeys did not reflect our individual theologies of how we are formed in Christ. What we found in reality was that individual investment—such as, for me, the pastor and banker in West Virginia—had contributed most to our personal formation. Recollection of these personal as well as community relationships—always centered in Christ and deeply rooted in His Scriptures—formed the first big learning moment for us in TACT.

There was, however, another important learning activity that opened our eyes in a different, tangible way. A pastor, who also served as a sensei at a local karate school, took us through the patterns and practices for earning a white belt. Though they were downright embarrassing and very humorous, we learned very quickly that after years of doing things "our own way," it was truly difficult to learn new patterns and practices. As we repeated the different patterns, it struck us that while some patterns came easily, others were not quite so natural. As we reflected on our experience, we realized that there was a direct application to our understanding of spiritual transformation.

We discovered that formation in Christ is undeniably rooted in our personal walks, community, and mission. But it is also a process of unlearning old patterns and relearning new patterns. Our hearts, wills, minds, and bodies have to be retrained in new patterns of thought and behavior. Romans 12:1-2 took on new meaning:

> Therefore, I urge you, brothers, in view of God's mercy, to offer your bodies as living sacrifices, holy and pleasing to God—this is your spiritual act of worship. Do not conform any longer to the pattern of this world, but be transformed by the renewing of your mind. Then you will be able to test and approve what God's will is—his good, pleasing and perfect will.

Dallas Willard's famous quote on grace also came into much sharper focus: "God is not opposed to effort but to *earning*."[3] We all realized that many new patterns of thought, emotion, and ways of acting might require much more effort than we initially realized.

For virtually all of us, TACT has been an incredible learning community. We have had the opportunity to sharpen our thinking and understanding. What we have experienced most is the transforming power of lives shaping one another as we live and minister together. We have become friends and are in the process of learning to be more and more like Jesus. We have sharpened one another in life-on-life relationships. Learning to love each other in the midst of some pretty big differences has been our greatest challenge. Conflicts have emerged in TACT that created great tensions and, regrettably, considerable heartache.

Learning and Growing Through Conflict

The first conflict arose regarding the term "spiritual formation." To some, it meant contemplative lifestyles, a leaving behind of the hustle and bustle that marks our twenty-first-century world. For others, it meant embracing the disciplines, such as prayer, fasting, Scripture reading, Scripture memory, and the like, and allowing such practices to renew their minds, hearts, and bodily responses. For still others, it meant following the ancients, learning from the likes of Thomas à Kempis and St. Anthony.

All of these streams of formation have contributed to the work that God has done in lives throughout the centuries. However, we were committed not to emphasize one stream over another but to focus on the broader overview of what it means to be developed as followers of Jesus. For some, this created personal tension as they sensed the very real disconnect between emphasizing a broader perspective over a particular stream of formation. We encouraged those who felt this tension to pursue their particular calling. Again, we already knew that we were not going to provide all the answers to the problems of spiritual formation, so we welcomed people to pursue other callings in order to provide additional light on the same subjects we were wrestling with when coming together. We remain in close contact with most of these individuals and have tried to learn from what they have discovered.

There was still a second conflict regarding the process of how to disseminate the things that we were learning together. Some desired to have conferences right away and act as a catalyst to a spiritual-formation movement that was already springing up all around us in the body of Christ. They wanted to fan the movement that God had already created. Most of us in TACT affirmed that such a movement did exist and that it needed to be fanned. We encouraged those who felt strongly about this existing movement to move ahead with what they felt God had for them. We continue to support their desires, and many in TACT do participate in that movement. But TACT remained a think tank to provide clarity for believers in the area of spiritual formation.

These first two conflicts helped to prepare us for yet another significant challenge. From the earliest days of TACT, we had been committed to reflecting a broad cross section of the body of Christ. By "cross
section" we meant to include differences in ethnicity, generations, ministry focus, gender, and temperament (we have a surprising number of
noncontemplative people for a group committed to spiritual formation).
Many of our early gatherings did indeed look like a good cross section of
the body of Christ. We were not seeking diversity for diversity's sake but
knew that if we were to tap into what God was telling us about spiritual
formation, it would be something that would connect with His whole
body, not merely small demographic strands of it.

For various reasons (some that were the fault of my own blind spots),
we began to lose that diversity over the next few years. Sometimes it was
merely the pressure to keep moving on, to "produce," that allowed me
and the rest of the group simply to miss that we were becoming more
and more homogeneous. By the time we gathered in September 2005,
believing we were empowered to begin publishing what you now hold in
your hands, we were stopped dead in our tracks.

As I have said, the environment we sought to create was one where
people could risk in relationship—including saying things that were
neither popular nor easy. At that meeting the environment was put to
the test as Paula Fuller (whose bio you can read at the end of this book)
stepped forward and told us that our group was entirely directed toward
writing to white baby-boomer males.

Now, of course, white baby-boomer males are not a bad group, but
they are hardly representative of the whole of the body of Christ. As
we looked around, we found that, with the exception of Paula and two
others, this described the attendees at our gathering. Clearly, that was
not an easy thing for Paula to point out, but it was equally hard to
hear.

We each individually and as a group stopped and reflected on
where we were and what we should do going forward. Each of us had
invested countless hours in TACT. Each of us was very busy. Did we
want to throw away all the work we had done? Did we want to press on

knowing that we had not stuck to the values of spiritual formation that we believed marked our group? Did we want to face up to our failures, or did we want to press on?

After some very painful tears and repentance, we faced our failures. It was not an easy time. In the end, though, we chose to humble ourselves and go back to those who had dropped out and apologize for mistakes we had made that had narrowed our group. We opened ourselves and our community to new people with vastly different backgrounds. We made the decision to become who we hoped we would be.

Saying it was not easy is an understatement. Creating community that is committed to mission and transformation for more than one slice of America and to advancing a whole gospel to the whole person is in many ways an incredibly difficult task. We are still learning and still making mistakes. Had it not been for Paula and the leading of the Spirit back in September 2005, we would never have embraced the challenge of living out who we hoped we would become.

REFORMING AND HEARING FROM GOD

The good news for all of us is that we did not stop. TACT moved forward. We met together in different locations. First we went to the inner city of Phoenix to see if what we were talking about was relevant to the poor. We met with pastors in Minneapolis to see if the Spirit was speaking to them as He was to us. We met in Los Angeles to see if an individual like Dallas Willard, who had dedicated his life to spiritual formation, was hearing from God as we were. We wrote; we battled with one another; we stayed in community; and we stayed committed.

What you are holding in your hands is not an "end product." We started out to see what the Holy Spirit was telling us as a diverse and committed community about how to tap into the dynamic of the gospel of the kingdom and be formed in Christ. We are still learning and still meeting. We have much more we would like to say, but we feel that what we are communicating here is most important for the body of Christ at this time. Our focus has been centered on key elements of spiritual formation rather than specializing on a particular dimension of spiritual transformation.

We have broken the elements of spiritual formation into two categories: process elements and theological elements. Process elements are those elements that have more to do with our practice of ongoing formation. The theological elements have to do with the major foundational biblical pillars of our being transformed into the image of Christ. Both categories overlap, but the broad outline is helpful in understanding the basic structure or design of the book.

Each chapter is built around one of these key concepts or elements. We list that element at the head of the chapter with a brief overview or summary of the content of that section of the book. The purpose in listing the element and the summary is to give you a sense of the relationship of that chapter to the other chapters. While the sequence of the elements is not intended to be linear, the elements are intended to be related. It is important to have an overview of the chapters before you begin. Therefore, I list them for you in this introduction in order to give you a sense of where you will be heading as you read.

Process Elements of Spiritual Formation

ELEMENT 1: The gospel of the kingdom is the realm of God's active goodness in forming us in Christ as we follow Him. The kingdom of God is grand, majestic, and full of beauty. We come to understand the kingdom by repenting and simply becoming apprentices of Jesus in His kingdom.

Description: Jesus said, "The time is fulfilled, and the kingdom of God is at hand; repent and believe in the gospel" (Mark 1:15, NASB). God invites us to repent, believe, and follow Him in discovering the beauty of His kingdom. We are privileged to step into eternal life as we enter the kingdom of God (see John 17:3).

The apostle Paul said, "For He rescued us from the domain of darkness, and transferred us to the kingdom of His beloved Son, in whom we have redemption, the forgiveness of sins" (Colossians 1:13-14, NASB). The kingdom of God is the realm of God's action, His resurrection life, and His mission. We are invited to be His followers and learn from Him as He is active in us and around us. We are called to enter into eternal life that begins the moment we enter the kingdom through Christ to be conformed to His image. We are His apprentices.

In Him are hidden "all the treasures of wisdom and knowledge" (Colossians 2:3). The complexity of the kingdom is the vastness and infinite beauty of God's realm that we will be discovering for all of eternity. The simplicity is that we discover all of the complexity of the kingdom by simply following Jesus. As we follow Him, we are also formed in Him.

ELEMENT 2: Spiritual formation is rooted in relationship with God and one another. Communities of grace and trust help us discover and define who we are and how we shall live in trust, love, grace, humility, dignity, and justice. Communities of grace and trust open the door to gaining permission to share truth among fellow believers and the unbelieving world.

Description: Those who receive this invitation will incorporate into their relationships with God and others the principles of grace that characterize the life of the Trinity. Safe communities of grace will be both the by-product of those who experience and live out these principles and the invitation for others to experience and live them out. The process of experiencing grace with God and others validates who I am, matures who I am becoming, and therefore is defining the way I should live.

ELEMENT 3: Spiritual formation into Christlikeness involves an intentional public, personal, and communal commitment to living as Jesus' disciples who are being transformed into His image in all aspects of our lives as we learn to obey His commands.

Description: Discipleship to Jesus Christ is a transformational process that begins with regenerated life as a person becomes Jesus' disciple, identifies with the community of faith, and engages in a purposeful pattern of life in which he or she learns to obey all that He commanded (see Titus 3:3-7). Transformation continues as the disciple intentionally pursues being conformed to Jesus' image, which is carried out in our everyday world of personal, public, community, and family life (see 2 Corinthians 3:17-18; Ephesians 5:21–6:9). As we align our lives with Jesus' example and commit ourselves to the purposeful pattern of life in which we learn to obey all that He commanded, all aspects of our lives are brought into conformity to Christ (see Matthew 28:20; Romans 8:29).

ELEMENT 4: Spiritual formation is a lifelong pursuit of being conformed to the image of Christ from the inside out and not a matter of external activity alone.

Description: Spiritual formation involves a radical internal change in which the spiritual heart directs the transformation of the entire person to reflect Jesus Christ (see Matthew 5:20; 15:18-20; Romans 6:17-19). This means developing congruency between inward transformation and external activity so that the entire person is obedient to Jesus (see Galatians 4:19; Romans 6:12-14; Ephesians 4:22-24). This kind of obedience intends to please God, not humans. Scripture extols effort but opposes forms of legalism that earn favor with God (see Matthew 6:1-18). Inside-out transformation is a lifelong process; while the outer person decays, renewal of the inner person continues throughout one's lifetime (see 2 Corinthians 4:16-18). This lifelong process requires tools and assistance in accomplishing holistic transformation into the image of Christ through every phase of life.

ELEMENT 5: Spiritual formation is a continual process of transforming the whole person, including the healing of woundedness and rebellion, by the power of God, not to be confused with mere technique or program.

Description: People have been created in the image and likeness of God. The Fall marred every part of that image and likeness and brought struggle and corruption into our experience so that we are deeply rebellious, alienated from God and one another, troubled, wounded, and our souls are in ruin.

The journey of the human life is a process of experiencing lifelong changes in our relationships, our physical maturation, our sufferings, and our goals, desires, and hopes. The Bible's primary metaphors for spiritual development likewise focus on long-duration concepts of growth: training for a race, wandering in the wilderness, and healing of woundedness and rebellion. In contrast to this, our culture's primary metaphors are those of quick fixes based on proper techniques, tools, and programs. Against this the Scriptures point us to the lifelong goal of transformation into the likeness of Christ using in the process techniques, programs, and life circumstances.

ELEMENT 6: Spiritual formation occurs when God, in His grace, invades the destructiveness of suffering that results from the fall of man and uses the pain of suffering for His redemptive purposes in His people. There is also a unique suffering that shapes the formation of believers as they enter into the call to love a lost world and the inevitable suffering that results from that love.

Description: For the follower of Jesus, no suffering is without meaning in our formation in Christ. All humanity suffers as a result of the Fall, but in the believer's journey of following Jesus, suffering takes on formational meaning when God, in His grace, enters into the pain of suffering to comfort and shape us into the image of Christ. Beyond suffering that is common to all men, followers of Jesus Christ are called to a particular kind of suffering as they embrace and live out God's love in the world and experience the inevitable suffering that results from that love (see John 15:18-20). This unique suffering opens the door to enter into the fellowship of Christ's sufferings, and we fill up what is lacking in Christ's suffering (see Colossians 1:24).

ELEMENT 7: Spiritual formation in Christ is a process of growing in kingdom living and participating in God's mission. This begins with our personal reconciliation with God and results in an irrepressible manifestation of God's good news. Disciples of the kingdom labor in community for reconciliation with God and one another as a central priority of mission. They also pursue justice and compassion for all people and work to correct institutional sin inherent in human structures.

Description: The kingdom of God is the reality of God's transforming presence, power, and goodness manifested in the community of Jesus' disciples (see Matthew 5:13-16). This community witnesses to the reality of the presence of the kingdom throughout this age (see Ephesians 2:1-21). Spiritual formation is not the end itself but is always pursued through and focused on the advancement of Christ's kingdom. We are God's chosen strategy for the world. The Spirit-energized community of Jesus' disciples is God's agency of reconciliation in this world as it calls all people to be reconciled to each other across divisions of class, gender, race, ethnicity, and nationality as they are reconciled to God (see Matthew 5:24; 9:35-38; 2 Corinthians 5:18-21). Witness comes both through the declaration of the gospel message and through the example of living out the gospel message as a family of faith characterized by humility, purity, accountability, discipline, reconciliation, restoration, and forgiveness (see Matthew 18:1-22). The task is profoundly beyond us, but God's invitation is to take what He gives and return it to Him in simple obedience. As we follow Him in His risky and costly call, we become the aroma of His life to a broken and needy world — and God works a miracle.

Theological Elements of Spiritual Formation

ELEMENT 8: The theology of spiritual transformation emerges from the Trinitarian nature of God — relational, loving, gracious, mutually submissive, and unified in will.

Description: This is the cornerstone statement. Everything that follows regarding spiritual formation flows from who God is. The God who is revealed in Scripture and who lived among us in Jesus Christ exists as a loving community of grace in three persons. From eternity past to eternity future, Father, Son, and Holy Spirit relate to each other with grace, love, mutual submission, and unity of heart and by honoring their roles practicing functional submission — the Holy Spirit to the

Son and the Father, and the Son to the Father. Marvelously, this triune God has invited us, in relationship with Himself, to participate in this culture of grace.

ELEMENT 9: Spiritual formation takes place by the direct work of the Holy Spirit, regenerating and conforming us to the image of Jesus Christ as the Spirit indwells, fills, guides, gifts, and empowers people for life in the community of faith and in the world.

Description: The best place to start in defining and understanding biblical formation is with Scripture passages about the Holy Spirit forming and transforming believers (see Romans 8:26-29). The Holy Spirit is at work to regenerate us and to progressively conform us to the image of Jesus Christ — reflecting purity, passion, and sacrifice and empowering us to live as salt and light in the world (see Romans 8:29; Galatians 4:19; Matthew 5:13,16). The Holy Spirit indwells and fills (see Ephesians 5:18) us as believers and communities of believers in order to guide us into all truth (see Romans 8:14; John 16:13), bringing forth the fruit of the Spirit in our lives (see Galatians 5:22-23), and gifts us for ministry in the church and in the world (see 1 Corinthians 12).

ELEMENT 10: Spiritual formation is based upon the Bible as God's reliable and authoritative revelation. The Bible, our primary source of truth, guides and informs the use of spiritual disciplines and models of spirituality as they have emerged worldwide and throughout time.

Description: The Bible is God's special revelation, so we need to rely on it and align with it as we study, practice, and teach spiritual formation (see Ezra 7:10; 2 Timothy 3:15-17). The Scriptures are living and active in penetrating, exposing, and transforming our hearts and lives as the Holy Spirit brings to bear upon us individually and together (see Hebrews 4:12-13). The Bible calls us to, and illustrates the use of, spiritual disciplines as invitations to grace and ways and means of living well in the kingdom and in the world (see Joshua 1:8; Matthew 11:28-30). The historical and contemporary models of spirituality from various traditions and ethnic contexts can be valuable sources for stimulating thought and progress in spiritual formation as they correspond to the teachings of Scripture.

AN INVITATION TO THE ELEMENTS OF SPIRITUAL FORMATION

Each member of TACT would say that these elements are vital to our lives in Christ. We believe that members of the body of Christ can safely follow the direction of these elements into healthy spiritual formation. This is not meant to be an exhaustive list but a collection of those key concepts we feel have universal application to formation in the life of any individual and in the formation of any spiritual-formation church.

We have chosen people from TACT who we feel are uniquely qualified to write on each particular element. As you read, keep in mind that all members of TACT are firmly agreed on each element, but as each author writes, he or she may express mildly different points of view on the actual implementation of the elements. We have not tried to push our unity to the point of uniformity but rather have allowed for individual expression. Although we have worked on this project as a group, we have not sought to be absolutely consistent in our views on spiritual formation. What we have sought to achieve is an overview of the important elements of formation without trying to be too insistent on conformity in the details.

Thank you for joining us on the journey of moving toward healthy spiritual formation. As you read this book and reflect on its content, consider yourself part of our TACT community.

The body of Christ in America has many strengths, but we must move from our consumer mentality to a more integrated and organic approach of spiritual formation. Best techniques and quickest results are not necessarily consistent with what is involved in being formed in Christ.

The apostle Paul made it clear that the objective of his ministry was to see those who had come to Christ also be formed in Christ: "My children, with whom I am again in labor until Christ is formed in you"

(Galatians 4:19, NASB). He said the same thing in a different way in Colossians 1:28-29: "We proclaim Him, admonishing every man and teaching every man with all wisdom, so that we may present every man complete in Christ. For this purpose also I labor, striving according to His power, which mightily works within me" (NASB).

We need a whole gospel for the whole person to the whole world. We need the fullness of the gospel of the kingdom! Do we have the courage to live it out?

FOR REFLECTION AND DISCUSSION

1. What barriers have you experienced in your desire to see spiritual-formation communities coming into existence?

2. What are your primary motivations for being concerned about spiritual formation? Are they externals (the culture), internals (the health of your ministry), or biblical (response to the Scriptures)?

3. What are the outcomes you expect as a result of a formed life and community?

4. As you read the elements of spiritual formation presented in this chapter, which ones were the biggest surprise? Which ones will be the most challenging to implement in your ministry context?

Part 1

Process
Elements of
Spiritual
Formation

Chapter One

The Gospel of the Kingdom and Spiritual Formation

Dallas Willard[1]

ELEMENT 1: The gospel of the kingdom is the realm of God's active goodness in forming us in Christ as we follow Him. The kingdom of God is grand, majestic, and full of beauty. We come to understand the kingdom by repenting and simply becoming apprentices of Jesus in His kingdom.

Description: Jesus said, "The time is fulfilled, and the kingdom of God is at hand; repent and believe in the gospel" (Mark 1:15, NASB). God invites us to repent, believe, and follow Him in discovering the beauty of His kingdom. We are privileged to step into eternal life as we enter the kingdom of God (see John 17:3).

The apostle Paul said, "For He rescued us from the domain of darkness, and transferred us to the kingdom of His beloved Son, in whom we have redemption, the forgiveness of sins" (Colossians 1:13-14, NASB). The kingdom of God is the realm of God's action, His resurrection life, and His mission. We are invited to be His followers and learn from Him as He is active in us and around us. We are called to enter into eternal life that begins the moment we enter the kingdom through Christ to be conformed to His image. We are His apprentices.

In Him are hidden "all the treasures of wisdom and knowledge" (Colossians 2:3). The complexity of the kingdom is the vastness and infinite beauty of God's realm that we will be discovering for all of eternity. The simplicity is that we discover all of the complexity of the kingdom by simply following Jesus. As we follow Him, we are also formed in Him.

⁂ ⁂ ⁂

There is a deep longing among Christians and non-Christians alike for the personal purity and power to live as our hearts tell us we should. What we need is a deeper insight into our practical relationship with God in redemption. We need an understanding that can guide us into constant interaction with the Kingdom of God as a real part of our daily lives. —Dallas Willard, *The Spirit of the Disciplines*

To enter into the fullness of human life as God intended it—and thus become the kind of persons we would expect from looking at Jesus and His teachings—requires us to live our lives in the kingdom of God. Constant and whole-life interaction with the kingdom of God is the *spiritual atmosphere* of steady progression in Christlikeness. The New Birth—the birth "from above"—is precisely birth *into* the kingdom of God (see John 3:5). The apostle Paul described it as being "rescued . . . from the domain of darkness, and transferred . . . to the kingdom of His beloved Son" (Colossians 1:13, NASB).

That is the *beginning* of new life in Christ. At that point we are *in* the kingdom. It has claimed us, but it is not yet in much of what we are. That is where spiritual growth or formation comes in. Jesus therefore directed us continually to seek the kingdom—which can be thought of as God in action, more than anything else—and to seek the kind of rightness or goodness characteristic of that kingdom. That is, we are called to intensely look for it everywhere. Then, Jesus said, everything else that we need will be provided (see Matthew 6:33).

You will notice that the emphasis here is upon what *we are to do*. Like many other key passages in the New Testament, we are called to *well-informed action in the process of our own spiritual growth*. The agencies of the kingdom—especially of the Word and of the Holy Spirit—are also essential. But we can trust them to do their part. What we must attend to is *our* part. The chapters that follow are designed to help us do that. They help us understand the relationship between living in the kingdom of God and spiritual formation. They help us understand what Christian spiritual formation is and how it develops. What is the nature of the changes involved, and what brings them about? In this first chapter, I want to pay special attention to several points about the kingdom of God that we must get right in order for spiritual transformation toward full Christlikeness to progress as it should.

Let us begin by noting that if we do not preach *the gospel of the kingdom of God* as Jesus did but preach some other gospel—of which there now are several—we cannot truly progress in the formation of character into Christlikeness. That is because *the message preached will have no essential connection with constant spiritual growth*. We need to announce (preach), teach, and manifest the good news that Jesus Himself announced. That good news is of *the availability of life now in the kingdom of God by placing our confidence in Jesus as the Lord of all* (see Matthew 4:17,23; 9:35; Mark 1:15; Luke 4:43; Romans 10:9-10; 14:17). Unfortunately, this is not the gospel generally given out by Christians today, and that is one reason why spiritual transformation into Christlikeness is *not* the routine or normal course of Christian life.

Here is an actual statement about what it means to trust Christ, by one of the most well-known evangelical ministers of our day:

When you trusted Jesus Christ as your personal Savior, here is what you did. You placed your trust in Jesus' death at Calvary, who bore your sin and your iniquity and your wickedness and your vileness on the cross, and as a result God punished Him for your sinfulness and made it possible for you to be forgiven because He is your substitute.

That is all. This very fine and influential Christian minister then proceeded to try to elaborate his view of atonement and of what it means to trust Jesus Christ into an account of our identification with Christ that *would* include a transformation into actual Christlikeness. But the facts of Christian living today simply do not bear out the connection he wished to make. Transformation through identification with Christ is not forthcoming for any but a vanishingly small percentage of those who have "placed their trust in Jesus' death at Calvary." Or else we must say that they did not *actually* so place their trust—an alternative that almost no one would be prepared to take.

WHAT IS THE KINGDOM OF GOD?

The deeper cause of the obvious fact that transformation into Christlikeness is not the routine or normal course of Christian life is our failure to understand *what the kingdom of God is and what it is like to live in it*. If we are to seek it in all we do, what exactly are we seeking for? What would it be like to find it in what is around us and in all we are doing? In order to answer these questions we have to return to the *source* of the idea of the kingdom of God, which is the historical experience of the Jewish people, recorded in the Old Testament. What the kingdom of God is stands out most strongly and clearly in the Psalms. Psalm 145:8-13 gives us some helpful perspective:

> *The LORD is gracious and merciful;*
> *Slow to anger and great in lovingkindness.*
> *The LORD is good to all,*
> *And His mercies are over all His works.*
> *All Your works shall give thanks to You, O LORD,*
> *And Your godly ones shall bless You.*

They shall speak of the glory of Your kingdom
And talk of Your power;
To make known to the sons of men Your mighty acts
And the glory of the majesty of Your kingdom.
Your kingdom is an everlasting kingdom,
And Your dominion endures throughout all generations. (NASB)

The basic teaching about God in the Old Testament is His dominion over *all* creation forever and *His immediate presence to all who call*
upon Him. Of course, this is a vast subject that had to be worked out
in detail through a slow historical process, and there were many misunderstandings that had to be resolved. But at least within the covenant
community of Israel, the idea arose that God's knowledge and power are
immediately available to those who call upon Him. The theological doctrines of the omnipresence and omniscience of God translate into real
life—a reality you see constantly throughout the Psalms and other parts
of the Old Testament. Consider that marvelous verse, 2 Chronicles 16:9:
"The eyes of the Lord run to and fro throughout the whole earth to show
Himself strong in behalf of those whose hearts are blameless toward
Him" (AMP). There you have both omniscience and omnipresence.

We also see this in the Twenty-third Psalm: "The LORD is my shepherd, I shall not want" (verse 1, NASB). Psalm 23 is a kingdom psalm;
it's about what life is like in the kingdom of God. But the reality of the
kingdom of God is His presence to all—to everyone and everything
on earth immersed in His loving care. We can think of many wonderful verses, such as Psalm 55:22: "Cast your burden upon the LORD and
He will sustain you; He will never allow the righteous to be shaken"
(NASB). Peter picked this up in 1 Peter 5:7: "Cast all your anxiety on him
because he cares for you." Psalm 34:15 says that "the eyes of the LORD
are toward the righteous and His ears are open to their cry" (NASB). In
Psalm 73:28 we read, "But as for me, the nearness of God is my good; I
have made the Lord GOD my refuge, that I may tell of all Your works"
(NASB).

A GOD OF ACTIVE CARE

At the center of biblical teaching, then, is the idea of an all-loving and all-powerful God who is *in action*, for us and with us. He is not passive. He is not distant. He is not indifferent. "He will not allow your foot to slip; He who keeps you will not slumber" (Psalm 121:3, NASB). All of these teachings are about the nature of a God who is in action. If you compare the pagan classical thought of Aristotle, Lucretius, and others, you will find variants of God in which He is aloof or He doesn't care or He can't act because He's limited. It is characteristic of the biblical teaching about God to fly in the face of such views — no doubt because of the experiences of God's ancient people — and to portray an active God who is not only at work in the universe but is always moving toward those who are open to receive Him.

Now the Jews had many problems in coming to understand all of this. When we look at their history not as a series of accidents but as planned out by God — from the Exodus to the wilderness wandering to the period of the judges to the assumption of the monarchy (which God said He didn't want in the first place) to all of the difficulties that the kings went through and the nation experienced and then finally to the Exile — we get a sense of their great discovery (especially in the exile from Jerusalem) that God is still God no matter what happens to you, and that *wherever* you are, God rules from the heavens. The idea of a "God of heaven" emerges in Daniel, 2 Chronicles, Ezra, and Nehemiah. You get from those Scriptures the notion of the "kingdom of the heavens," and after a few centuries, the fruit of this idea is harvested in the gospel of Matthew. Matthew used that phrase — "the kingdom of the heavens" — over and over to express the fact of the direct, immediate *availability* of God to those who call upon Him and especially, of course, to His covenant people. It is the favored way in Matthew of expressing the message of Jesus — the good news.

The idea that God is God of the "heavens" — that is, *of the surrounding atmosphere* — is a primary part of the revelation of Jehovah to His select people, from Abraham on. The texts of Genesis and following make this clear. For example, even those who from afar knew of Israel's experience with God understood this. Rahab told the spies sent into Jericho how she and her people had heard of them and how "our hearts melted and no courage remained in any man any longer because of you; for the LORD your God, He is God in heaven above and on earth beneath" (Joshua 2:11, NASB). What God had done in Egypt and in the wilderness was widely known. In the final song of Moses he said, "There is none like the God of Jeshurun, who rides the heavens to your help, and through the skies in His majesty. The eternal God is a dwelling place, and underneath are the everlasting arms" (Deuteronomy 33:26-27, NASB). That was a vital part of God's revelation: not just to Israel but to the whole world. But it took the harrowing events of the destruction of Jerusalem and the Babylonian exile to bring to the Jews an understanding that God was not bound to a special place (Jerusalem, cp. John 4:21) and that He was still present and in action where there were no visible manifestations in the surrounding heavens. That is the lesson of the interbiblical period, which ripens in meaning until it comes out of the mouth of John the baptizer.

THINK ABOUT YOUR THINKING

Now, a problem arises in how to move our understanding of the kingdom of God *beyond* the covenant people and deal with the kind of ethnocentricity that comes from being publically marked out as God's special people on earth. Being chosen by God is a huge burden to carry. One reason the world is chronically angry with the Jewish people is that they are God's chosen people. They *are* the chosen people, and they stand in the midst of the earth *as* a chosen people. Those not chosen have trouble getting over that fact. They resent it and resent the Jews. But God's intention with Israel *always* lay beyond Israel, for He said, "It is too small a thing that You should be My Servant to raise up the tribes of Jacob and to restore the preserved ones of Israel; I will also make You a light of the nations so that My salvation may reach to the end of the earth" (Isaiah 49:6, NASB). This calling lies in God's word to Abraham: "In you all the families of the earth will be blessed" (Genesis 12:3, NASB). Israel is not for the sake of Israel, but for the sake of the world, as today the church is not for the church, but for the world.

We must come back to this outward movement of the kingdom of the heavens, but for now we must be clear that Jesus emerged into world history from among this chosen people of God. He didn't come to the Greeks or to the Egyptians. He came to a people that had been prepared *by their experience* to understand what the kingdom of the heavens and the kingdom of God are all about. As we have seen, if you read the Psalms with an eye to the kingdom, you'll see they invariably are testimonies to the nature and reality of the kingdom. They are excerpts from the lives of people who loved that kingdom, though often in misguided ways. At the center of the Psalms, you see the beauty of kingdom life. Jesus came after a period of time when all this had been slowly developing. The interbiblical period plays a crucial role in driving home the message that there is always a kingdom of the heavens, even in the absence of a place and a political kingdom through which it rules.

There *is* a kingdom of the heavens, a present governance by God, and understanding of it had matured to a high point (with still a ways to go) when John the baptizer came to speak in Matthew 3. His message was "Repent" (verse 2, NASB). One can hardly say that word today because of misunderstandings and false images. When we hear the word, we are apt to think of some man walking back and forth on the sidewalk with a placard that reads, "The end is near." But biblical repentance is a very important and instructive concept, and we cannot let it go. I like to translate *metanoeite* this way: "Think about how you have been thinking." Or "Get a thought about your thoughts, a thought beyond your thoughts." Think in the light of the fact of God's immediate presence and availability through Christ, so that you can *now live in the kingdom of the heavens*. Psalm 23 can be your daily existence. And that is open to everyone. "Whosoever will may come." Reconsider your way of thinking about your life—your plans, your fears, your hopes—in the light of that.

OPENING THE DOORS OF THE KINGDOM

The great change that Jesus brought in His person and His gospel was *the openness* of the kingdom to everyone, and first of all to those who were the rejected, the unacceptable, *within* Israel. That is the heart of His gospel. Jesus was bringing the kingdom of God to those whom the authorities—the religious leaders, scribes, and Pharisees—thought were hopeless and should be shut out. And so on page after page of the Gospels, we find Jesus sitting down with publicans and sinners, fellowshipping with them, and offending the authorities (see Luke 15:1-2).

With the doors of the kingdom wide open, the gospel of the kingdom of God came as a power into the world and began to do what Daniel said was going to happen. You will remember that in Daniel 2, King Nebuchadnezzar dreamed of a great idol or statue. At its top was a golden head (Babylon) and at the bottom clay and iron for the feet and toes (the Roman Empire). And then, all of a sudden, a stone cut "without hands" struck the idol (verse 34, NASB). It smashed the idol, became a great mountain, and filled the whole earth. It was a kingdom that would "endure forever" (verse 44, NASB). That stone, Daniel told the king, was the kingdom of God. "The God of heaven will set up a kingdom" (verse 44, NASB). That was the vision of the kingdom of God that came to Daniel even in exile. There the Israelites had begun to understand the true nature of the kingdom of God—"cut out without hands" (verse 34, NASB). It is independent of all human government or arrangement.

SEEK FIRST THE KINGDOM

As we have noted, the kingdom of God is just God in action. Theological books like to use the word *reign* for it and that is fitting, but *reign* doesn't mean very much to ordinary people. *Rule* might be a substitute, but it is more informative to say that the kingdom is *God in action*. The kingdom of God is where what God wants done is done. In order to achieve that, He doesn't always have to be micromanaging it. Consider, for example, the *laws* of God—the order He has established in reality and in human life. They too are what God wants done. They are a power that, especially in the natural world, accomplishes what God wants. And the moral law—that also is what He wants done. To seek the kingdom of God is to seek to know and conform to the laws that God has established for nature and for human living.

For this reason, we must take seriously verses like Joshua 1:8: "This book of the law shall not depart from your mouth, but you shall meditate on it day and night, so that you may be careful to do according to all that is written in it; for then you will make your way prosperous, and then you will have success" (NASB). When you line up with the laws of God, you are lining up with what God Himself is doing. The laws of God express the character of God in His kingdom. When Jesus said, "Seek ye first the kingdom of God" (Matthew 6:33, KJV), we might ask, "How do you do that?" One way is to find and follow the laws of God. We need plenty of help to follow those laws, and the help is actually available. God's laws were never imposed without the supply of His grace for us to follow them.

Notice that there are many instrumentalities of the kingdom of God. There is God Himself. There are the Son of God and the Spirit of God. There is the Word of God. There are the people of God. There are God's acts in history. All that is a part of the kingdom of God. But what is the central reality of the kingdom of God? Once again, the kingdom of God is *God in action*. That's why the kingdom of God has been around forever and will always exist, because God has always been and will always be acting. Some people wonder what God was doing before He created the world—as if He didn't have anything to do. I often get asked that question on college campuses. I always reply, "He was enjoying themselves." People seem to think that the physical universe dwarfs God. But no. We don't have a big physical universe with a little God flitting around here and there. We have a physical universe that fits on the little finger of a great big God who has been here always and will be here forever.

OUR GOD REIGNS

But this great God has to deal with the problem of the *mediation* of His presence to free persons whom He has made and who have nevertheless adopted a posture of hostility and rejection toward Him. His response to that situation is, roughly, human history, with Christ at the center. When Jesus came, He announced the availability of God's kingdom and made it present in a gentle way. It was not, strictly speaking, a new message, but it had some new implications. Most of us are familiar with the praise song that says: "Our God reigns." That's from Isaiah 52:7, the same passage that contains the phrase, "How beautiful are the feet of those who bring the gospel of peace" (PAR). And what is the gospel of peace? Our God reigns. Of course, in that verse Zion is looking for deliverance and the reigning of God. But God has something much larger in mind—humanity and the physical cosmos. This expansiveness comes out in many wonderful passages from the prophet Isaiah, who had a great vision of the kingdom of God. Though this passage from Isaiah 52 says, "Say to Zion, 'Your God reigns!'" (verse 7), it applies far beyond Zion. We here today aren't Zion. We are something more. The call to Zion was not just to be a light upon Zion but also upon the whole world, even the whole universe.

So, we see the breaking out *within* Israel of the gospel of the kingdom. But when Jesus said in Matthew 4:17 and elsewhere, "Repent, for the kingdom of heaven is at hand" (NASB), He was announcing the availability of the kingdom of God *beyond all existing assumptions*. Paul called this worldwide availability a "mystery which has been hidden from the past ages" (Colossians 1:26, NASB). And this hiddenness was necessary because the kingdom of God had been committed, in a special way, to the people of Israel. Others did not share in it prior to Jesus' announcement. The people of Israel had been appointed to be what you might call the "street address" of the kingdom of God on earth. God was always beyond Israel, of course, but they had a special calling, and anyone who wanted to find God could find Him through coming to Israel. God intended to bring the kingdom to earth through the people of Israel. And He did just that!

BLESSED ARE THE POOR?
WHAT'S GOING ON HERE?

The great change that came with Jesus—the "good news," according to Him—had to do with *its availability*. It first reached out to those *within* Israel who were ordinarily understood *not* to be blessed. You see this constantly in the gospel stories, and it is systematically driven home in the Beatitudes (see Matthew 5 and Luke 6) and in the Woe Bes (see Luke 6). There we see the great kingdom inversion of who is blessed and who is not. And that inversion is always tied to the kingdom of God. "Blessed are you who are poor," Luke 6:20 says, "for yours is the kingdom of God" (NASB). This is a proclamation of the gospel as well as a teaching about what the kingdom of God is like. It doesn't tell anyone to become poor in order to be blessed. It doesn't suggest that there is anything especially good about poverty. "Blessed are you who weep" (verse 21, NASB) doesn't tell anyone to go and weep. The Beatitudes just announce and explain, "You over here who are (on the human scale) normally thought *not* to be blessed *are* blessed anyway as you live in the kingdom of God—in spite of all humanly deplorable conditions." The gospel of Jesus is the good news of the availability of the kingdom of God to everyone—to Romans, to people who are unclean because of disease, to the poor who are thought to be cursed.

This remarkable shift in the *availability* of life in the kingdom is driven home by the poignant scene from Matthew 11 where John the baptizer, who first began to preach Jesus' message of kingdom availability (see Matthew 3:2), is in prison facing death. He is there coming to grips with the fact that what the availability of the kingdom meant is not what he thought. He sent his disciples to Jesus to ask, "Are You really the One? I thought You were, but things aren't looking so good for this kingdom." Jesus returned a message. And if we look at that message, we see it is precisely a message of the availability of the kingdom of God to people who were not thought to be included. Jesus' answer is, "Go and report to John what you hear and see: The blind receive sight and the lame walk, the lepers are cleansed and the deaf hear" (Matthew 11:4-5,

NASB). What is that? That's the power of God available to needy people, those of no qualifications. It is God in action. Jesus added, "The poor have the gospel preached to them" (verse 5, NASB). But it was a kingdom that John the baptizer never understood. And that's why Jesus, continuing His discussion of John, said, "Truly I say to you, among those born of women there has not arisen anyone greater than John the Baptist! Yet the one who is least in the kingdom of heaven is greater than he" (verse 11, NASB).

PEOPLE OF VIOLENCE?

Jesus gave the poor some good news for a change. That was indeed a great sign of the kingdom, perhaps even greater than healings and other miracles, certainly greater than a government takeover by the Jewish people. But it really hit the Israelites hard in their theology. You may recall Jesus' discussion about riches and poverty after the incident with the rich young ruler. It's crucial to understand that discussion correctly because it is integral to the major change that emerges in Matthew 11:12 (see also Luke 16:16.). Listen to this: "From the days of John the Baptist until now the kingdom of heaven suffers violence, and violent men take it by force" (NASB). This is not what some liberation theologians took it to mean. It's not talking about taking up arms and reversing the cultural standards, exalting and empowering the poor over the rich. It is talking about something you see on every page of the Gospels—namely, access to the kingdom of God by people who do not do what is proper, who do not stand on proprieties in dealing with the kingdom, especially the Jewish proprieties.

It is talking about a little leper who came to Jesus (see Matthew 8:1-4). Lepers were not supposed to be coming to people. But no doubt, he had heard Jesus speak and watched Him heal. Finally, the leper got up his nerve, came to Jesus, and said, "Lord, if You are willing, You can make me clean" (verse 2, NASB). And Jesus said what? "I am willing" (verse 3, NASB). The kingdom reached out in Jesus, who not only spoke to that man but also *touched* him. And if you understand what that would mean to a leper and what it would mean to those standing around watching Jesus, you begin to get the idea of what violence is in this verse. Violence means you don't stand on the proprieties, whatever they may be. You just come to Jesus, and He brings the kingdom of God to bear on you whether you are unclean by disease or by being a Gentile. He brings it to bear on anyone, whether the person is a tax collector, a woman of the street, a Roman centurion, or whatever. Those are the people of violence. They didn't take the proper path to relationship with God; they just came to Jesus as they were.

You must update that for our world because we have our proprieties too. And they routinely stand in people's minds as barriers to life in the kingdom. Always, if you watch, you will see Jesus breaking through those proprieties and doing something that people *within* their proprieties — the self-righteous scribes and Pharisees — don't understand. Matthew 21:43 emphasizes the abrupt departure that is occurring around Jesus. There were some harsh encounters between Him and the people in charge (or who thought they were in charge). Jesus said, "The kingdom of God will be taken away from you and given to a people producing the fruit of it" (NASB). Jesus was announcing the great movement to come right after His death. Jesus had developed a small group of people who could carry the kingdom to the ends of the earth. They bore the kingdom in themselves (see Luke 10:9,11) to the rest of the world. And it was not just the word *about* the kingdom that they brought, but the reality of the kingdom itself. "The kingdom of God does not consist in words but in power" (1 Corinthians 4:20, NASB). However, what set Jesus against the religious leaders of His time was that they did not adopt this non-Jewish, worldwide missional emphasis of the kingdom. They thought only of themselves and their positions. In Matthew 23:13, Jesus spoke about Israel's spiritual leaders who had shut up the kingdom of heaven: "You do not enter in yourselves, nor do you allow those who are entering to go in" (NASB).

Caught Up in God's Life

The words of Jesus in Matthew 5:20 illumine the condition of those leaders: "Unless your righteousness surpasses that of the scribes and Pharisees, you will not enter the kingdom of heaven" (NASB). Jesus was not talking here about "going to heaven" after death, about who will get in and who won't. He was talking about a present relationship, about entering into a real life now — a life with God in the present, this God who is in action spreading His kingdom among humanity. Jesus was saying that if you stay at the level of the scribes and the Pharisees, you will not interactively engage the yeastlike spread of the rule of God. Your life will be limited to what you think is proper and to what you can accomplish by your own powers. And that is not very much.

Jesus now stands in the midst of the world. The King is saying, "Whosoever will may come." There is no preexisting condition that eliminates you from this policy. None. It doesn't matter if you've got leprosy or AIDS, whether of the soul or of the body. It doesn't matter what your race or your gender is or your economic condition. You can come. You're rich? You can come, too. But you're going to need more than your riches. They are not your blessing. You're poor? You can come, too. And you'll have everything you need. Your life becomes caught up in God's life, and that makes your life an *eternal* life. As Jesus said in John 17:3, "This is eternal life, that they may know You, the only true God, and Jesus Christ whom You have sent" (NASB). That is eternal life — an active relationship with Jesus, eternal living.

Paul and the Kingdom

Let's look now at the kingdom of God in the apostle Paul's thinking as he moved out into the Gentile world. It is often thought that Paul preached a different gospel than Jesus did. But we have already noted how, in Colossians 1:13, Paul spoke of our being "transferred," in the birth from above, out of the kingdom of darkness and into the kingdom of the Son of God's love. Kingdom language is Paul's language. And

Paul's gospel is centered on spiritual formation, just as Jesus' was. If you grow into doing what Paul said, you will take the teachings of the Sermon on the Mount at a walk.

Colossians 1:9-12 contains a profound prayer for what Paul longed to see in the lives of the Colossians:

> That you may be filled with the knowledge of His will in all spiritual wisdom and understanding, so that you will walk in a manner worthy of the Lord, to please Him in all respects, bearing fruit in every good work and increasing in the knowledge of God; strengthened with all power, according to His glorious might, for the attaining of all steadfastness and patience; joyously giving thanks to the Father, who has qualified us to share in the inheritance of the saints in Light. (NASB)

This, of course, is nothing but the result of spiritual formation or growth in grace. It lay at the heart of Paul's intentions, for himself and for those he taught.

This prayer is based upon the reality of Christ the King:

> He is the image of the invisible God, the firstborn of all creation. For by Him all things were created, both in the heavens and on earth, visible and invisible, whether thrones or dominions or rulers or authorities—all things have been created through Him and for Him. He is before all things, and in Him all things hold together. He is also head of the body, the church; and He is the beginning, the firstborn from the dead, so that He Himself will come to have first place in everything. For it was the Father's good pleasure for all the fullness to dwell in Him, and through Him to reconcile all things to Himself, having made peace through the blood of His cross; through Him, I say, whether things in earth or things in heaven. (Colossians 1:15-20, NASB)

Once you get Paul's meaning, it enables you to see the scope of God's plan, and after these words about who Jesus really is in the cosmos, there comes the glory of our lives now in Christ: "If you have been raised up with Christ, keep seeking the things above, where Christ is, seated at the right hand of God. Set your mind on the things above, not on the things that are on earth. For you have died and your life is hidden with Christ in God" (Colossians 3:1-3, NASB). This and the following verses are *pure spiritual-formation* verses. But notice how being risen with Christ beyond death is the assumption of it all. This is the kingdom as it expresses itself in Christ and, above all, in the resurrection. Remember what Paul said in 1 Corinthians 15:17: "If Christ has not been raised . . . you are still in your sins" (NASB). Well, what about the Cross? The Cross must never be presented without Resurrection. We must have both Cross *and* Resurrection, or we do not have a kingdom or the Christ of the kingdom, and then we will also have a mistaken view of salvation — one that does *not* relate to the present spiritual life of the believer, which is to be precisely a resurrection life. Spiritual formation or continual growth in grace is not part of such salvation.

RESURRECTION LIFE

To truly engage in the spiritual life, then, we have to get past a view of atonement in which *all that matters* in salvation is Jesus taking the punishment for our sins. The problem with such a reductionistic view is that once salvation is taken care of and heaven after death is assured, that is the end of it — period. It's all done *for* us, and it's all over and done with. So, what are we going to do now? What about discipleship? Not required, and not even natural to the "saved" condition. "Saved" in the reductionist view just means my sins are forgiven. Let me assure you, lest you misunderstand me, it certainly means that. It certainly means your sins are forgiven, but remember that the basic act of salvation from God's point of view is *the impartation of life*. It is regeneration. And that life imparted is resurrection life, an ongoing, developing reality.

So, let's go back to Colossians 3:1-4:

If you have been raised up with Christ, keep seeking the things above [there's that word again—*above*], where Christ is, seated at the right hand of God. Set your mind on the things above, not on the things that are on earth. For you have died and your life is hidden with Christ in God. When Christ, who is our life, is revealed, then you also will be revealed with Him in glory. (NASB)

Glorious! The theme of *who we are becoming* appears over and over in the New Testament. Remember what John said in his first letter:

See how great a love the Father has bestowed on us, that we would be called children of God; and such we are. . . . Beloved, now we are children of God, and it has not appeared as yet what we will be. We know that when He appears, we will be like Him, because we will see Him just as He is. And everyone who has this hope fixed on Him purifies himself, just as He is pure. (1 John 3:1-3, NASB)

That great theme—that we are becoming like Christ—makes plain the glorious life we are entering into now. *We are purifying ourselves as He is pure—a precise description of spiritual formation.*

Thus the apostle Peter wrote, "According to His great mercy [God] has caused us to be born again to a living hope through the resurrection of Jesus Christ from the dead" (1 Peter 1:3, NASB). If we don't get the vision for this kind of life *as* salvation, spiritual formation will appear as something odd and basically irrelevant—which is precisely how it does appear to most professed Christians today—because spiritual formation is precisely formation *in* this life and *of* this life from above. The gospel of the kingdom opens us to progressive *transformation* in this life.

THE WORLD, THE FLESH, AND THE DEVIL

Though spiritual formation is a natural part of salvation in Christ, correctly understood, we would make a mistake if we thought there was no battle involved in our transformation. Ephesians 2 gives us a full picture of what's at stake. And it's not a very encouraging picture, to tell the truth. It starts off, "You were dead in your trespasses and sins, in which you formerly walked according to the course of this world" (verses 1-2, NASB). There you find the first member of the trinity of evil: *the world*. Then we read, ". . . according to the prince of the power of the air, of the spirit that is now working in the sons of disobedience" (verse 2, NASB). There is the second member: *the Devil*. Then, "Among them we too all formerly lived in the lusts of our flesh, indulging the desires of the flesh and of the mind, and were by nature children of wrath, even as the rest" (verse 3, NASB). That's number three: *the flesh*. If you've ever wondered where that expression comes from — "the world, the flesh, and the Devil" — here is Paul's statement.

So, you've got all these factors working against you: the world, the flesh, and the Devil. What are they? You have the social and historical organization of evil in the midst of which you must live: that's the world. You have the personal spiritual power behind that: the one who is the prince of this world, the one who in a certain manner governs it. He came to Jesus in the great struggle before His crucifixion. Jesus said at the end of John 14, "I will not speak much more with you, for *the ruler of the world* is coming" (verse 30, NASB, emphasis added). The world is one of the elements that is generally missing in our understanding of the whole story of redemption and spiritual formation. And then there is the flesh. The flesh is primarily to be identified with the natural desires of human beings, and the flesh within the human being wars with the human spirit. The human spirit is the *will*, and the will, if not totally enslaved by desire, is always contemplating alternatives, seeking *what is best*. But desire does not contemplate alternatives. It says things like, "I've just got to have a doughnut." No, you don't have to have a doughnut. But your desire for a doughnut says, "Forget about your blood sugar.

Forget about your weight. Forget about the fact that you're addicted to this junk. *You want a doughnut!*" That's the flesh speaking.

Paul said in Galatians 5 that the flesh wars against the spirit, and the spirit wars against the flesh. That's the natural condition because flesh gives rise to desire, and desire has the power to obsess you. Again, *desire does not contemplate alternatives.* It simply says, "I want that!" And if you sign over your will to desire, then you will become an addict. An addict is a person who has basically resigned his spirit and his will to a desire. He has said, "Yes, I must have this!" Whereas actually he doesn't have to have it. There are some things you have to have, but they are very few and often we don't pay very much attention to them. Spiritual formation is a matter of ordering desires and putting them in their place with reference to what is good under God.

POWERS, IDEAS, AND IMAGES

The apostle Paul warned us that "our struggle is not against flesh and blood, but against the rulers, against the powers, against the world forces of this darkness, against the spiritual forces of wickedness in the heavenly places" (Ephesians 6:12, NASB). These higher-level powers and forces are spiritual agencies that *primarily work within the idea systems of our culture.*

Idea systems are commonly held assumptions about reality. They are patterns of thinking and interpretation, historically developed and socially shared. Examples of ideas are freedom, education, happiness, the American dream, science, progress, death, home, the feminine or masculine, religion, church, democracy, fairness, justice, family, evolution, God, and the secular. Ideas such as these are so pervasive and essential to how we approach life that we often do not even know they are there or understand how they work. Our particular idea system is a cultural artifact, growing up with us from earliest childhood out of the teachings, expectations, and observable behaviors of family and community. These idea systems can be manipulated by evil forces; they are, in fact, evil's main tool for dominating humanity.

By contrast, we who have been rescued "from the power of darkness and transferred . . . into the kingdom of his beloved Son" (Colossians 1:13, NRSV) are to "let this mind be in [us], which was also in Christ Jesus" (Philippians 2:5, KJV). This is an essential way of describing the substance, the underlying reality, of Christian spiritual formation. We are, in Paul's familiar language, transformed precisely by the "renewing of [our] mind" (Romans 12:2, NASB).

Closely associated with these idea systems are *images* that occupy our minds. Images are always concrete and specific, as opposed to the abstractness of ideas, and they are heavily laden with feeling. They frequently have a powerful emotional and sensuous linkage to governing idea systems. For example, hair (long, short, skinhead, green, orange, or purple), body piercings, tattoos, flags (and their desecration), and clothing styles have provided powerful images and symbols for conflicting idea systems. These images are often adopted by one generation, ethnic group, or locale to set itself off from another.

Of course, Jesus understood the great significance of images. He carefully selected an image that brilliantly conveys Himself and His message: the Cross. The Cross represents the lostness of man as well as the sacrifice of God and the abandonment to God that brings redemption. No doubt it is the all-time most powerful image and symbol of human history. Need we say He knew what He was doing in selecting it? He is the master of images. For their own benefit, His followers need to keep the image of the Cross vividly present in their minds. In fact, learning to keep the Cross constantly in mind is a major factor in spiritual growth and maturity.

Ideas and images are the primary focus of Satan's efforts to defeat God's purposes for humankind. They form the primary arena of the battle of spiritual formation. When we are subject to Satan's chosen ideas and images, he can take a holiday. When he undertook to draw Eve away from God, he did not hit her with a stick, but with an idea. It was with the idea that God could not be trusted and that she must act on her own to secure her own well-being.

THE IDEA BEHIND ALL TEMPTATION

Here is the basic idea behind all temptation: God is presented to our minds as depriving us of what is good (or at least of what we want) by His commands, so we think we must take matters into our own hands. This image of God leads to our pushing Him out of our thoughts and putting ourselves on the throne of the universe. We can see that the single most important thing in our minds is our idea of God. The process of spiritual formation in Christ is one of progressively replacing our destructive images and ideas with the images and ideas that filled the mind of Jesus Himself. We thereby come increasingly to see "the light of the gospel of the glory of Christ, who is the image of God" (2 Corinthians 4:4, NRSV).

An illustration of the great difference of outlook in the Christ-formed mind is found in Paul's letter to the Colossians. There he contrasted the way of earth, or the flesh, with the way of the new person. The human way is one of anger, wrath, malice, slander, abusive language, and lying (see Colossians 3:8-9). Think for a moment how true this is to human life. But Paul said, "Lie no more, since you have stripped off the old self and its characteristic behavior and put on the new self, which sees things as they really are in God's view" (verses 9-10, PAR). In that view, the usual human distinctions (between Greek and Jew, circumcised and uncircumcised, barbarian, Scythian, slave or free person, and so on) do not matter in how we relate to people, because Christ is (or can be) in all alike (see verses 10-11).

What is more *unlike* humans than to *treat all kinds of people with equal truth and love*? Imagine the difference it would make as you go through just one day. In a significant manner, the antidiscrimination of which we now hear so much is a profound truth of kingdom living. The ideas and images that govern unredeemed humanity make it impossible, except in highly selective circumstances and in very recent societies strongly influenced by Jesus and His followers. Paul knew we can only escape being conformed to a fallen humanity by receiving the mind of Christ Himself (see 1 Corinthians 2:16; Philippians 2:5). Spiritual formation in Christ moves toward a total interchange of *our* ideas and images for *His*.

How is this to come about? This question is answered when we see how grace and human initiative work together to break the power of the toxic system of ideas and images that makes us dead to God. After God has implanted new life from above in us by word and Spirit, we can begin to take initiative in progressively retaking the whole of our thought lives for God's kingdom. That is a major part of what it means to "seek first His kingdom and His righteousness" (Matthew 6:33, NASB). God's grace will accompany us every step of the way, but it will never permit us to be merely passive in our spiritual formation in Christ.

THE WORK OF GRACE

The context of the battle of spiritual formation is resurrection grace. "But God, being rich in mercy, because of His great love with which He loved us, even when we were dead in our transgressions, made us alive together with Christ (by grace you have been saved)" (Ephesians 2:4-5, NASB). The context of our struggle is *grace*. What makes us alive? Grace. What is grace? *Grace is God acting in our lives to accomplish what we can't accomplish on our own.* Is it unmerited favor? Of course it is. But if that's all we know about grace, we still have problems. I have heard distinguished Christian speakers say, "Grace is only for guilt." A candid search of the Scriptures would never teach you that. Grace is also for life. That's why you can grow in grace without growing in guilt. Grace is for life. *We would still have needed grace if we had never sinned.* You will understand that once you realize that grace is God acting in your life to accomplish what you can't accomplish on your own. We find the kingdom as we experience this action with us in life. We were created by grace for grace.

SPIRITUAL FORMATION REQUIRES
OUR INITIATIVE

God's plan allows for a kingdom of darkness to exist. Paul indicated in Colossians 1:13 that we were in "the domain of darkness" before being brought into "the kingdom of His beloved Son" (NASB). We were dead in the kingdom of darkness—not alive to God. This means that our basic nature was not working. We had to have the birth from above to reestablish contact with the kingdom of light. After that we have choices about how we move within that kingdom of light. This is crucial to the details of spiritual formation, because this transformation is not a passive process. It is a process in which we continue to make choices and our character develops, and sometimes the experience is hard.

St. Anthony, when he went into the desert, had some horrendous nights in which Satan approached him in all kinds of visible and auditory forms. He held on and resisted and would not give in. Finally, Jesus came to him. (I'll leave you to figure out what this means. I'm inclined to be pretty literal about it.) The first question St. Anthony asked Jesus was, "Why didn't You come sooner?" And Jesus replied, "I wanted to see how you would do."[2] Now, actually, that is a biblical theme. God did it with Abraham (see Genesis 22:12) and with the Israelites in the wilderness (see Deuteronomy 8:2), for example. Jesus did this with the disciples (see Mark 6:37,48-51). You can be sure He will do it with you and me. It is indispensable to our growth in grace.

This throws light upon the course of our own spiritual development. God will make the darkness praise Him, but we often don't experience that at the moment. We're in a world in which people make choices, and they often make wrong choices. And there is an enemy of God who fought with God and couldn't win. So now he focuses on one of God's major projects: humanity—namely, you and me. We struggle on in a world of darkness, and some of that darkness is in us. We are in the process of spiritual formation, which a disciple of Jesus goes through to progressively remove the darkness within us and around us. Remember how much is made of light and children of light in the Scriptures. It is our destiny to be children of light and live fully in the light. Consider this statement from Ephesians 5:8-9: "You were formerly darkness, but now you are Light in the Lord; walk as children of Light (for the fruit of the Light consists in all goodness and righteousness and truth)" (NASB). We know what importance the apostle John gave to light in his writings and how crucial for him light was in spiritual formation. To move out of darkness, we need to move out of places where we hide and away from activities we do not want to be known for.

SATAN IS UNDER GOD'S CONTROL

The kingdom of God allows space for a lot of things that God wouldn't have preferred. He permitted—as I've already mentioned—the monarchy in Israel. That's an illustration of something God did not want but He permitted. And in that sense, it was with His approval. But He said to Samuel, "They have not rejected you, but they have rejected Me" (1 Samuel 8:7, NASB). That is one of the most instructive verses in the Bible for understanding what the kingdom of God is like—what God blesses and what God permits and uses may radically differ. What are the things in my life that God permits but does not want? That is one of the most important questions to keep before us in spiritual formation. Does God actually approve of everything He permits? I think the answer is obviously no, He doesn't. But everything God permits, can He use it? Yes, He certainly can, and He will for those who continually seek the kingdom.

THE LIFE OF FAITH

As we live in the experience of the new life from above, we begin to see regeneration in a different light. We understand, for example, from 1 Corinthians 12:3 that no man can call Jesus Lord except by the Holy Spirit. There are problems with metaphors, but in a similar way birth is not something that I do. Birth is something that is done to me, and the birth from above is entrance into a new realm. Abraham believed God and it was reckoned to him as righteousness. If I can paraphrase what's going on there, I believe that God looked at Abraham's faith, which no doubt was dependent on God as well as on Abraham (Abraham at least had to be willing), and said, "I would rather have this trust in Me than perfect obedience. I would rather have the confidence that this man has in Me than some kind of legal conformity." And we must recall that the confidence in question had no fancy theological garments on it. Abraham's confidence was that God would give him a male heir. That's the faith that God looked at and accepted as righteousness. That's the life of faith. That's counting on God for life. That's the kind of faith—Abraham's kind—that Paul spoke of in Romans 4. This awakening of faith—which, by the way, need not be just a moment but can also be a process—is, in fact, regeneration. In regeneration and the impartation of new life, forgiveness is one essential part of the grace of God moving toward us.

THE GOSPEL IN THE EARLY CHURCH

Let me now call attention to how the gospel looked in the early church. One of the best places to do this is with Philip in Acts 8:12: "But when they believed Philip preaching the good news about the kingdom of God and the name of Jesus Christ, they were being baptized, men and women alike" (NASB). Now, wait a moment. Here is something new. Philip was preaching the good news about "the kingdom of God and the name of Jesus." What's that? The gospel is about the name of Jesus? Actually, when you begin to study this in the New Testament, you find that there are a lot of different ways of putting the gospel. Here we see the relationship of the disciple to Christ and His kingdom through "the name of Jesus." The very name of Jesus is "good news." One finds the kingdom of God by acting *with* the name of Jesus (see John 14:13-14).

Now, think about this: If you have a Christ without a kingdom, you don't have a Christ. And if you have a kingdom without Christ, you don't have a kingdom of God. You have to keep those two together. How they came together for Jesus' early disciples and their disciples is made plain by the book of Acts. Jesus put a face on the kingdom of God. But the phrase "the kingdom of God" went wild in the nineteenth and twentieth centuries. I don't just mean in a theological context but in the political as well. The great threat, especially among the more liberal-leaning branches of the church and of Western society, is to forget about Jesus. Then you will have a kingdom of man parading itself as the kingdom of God. But we can't really forget about Him. He won't go off the page. Consider John 12:32: "And I, if I am lifted up from the earth, will draw all men to Myself" (NASB). You can't get rid of that. Pull that out and history disappears. Jesus and His teachings are the focus of the Western world. We are in a tragic experiment with regard to Jesus in our culture in America today. We're trying to put something in the place of Jesus: the empty shell we call secularism.

Still, here is the gospel: the kingdom of God and the name of Jesus. What is the name of Jesus? It is access to the kingdom of God. Jesus taught His disciples how to act in His name. It is in His name that we overcome the darkness and its prince.

Spiritual Formation for Disciples of Jesus

If we were to move carefully through the book of Acts, we would see that the kingdom of God stays right there, from beginning all the way to the end. It shows up in wonderful passages, like Paul's parting from the Ephesian elders in Acts 20. And when we come to the end of Acts, we have "preaching the kingdom of God and teaching concerning the Lord Jesus Christ with all openness, unhindered" (Acts 28:31, NASB). That's the last verse of the book of Acts. This passage is about Paul in Rome, and, symbolically at least, this is the fulfillment of Matthew 21:43 where "the kingdom of God will be taken away from you and given to a people, producing the fruit of it" (NASB).

In the light of all this, what is spiritual formation? Spiritual formation is the training process that occurs for those who are disciples of Jesus. Spiritual formation and discipleship are all about development of the life in the kingdom of God that comes to us through the risen

Christ. As a disciple of Jesus, I am living with Him, learning to live in the kingdom of God as He lived in the kingdom of God. Spiritual formation is taking the explicit statements of Jesus and learning how to live this way. Jesus did tell us, did He not, that we should make disciples, submerging them in Trinitarian reality? Baptizing them in the Trinitarian name doesn't just mean saying the names "Father," "Son," and "Holy Spirit" over them while you get them wet. The name in biblical understanding is reality, and to baptize them is to submerge them in the Trinitarian reality. We must understand the relevance of the Trinity to the gospel! The gospel is about life with the Trinity.

ENTERING THE KINGDOM

Perhaps now we have a deeper understanding of Matthew 5:20. Jesus said, "For I say to you that unless your righteousness surpasses that of the scribes and Pharisees [and you can insert here your own particular variety of goodness], you will not enter the kingdom of heaven" (NASB). Now when you read the statements about entering the kingdom of heaven, perhaps you will think in this way: *Maybe they are not talking about going to heaven after I die. Maybe this is a reference to* this life. There you have it. But if you are living in the kingdom of heaven — living it in a moment-to-moment experience — you can forget any concerns you may have for what happens *after* this life. They will be taken care of.

We have, then, moved *beyond* the righteousness of the scribes and the Pharisees. That means we've stopped thinking in terms of what we do or don't do and started thinking about *who we are*. Our identity and nature are provided by a life that is given to us in the kingdom of God. Spiritual formation shines all through the Sermon on the Mount. How do I manage not to be an angry, contemptuous person? That's spiritual formation. The scribe or Pharisee will say, "I didn't kill anybody." Or "I didn't commit adultery." But the issue is: What kind of person am I? Can I come to the place where I love people so much — for example, I love the women I see, meet, and deal with so much — that I would not use them to excite my lusting or in any other way? Because the real issue is: How do you think about people? It is not: Did I have sex with somebody or did I kill somebody? Instead, it is: How do I actually think about people? Where do they stand in my heart and mind? That is where spiritual formation really takes hold. It's not about external proprieties or improprieties but about the development of the inner person in Christlikeness.

THE GOSPEL OF THE KINGDOM AND SPIRITUAL FORMATION

The gospel of the kingdom is the availability of life from above through reliance upon Jesus, the Living One, the Master of the Universe. Those who receive this gospel, throwing themselves upon the mercy of the risen Christ, *live* in God's action—which is grace moving in them. In John 1:12 we read, "As many as received Him, to them He gave the right [or the authority, if you wish (the Greek is *exousia*)] to become children of God" (NASB). John continued, ". . . even to those who believe in His name, who were born, not of blood nor of the will of the flesh [natural abilities] nor of the will of man, but of God" (verses 12-13, NASB).

That impartation of kingdom life is the open door to spiritual formation. But today we often bring people into the church on a nondiscipleship basis and without natural entry into a life of spiritual formation. Then, if we try to bring up the subject, they are thinking bait and switch because what they were told coming in the door had nothing to do with this new idea. Many—most, I find—just turn off or get mad or get going. They were perhaps asked something like, "Don't you feel a need for Jesus?" And they would be fools not to, wouldn't they? But what exactly is the need they feel? Unless you understand the gospel as I've explained it here, on the basis of the New Testament, that "need" may be any one of many different things, perhaps not even a need for forgiveness. But the authentic gospel of Jesus says, "I offer you life, but you have to give up yours. Yes, that life you think you're in charge of—the one you complain so much about—you have to give it up." Our task then is to present Jesus in such a way that people are ready to seize *Him* as their constant companion, Lord, teacher, mediator. We must present Him not just as the person who died on the cross, but also as the person who lives beyond the cross. He is the One who comes to reconcile us to God so we can begin a new life in God's close company, with an unending destiny in His cosmic future—call that heaven.

In presenting this gospel we have to remember that the mind of the flesh is hostile to God. Human beings, right down to their muscles and bones, do not like God. That is something only a new life can redeem them from. It can bring them out of the grip of sin and the world, the flesh, and the Devil and replace their hostility to God with agape love—again, down to their muscles and bones. We do not simply wait for that new life to act in people. Through the Word, the Spirit, our own lives, and the lives of the church, we bring fruit and faith and repentance to their minds and their hearts. *Spiritual formation and discipleship then become natural responses to the gift of life in the kingdom of God through faith in Jesus Christ.* The kingdom of God becomes the texture and the energy of our spiritual formation in Christ.

FOR REFLECTION AND DISCUSSION

1. In your own experience, why would you say that an understanding of the gospel of the kingdom is foundational to formation into the image of Jesus?
2. How would you characterize the gospel of the kingdom as opposed to a gospel directed primarily at assuring the afterlife?
3. Reflect on the current model(s) of ministry that you are using or engaged in. How central is the gospel of the kingdom of God to its ethos and manner of ministry?
4. Given the values of the kingdom of God, what would a formational ministry based on this do differently? Do the same? What part of the gospel of the kingdom represents the most radical challenge for your ministry and the people involved?

FOR FURTHER READING

Bright, John. *The Kingdom of God: The Biblical Concept and Its Meaning for the Church.* Louisville, KY: Abingdon, 1957. (Bright takes a later turn toward theological liberalism, but it is still the best book on the biblical elements of the kingdom.)

Lloyd-Jones, Martyn, and Christopher Catherwood. *The Kingdom of God.* Chicago: Crossway, 1992.

Wakabayashi, Allen Mitsuo. *Kingdom Come: How Jesus Wants to Change the World.* Downers Grove, IL: InterVarsity, 2003.

Willard, Dallas. *The Divine Conspiracy: Rediscovering Our Hidden Life in God.* San Francisco: HarperOne, 1998.

Chapter Two

COMMUNITIES OF GRACE

Bill Thrall and Bruce McNicol

ELEMENT 2: Spiritual formation is rooted in relationship with God and one another. Communities of grace and trust help us discover and define who we are and how we shall live in trust, love, grace, humility, dignity, and justice. Communities of grace and trust open the door to gaining permission to share truth among fellow believers and the unbelieving world.

Description: Those who receive this invitation will incorporate into their relationships with God and others the principles of grace that characterize the life of the Trinity. Safe communities of grace will be both the by-product of those who experience and live out these principles and the invitation for others to experience and live them out. The process of experiencing grace with God and others validates who I am, matures who I am becoming, and therefore is defining the way I should live.

❧ ❧ ❧

NO TOGETHER PEOPLE

Grace and I (Bill) had been married five years when one day as I arrived home from work, Grace met me at the front door. In those days I was a CPA and management consultant in Phoenix. My mild-mannered wife gave me a blunt directive: "We need to go for a ride."

Grace's strained tone and piercing eyes told me she had something important and uncomfortable in mind. Very astutely, I reasoned, *I'm in trouble*, and tried to stall by asking, "What about the kids?"

"I took care of them," Grace replied. "They'll be fine."

Heading for the car, I worried, *What did I do? What did she find out about me that I haven't told her?* By the time I had settled behind the steering wheel, I was already perspiring as I compiled my mental list of initial defenses and alibis. "Where to?" I asked with cucumber-like cool-ness and cheer.

"Drive north," she said.

We drove for what seemed like the longest thirty minutes of my life. Neither of us said a word until she instructed me to pull over into an almost-empty parking lot in Scottsdale. Although my sweat had now soaked through my suit, I wasn't about to let her see my nervousness, so I kept quiet. Grace had never done anything even remotely like this before. This was her call.

I could see she had prepared well for this moment. Her peace and clear presence of mind further unnerved me. After a long pause, Grace finally spoke.

"I want you to know that I am extremely unhappy in our marriage."

"What?" I interrupted. "I'm a good father. I work hard for my family. We're making a lot of money. We're deeply involved in youth ministry. How can you say you're not happy?" I was momentarily relieved as I thought, *This isn't about me. It's about her. She's unhappy.*

Continuing to vent my angry response, I blurted out other personal accolades to elicit remorse from her. But they didn't work. So I got out of the car and stormed around, playing the wounded-spouse role to the hilt. *How dare she!* I grumbled to myself. When I finally got back into the car, Grace was still peaceful, completely unmoved by my antics. Then, very simply, she asked, "Don't you want to know *why* I am so unhappy?"

"Well . . . uh . . . yes," I responded. "That would be a good place to start."

"You will not let me love you," she replied. Then, after a brief pause, "You do not even try to trust me. I love you. I want to be all I can for you, but you won't let me. Please hear me."

Tears filled her eyes. "This is so serious," Grace continued. "You cannot just love me. To have a relationship, I have to be able to love you!" She explained how my inability to trust was slowly decaying our marriage, my relationship with the children, and my influence.

For five years I had kept my life hidden from Grace. I tested her love in many ways, not willing to believe it could be trusted. I felt she would not be able to handle the real me. Each rejection of her sincere, loving attempts to win my heart caused Grace tremendous pain. Yet instead of condemning me or putting me down, she responded with strength and commitment. She gave me a safe place to trust, to give her access to my life, to be loved. For the first time, I chose to trust Grace with me. This began the journey of resolving my issues of mishandling our funds, my attempts to "look good," and my addiction to pornography.

Since then we have met thousands of people, including many leaders in various walks of life, who are suffocating in the toxic wasteland of a two-faced life. Most Christians, especially Christian leaders, are committed to *giving* love. They evangelize, teach, preach, study, serve, lead, work for justice, and so forth. Using these gifts demonstrates God's grace, which is expressed in love. However, all this activity can be executed while the Christian leader, as Bill illustrated, lives in isolation, in hiding, in vacant relationships, and in unresolved life issues. This unhealthy condition occurs when the Christian learns only to give love rather than *receive* love. Most Christians rarely, if ever, experience this protective love. Yet it is absolutely essential for freedom from sin, healing from wounds, and spiritual and emotional health. In fact, this is how an *culture*

...onment of grace grows and develops among the followers of Jesus.

Reflect on Jesus' promise: "By this all men will know that you are my disciples, if you love one another" (John 13:35). What comes to mind? If you thought, *This means I must love more*, you were right. But you are also right if you thought, *This means I need to learn how I can receive more love from others*. If you didn't think that, then you missed the foundation of how to love more and better. This promise cannot function unless and until we learn to *receive* love. In God's world, receiving love comes *before* giving love. We learn how to love only when we first learn how to receive the love of God and others. "We love because he first loved us" (1 John 4:19). And that takes trust.

So, here is a core principle for learning how to receive love: *The degree to which I trust you is the degree to which I am able to receive your love, no matter how much actual love you may try to give me.* People who are unable to trust will never experience love—not ever. None of us can find a way out of that particular cul-de-sac. We have the need for love, but we are unable to receive it. Learning to let others love us on their terms is part of what it means to "submit to one another out of reverence for Christ" (Ephesians 5:21).

What does receiving love have to do with a community of grace? And how does such a community define me and teach me how to live?

A SIMPLE LAW OF COMMUNICATION

Before studying communities of grace, it is important that you know what TACT members believe about communities in general. (For this book's purposes, we'll use *community, environment,* and *culture* interchangeably. We define *community* or *culture* as "how we do things around here." We define *climate* as "how we feel about how we do things around here.")

An assumption underlies this chapter—indeed, the entire book: *Environments are more powerful than words, no matter how carefully those words are crafted.* Another way of putting this is, "Actions speak louder than words." When you say you believe something but act as if you don't, other people see the inconsistency. They don't believe you. Another variation of this law states, "What we see about a person can defeat the words we hear from him." Words are powerful for building up or tearing down. But we only believe what we actually experience in the community (how people treat one another). This is more than what they say.

What are the implications of this law for spiritual formation? Ponder this. If you attend a church, what is the most carefully crafted message of your week? Probably the weekly teaching session. So, our law of communication says that over time, sermon truth will lose out to environmental truth *when* the two conflict. Therefore, if your church eloquently teaches forgiveness, yet your environment is critical, blaming, and cynical, church members learn alienation rather than reconciliation. The obvious implication for all of us is to ensure that our church environments align and conform to, rather than conflict with, our well-intentioned messages. In either case, a community of grace or a community of ungrace will shape (or misshape) Christians—even more than words.

YOUR BLOOD AND YOUR EMOTIONS

This law of communication is not the only reason an environment is more powerful than words. From a scientific perspective, God designed the emotional centers of the human brain to work in what are called open loops. A closed-loop system, such as the circulatory system, is self-regulating, which is why what's happening in the circulatory system of others around you doesn't affect your own system. But the emotional system doesn't work that way. It is an open-loop system that depends largely on external sources to maintain health. For example, American Medical Association surveys show that "cardiac care units where the nurses' general mood was 'depressed' had a death rate among patients four times higher than on comparable units."[1] So, choose your cardiac care unit for the health of its relational and emotional community! And make this a nonnegotiable criterion in your church selection as well.

When you walk into some churches, you can feel freedom, joy, and safety before anyone has spoken to you—it's an atmosphere. You can also sense intimidation, fear, or power in a room. Environments are determinative for either good or evil, growth or degradation. Therefore, it not only matters what we as parents, presidents, and pastors say and do, but *how* we do what we do in community. A healthy community is determinative for security, trust, integrity, freedom, creativity, maturity, joy, and even physical safety. In other words, community drives forma-tion—either positively or negatively. As Dr. Daniel Goleman pointed out, we count on connections with other people for our own emotional stability and growth.[2] Healthy spiritual formation happens only in a communal context. Now, let's define grace from that community or environmental perspective.

GRACE IS A COMMUNITY YOU ENTER

The axiom that environments are more powerful than words (when the two differ) helps us pay attention to a principle of grace that is seldom taught: *Grace is a community you enter.* If this truth were obvious to the majority of Christians, they'd be looking for a door—an entrance to this realm. But since for most people grace is primarily an experience of salvation or a doctrine to be learned, it is pointless to search for a way into such an environment.

Grace has been buried under the rubble of misunderstanding. Grace is one of the most overused and abused terms in the world. Many of us understand grace as a theological position. And it is delightfully that. Undeserved, unending, unearned, unwavering grace is God's inexhaust-ible love and absolute acceptance of us, coupled with His unabashed delight in us. Grace brings us wholehearted adoption into God's family and a new identity, new life, new power, new capacity, and God's full protection.

GRACE: A PLACE WHERE GOD LIVES

But grace is much more than a theological position. Grace extends a long way beyond the means of our salvation; grace is the very basis for our maturing and our life together. Grace is a realm, a present-tense reality that weaves around and through every moment of even our worst day. God's gift of grace continuously and always surrounds us.

We have seen thousands of people experience a new quality of life, healing of wounds, reconciled relationships, and the joy of living out God's dreams for their lives simply because they have entered into and experienced over time this realm of grace. Many have told us it is their "Narnia experience." This environment powerfully informs us about the Trinity and forms us into the likeness of Christ (see Hebrews 4; Colossians 1).

God is not sitting on a throne made out of grace. The Trinity actually lives, loves, and leads together *in a realm* of grace, a community of grace where truth and trust are flowing in relationship (see Hebrews 4; John 17:20-24). Hebrews 4:16 is God's way of inviting His children to love and lead from within that same environment. The Christian faith is a faith of relationship, and the environment of grace is where we learn what those relationships are like. It all starts and ends here. How amazing that the Trinity has invited *us* into their presence, *their community*!

THE CENTERPIECE OF THIS COMMUNITY IS JESUS

Jesus came to us full of grace and truth. By faith, we gain access through Jesus into this grace (see Romans 5:1-2). His sacrifice made possible our entry into this mind-boggling place of grace, this holy of holies. Paul said, "You know the grace of our Lord Jesus Christ, that though he was rich, yet for your sakes he became poor, so that you through his poverty might become rich" (2 Corinthians 8:9). He is the centerpiece of this community of grace, and He invites us in. Jesus is our Vision, our Inviter, our Savior.

Yet many Christians desperately and incessantly strive to prove to Jesus that they deserve to be close to Him, not stuck in some corner far away from Him. Some don't believe they're good enough for this realm, this holy of holies. They know God loves them and wants to be with them, but they also believe their sin has put an impossible mass between God and them.

We used to believe the very same things. We knew that Jesus made a way for us to one day be together in heaven, but we thought, *Right now — until we get better, do better, or start to take things seriously — we'll have to settle for rare moments of intimacy with Him.* We, too, used to live in hiding because we looked at ourselves this way; we lived two-faced lives. We knew ourselves too well, and there was no way we were ever going to keep from sinning. We believed God loved us, but we also knew He was pretty disappointed in us. We expected to see Him someday but for now were separated from Jesus by this mass of sin. We could only hope that some days we would feel His touch in our lives. We realized that was as good as it gets on this earth. Or so we came to believe.

Imagine our amazement, our utter shock, when we finally understood that Jesus actually loves us and never leaves us! That our sin does not stand between Jesus and us. That Jesus, who is the centerpiece of this realm of grace, actually walks around our sin, stands with His arm around us, with our sin in front of us, and gives us His perspective on our sin. He never leaves. Well, this changes everything!

To many, this truth of Jesus standing with us sounds presumptuous, even careless. Imagining God with His arm around *me*, as we view my sin together? Come on! Surely they've written it down wrong. I've always been told that my sin is still a barrier between God and me. If it could be true that God actually stands with me, in front of my sin, well, that intimacy would change everything. If it is true, God has never moved away from me no matter what I've done! And I'd have to rethink everything.[3]

As Christians, we realize we were born with zero capacity to save ourselves. So, we trusted a Savior. Jesus died for *every* sin because we could not deal with *any* sin. But somehow, after we became Christians, many of us imagined that we gained some special capacity to manage our own sin, to somehow put it in its place. How incredibly naive and arrogant!

This sin-management theology comes with another significant problem: It sets us up to fail and live in hiddenness. It disregards the godliness—righteousness—that God has already placed in us, at infinite cost (see Ephesians 1:3-14), and will sabotage our journey. Once we choose this path, the bondage of performance persistently badgers us. Sin-management theology reduces godliness to this formula:

More right behavior + Less wrong behavior = Godliness

The apostle Paul tried to help us think our way out of this trap:

> Have some of you noticed that we are not yet perfect? (No great surprise, right?) And are you ready to make the accusation that since people like me, who go through Christ in order to get things right with God, aren't perfectly virtuous, Christ must therefore be an accessory to sin? The accusation is frivolous. If I was "trying to be good," I would be rebuilding the same old barn that I tore down. I would be acting as a charlatan. (Galatians 2:17-18, MSG)

So, how do you enter this realm? How do you experience the Jesus who never leaves and always has His arm around you? What is the key to entry?

THE KEY TO ENTERING THE COMMUNITY IS HUMILITY

First Peter 5:5, James 4:6, and other Scriptures show us the door to the realm of grace. God generously gives grace to a certain kind of person: a humble person. He resists another kind of person: a proud person. These verses and others like it imply that while I cannot earn grace, I can grace. While grace is always unmerited, it is not always uninvited because humility attracts God's grace. The key for entering God's community of grace is humility.

This is not the pretend humility of pseudospiritual relationships where I act like I am less than who I really am. Neither is this the humility that causes me to imagine in my own mind that I am humble, when everyone around me knows differently. Such humility is misnamed and worse than useless for it keeps me spiritually malformed.

Biblical humility is noticeable. You can tell when someone has humility and when he or she doesn't. You don't have to say foolish things like, "As soon as you claim to have humility, you lose it." No, humility is simply trusting God and others with me. If you encounter a definition of humility without the concept of healthy interdependency, the idea of trusting others, you have found a definition that is inadequate, does not function, and does not reflect the community of the Trinity. Humility is not only how you enter this community, it is how you live in it every day.

Humility is trusting God and others with me. This is perhaps the most basic of all spiritual disciplines. We gained initial entry into the environment of grace by trusting God. Now, we live our lives in God by trusting Him. When you trust God and others, you attract God's grace, which is where divine power resides. It is the power of *His* grace (see Romans 5:20; 11:6). Therefore, if you ever hope to routinely nurture a community of grace in which you can live and work, you must learn to trust others with yourself.

Humility is not codependency. But humility spawns an interdependency where those in the community routinely say, "I need others to get healthy. Without others I cannot get well, I cannot mature. And I can do all of this without losing my identity and unique temperament; in fact, it is in this community that my personality and strengths can reach their full expression."

In our own relationships and community, we are continually learning this basic truth. It is messy, inefficient, and wonderful. Bill is strong but grows passive if he feels devalued by Bruce. Bruce is strong but grows controlling if he feels overpowered by Bill. We are both type As who have given up on drivenness, controlling life, and being right. We know that neither of us can resolve our life issues or mature spiritually without trusting others with ourselves. In our community we are on a lifelong pursuit of trusting others with how they see our weaknesses and limitations. We let them protect us from what we are unable to see or be. Sometimes we do it well and sometimes we mess it up, but we know this is the bedrock of a community of grace. We are not going back to the old ways. As the descriptor states, "Communities of grace open the door to gaining permission to share truth among fellow believers." We are back to the principle of *receiving* love, which we learned about with Bill and Grace in the first story. In the community of grace, I cannot receive love apart from humility. And without experiencing love I cannot get healthy.

All environments contain particles that produce the unique quality of that environment. Sunny and snowy days differ because of the contrasting parts in their environments. Humility is the first and most important particle in a community of grace because, more than any other, humility is both the way into and the means for living in the community.

THE COMMUNITY OF GRACE TEACHES ME WHO I AM

Ever since we were young, how we see ourselves has been shaped by our environments and circumstances — some mild, others dramatic. The following traumatic event occurred in the life of our coeditor, Marion Skeete. Think about how this story would affect how you see yourself.

Tires screeched loudly as two white armed troopers jumped out of their vehicle and surrounded our tiny Chevy Camaro, ordering all of us to put our hands on the dashboard. Their guns were drawn and aimed at our temples. Twenty-four-year-old Lincoln, my thirteen-year-old brother Sean, and me, as a black woman, were about to receive a lesson in the cruel stereotype, where society had confined me to a caste system with the label "double minority."

One of the officers grabbed Lincoln out of the car and began to frisk him violently. I prayed, "Lord, please don't let them kill my brother!" When the trooper could no longer get the answers he wanted from Lincoln, he dragged him to the cruiser, as the other trooper guarded Sean and me. Sweat beaded this officer's face, and his hands shook with fear. In fact, that moment was so intense as we stared at each other in silence that it was only the grace of God that he didn't pull the trigger, if just to get some relief. A few minutes later, this near-death trauma was over. A case of "mistaken identity."[4]

When someone experiences an event this shocking and distressing, where the person realizes the color of his or her skin led to a case of "mistaken identity" and near-death, how does that person adopt another "true" identity? Marion Skeete, now a pastor in an influential church, lives with a new identity because she knows the power of living in an environment of grace. Humility says to God, "I trust who You say I am." The formation of a community of grace always starts with trusting others, and the first among others is always God.

TRUSTING YOUR CIRCUMSTANCES

Most Christians live out of their "mistaken identity," not out of who God says they are. So they feel the need to create an identity by *trying to live out of who they think they should become.* They strive to reform themselves. They attempt to identify themselves by their periodic successes in spiritual formation, even though those are usually less than hoped for. Generally, they trust their assessment that they have failed God, which triggers a belief that He is disappointed with and condemning of them. That leads to mask wearing in the community. Still others in the community cannot bear the thought of their own failure, so they deceive themselves into believing that their own efforts have brought them into a state of astonishing spirituality. Either of these false extremes gradually becomes a "mistaken identity." This theological root cannot produce the fruit of authenticity; it can only yield hiddenness.

Complicating this situation, many live in environments that reinforce the erroneous message that they are fairly lame Christians, sinners hoping to do better, failures hoping to one day earn God's acceptance. Their family environments or church cultures cause these Christians to actually believe and live by this message, even if their church pulpit declares that they are righteous. (Remember, environments are more powerful than words.)

When Christians see themselves as "sinners saved by grace," they have no choice but to live life as sinners, strenuously striving to become saints. Naturally, this effort leads to failure because we're not in charge of our sainthood. Our sainthood has already been accomplished by our loving Savior, Jesus Christ. Therefore, when Christians are able to see themselves as "saints who sin," as Christ-in-me creatures, as clothed with robes of righteousness, they have the only basis to grow up into what is already true of them. God says we are righteous, and this becomes the context or the condition that allows Christ to dwell in us. If my vision of what I can become is based on my vision of who Jesus says I already am—righteous—I can relax and mature into something I already am. When we trust God (remember humility?), our self-identity builds on His assessment, not ours—on His righteousness, not our own "righteousness."

BUTTERFLY THEOLOGY

Sometimes when we lose our grip on who God has made us to be, we must remember the butterfly. Nature provides many examples of this incredible discrepancy between who we appear to be and who we truly are. Consider the caterpillar. If we brought a caterpillar to a biologist and asked him to analyze it and describe its DNA, he would tell us, "I know this looks like a caterpillar to you, but scientifically, according ry test including DNA, this is fully and completely a butterfly." Wow! God has wired into a creature that looks nothing like a butterfly a perfectly complete butterfly identity. And because the caterpillar is a butterfly in essence, it will one day display the behavior and attributes of a butterfly. The caterpillar matures into what is already true about it. In the meantime, berating the caterpillar for not being more like a butterfly is not only futile, it will probably hurt his tiny ears!

So it is with us. God has given us the DNA of godliness. We are saints — righteous. Nothing we could do will make us more righteous than we already are. Nothing we could do will alter this reality. He knows that we are "Christ in me." And now He is asking us to join Him in what He knows is true.

FLIPPING FOUNDATIONS IN SPIRITUAL TRANSFORMATION

We are arriving at a very crucial formation juncture, so we will linger longest in this section. Many of us have spent too much of our lives serving God while embracing a theology of "rebuilding the same old barn" as it says in Galatians 2:17-18 (MSG). We have placed all our efforts in "trying to be good." Yet we are broken, defeated, lonely, and despairing. By contrast, the theology of grace invites us into a community where our worldview (how we see ourselves and others) and our sin-view (where we see sin residing and how sin is handled) change the foundations of how we are formed into Christlikeness.

In this life, we who have trusted Christ will always have these two constants: our sin issues and our new identity. They are unchanging realities. They are pictured with these two lines below.

Working on My Sin Issues

Trusting Who God Says I Am

Here's a key question: Which one of these two constants defines your life focus? Which line do you start with to get to the other line? Which line offers you the hope of experiencing the other? If you opt for the top line, you will never experience the bottom line. But if you start with the bottom line, you will experience unparalleled transformation regarding your sin issues in the top line.

It's a whole new way of seeing, not unlike those unusual pictures that were popular a few years ago. At first glance you just saw patterns. Yet, if you squinted and looked "through" the picture, you eventually saw shapes in three dimensions, revealing a beautiful and astounding picture. The first time you broke through to see such images was truly a remarkable moment. It is the same with seeing all the way through the patterns of our sin issues into the beautiful and astounding reality of who God says we are. Suddenly life is in three dimensions—alive, rich, and full of hope.

Too few Christian leaders understand this truth because, like numerous biblical truths, it is counterintuitive. It appears that if you were really serious about your sin issues, you'd start on the top line, working on them with all the sold-out commitment possible so you could become godly. Actually, the opposite is true. As TACT authors, we understand the critical role of intentionality in our spiritual formation. As the apostle Paul indicated in Colossians 1:29, grace is not devoid of effort. However, our intentionality does not reform us into more righteous people. Rather, we intentionally trust that God is right when He says we are righteous, and we intentionally trust Him for direction to mature into what is already true—that righteous identity, which is our new heart. This is the basis for our becoming like Christ.

Here's an example of how this works. About two years ago, someone deeply offended me (Bruce), damaging friendships and reputation and causing a loss of funds, among others things. At that point, I had a choice: forgive or not forgive. If I decided to forgive, I had another choice: to *will myself* into forgiving because I'm supposed to or to *trust the vision* and counsel of Jesus, rest in His wisdom, and let Him determine the outcomes. Remember, Jesus is standing with me whenever I sin or am sinned against. Even if I decided not to forgive, Jesus stayed with me through all my resentment and bitterness. Jesus was close enough for me to hear Him say, "If you ask Me—and I hope you do—you will forgive this person as I have forgiven you. Trust Me with this advice, and I'll heal you, restore you, and free you with the truth it brings to you." Since I trusted Jesus, I forgave. This did not come from willpower, which for me is like no-power, but out of trust. Notice how trusting Him fulfills the command "put to death the deeds of the body" (Romans 8:13, NKJV). Thus, I participated in God forming me. Yet even before I decided to forgive, Jesus was still standing with His arm around me. Because I chose to forgive, I've experienced genuine freedom from any residual bitterness.

This new heart also creates an intentionality that is about living for the sake of others. It becomes an intentional mind-set that will profoundly stimulate our awareness of and openness to our life issues. When we believe that love covers a multitude of sins in a community of grace, we invite others to love us by protecting this new heart in us. We no longer need to hide. When we misplace our intentionality in trying to manage our sin, we remain bound in our sin issues.

Therefore, when you start from the top line, your faith becomes a law-driven effort. Launch from the bottom line (the line of trust), and you experience grace. The top line depends on your power, while the bottom line depends on God's power. It's self-effort versus God's effort.

Going from the top line down, you attempt to become your own savior. But moving from the bottom line up, you invite Jesus to be your Savior. (Remember, you became a Christian in the first place by finally admitting you couldn't do anything about your sin. We can do nothing—absolutely nothing—to make provision for our sin.) Do you think you're going to please God by first proving through your behavior how much you love Him? He knows better. You will not please Him that way because it devalues His greatest gift to you—His Son, the Savior. He wants you to trust Him first (bottom line); then you'll please Him (top line). Therefore, He says, "without faith [the noun form of the verb 'to trust'] it is impossible to please God" (Hebrews 11:6).

If you start with the top line so you can become more godly, you will get hopelessly tangled up in trying to sin less. That's attempted sin management. Welcome to failure. It's like rearranging the deck chairs on the *Titanic* so you can get a better view as the ship goes down. A sin-management system shuts off the only resource that can deal with sin: our trust in who God says we are, a trust that attracts the power of His grace. But if you launch from a place of trusting who God says you are, you'll replace your sin management with Christ's sin atonement. You will love more and sin less. If you try to work on your sin issues (top line) so you can become godly, you will end in hiddenness. But if you trust who God says you are so together you and God can address your sin issues, you will become openly authentic in your faith.

Entry into a community of grace will require that despite these risks, despite your circumstances, despite who society may say you are, you trust God's declaration of who you are. You are righteous in Christ. While no one else in society may affirm or clarify your identity, those in a community of grace will affirm who God has already made you to be.

Will others meet our needs perfectly and will we trust perfectly? No. But in this new community, "Grace is the face love wears, when it meets imperfection."[5] Learning to love perfectly or trust perfectly is not the point; rather, it's learning to receive love. We can't wait for perfect people before we trust one another with ourselves or we'll wait until we get to heaven.

At this point, you may be wondering if you really want to enter the community of grace. If you're like us, you will be conflicted, weighing a deep desire to enter this amazing community against your concern that it may make you too vulnerable or cost you too much. As Dietrich Bonhoeffer proclaimed: Grace is free, but it is not cheap. If you're like us, you will simultaneously want to know more of God's grace while fearing that it might let you down. But once you experience this life for very long, you will never want to go back.

If it is unerringly true that each of us enjoys only the love we will allow in, and if it is equally true that God went to unending lengths to bring us love in a way that we would allow in, then it becomes stunningly obvious that the carriers of God's love ought to be wildly driven to learn to give His love in a way that can be easily put on.

HOW A COMMUNITY OF GRACE FORMS ME

How shall we describe the way a grace-filled community works, especially if it is a world away from where most of us live? The task is a little like Peter and Susan trying to describe Narnia to their London family. The sights and sounds and places and customs of this new world are almost completely different. Here is a summary of what we've attempted to describe in the preceding paragraphs about *how* a community of grace forms me.

First, trusting God and others with me (humility) is the starting block for my sanctification, just as it is the starting block of my justification. Such trust grows, wanes, and thrives again. It's a fluid experience in my life, where there is no end point. I trusted God instead of my own solutions when I first met Jesus, and this life in Christ is no different. When I trust Him instead of trusting my self-assessments or my shame-driven inner self-story, I actually begin to trust that what God says about me is *more accurate* than what I say about me. And because I trust a perfect God, I can afford to trust some imperfect others in my life.

The reason many people fail to realize how powerful *trusting others* is in forming them spiritually is that they have always lived in an environment of moralism with its exhortations to be better, to buck up. That environment does not highly value humility. Humility may be a topic addressed in their community, but their greater values are knowledge, competency, and trying harder. Notice, then, that there are two contrasting cultures resulting from two conflicting value systems: humility versus competence or trusting versus pleasing.

People who have lived many years in such good-intentions environments will be quizzical about the power of humility because they have not experienced humility—trusting God and others with me—in ongoing relationships. They talk about humility, certainly, but they'll continue to say, "Tell me the next thing; tell me what to do." This is their "how." But, a community of grace is driven by trust, not primarily by a moralistic "ought."

Second, when my failures become particularly acute, I get the opportunity to be loved in real time by others who actually treat me accurately—as a righteous saint who sins. This changes everything! Recall that such a relationship of trust in an environment of grace is more powerful than words. This environment of grace relaxes me. This love from others reminds me of who I am in the middle of the failure. *If* I trust this love, it tells me that I am actually "Christ in me" right now on my worst day. This environment also contains relationships in which I invite others—I give access to others—to talk with me about my weaknesses, my flaws, my sin. Yet, since this community of grace no longer measures righteousness by how much or how little I sin but by how well we experience love, people stand with their arms around me, even when I need to repent or forgive or seek reconciliation. They don't wink at sin, but they know love can handle sin and they help me trust God's grace as I learn to repent or forgive or as we together experience reconciliation.

Other people in this environment of grace are no longer using a measuring stick that fixates on my sin or fastens on my futile moralistic attempts to be better. Their love is freeing me, and I am sinning less. I discover that attempting to sin less doesn't guarantee that I will love more, but loving others will definitely result in less sinning. A major reason this is true is that when I experience the love of others because I trust them, this action actually diminishes the power of my shame, which drives my sinning. Only grace through love can overcome my shame. When I let others remind me that I have a shame-free identity, I heal, I grow, I mature. The Holy Spirit's counsel and encouragement to me is better trusted in this safe place, and His fruit, primarily love, is being produced in me.

Third, trusting others, according to 1 Peter 5, attracts God's grace. There is much more grace in a community where humility is prized, because humility attracts God's grace. Grace is formative because it nurtures safe places for our relationships, which are superior environments in which to experience love, submit to truth, and trust each other's guidance. Such grace is both practical — or logical and understandable — and mysterious. There is actually a "how" in the way grace matures me into the person I already am. I am being reoriented by the grace of God, which God gives me in response to my humility. I am *in community* being formed into the image of Jesus.

THE COMMUNITY OF GRACE IS NATURALLY MISSIONAL AND ATTRACTIONAL

Thousands who are spiritually searching keep a safe distance from Christians. Paradoxical, isn't it? Many seekers consider numerous Christian enclaves, such as churches, organizations, and institutions, unsafe. Further, many believe that Christians live superficial lives that don't match their broadcasted claims. Others stare right through thinly veiled evangelical masks to the weaknesses, flaws, and warts. The blemishes they can accept, but not the masks that attempt to hide them. So, they move on to something that is more authentic. Many outside the church don't like the way Christians treat one another — nor do they like the way Christians treat those who, like themselves, are not followers of Jesus. This explains why a high percentage of teens who grow up in churches leave those communities after they graduate from high school. Beyond the lack of authenticity, many feel as if they are "projects" of the Christians; they're not treated with the honor and dignity of a genuine relationship. Those approaches don't attract. The community of grace is designed by God to innately resolve such roadblocks to mission.

Millions of North Americans long for authenticity. If you travel to other continents, you know this yearning holds true there as well. People everywhere want what is real. Everyone craves being known, being loved, being who they really are. When we realize we are designed in the image of God, such relational longings follow.

ATTRACTIONAL COMMUNITIES

Grace is always missional, and in a missional community of grace, attraction trumps everything. Communities of grace are unavoidably attractional because they are authentic, generous, and freeing (see 2 Corinthians 8–9). Attraction inevitably flows from such qualities. Institutional churches bias toward becoming programmatic. Communities of grace move naturally and continuously in relationship among seeking people. Not surprisingly, seekers are drawn to the authenticity and love of those carrying the message. In other words, *if you are being formed in Christ, mission will take care of itself.* Too few people understand that transformation organically leads one to care for others. A transformational community is missional. Recall this as you read chapter 7.

First Peter 5 says that God gives us grace so that at just the right time He can lift us up, expand our influence, and show us our destiny. This is true personally and corporately. God's ultimate goal in the community of grace is to release the mature into the dreams He designed for them before the world began. Those dreams will always involve serving people generously, creatively, and sacrificially in relationship. The servant is like his Master, and Jesus did not come to be served, but to serve (see Matthew 20:28; Mark 10:45). If you experience the grace of our Lord Jesus in your environment, you will enjoy fresh and unexpected mission flowing from your life.

CUSTOMIZED DESTINY

One of the most beautiful aspects of a functioning community of grace is that you personally get to enjoy your custom-fit destiny. Communities of grace are diverse because they honor the dignity of each individual. In such a culture we learn how to submit to one another's strengths while protecting each other's weaknesses.[6] In such a place, you luxuriate in the form-fitted service that God has planned for you before the world began.

Throughout this chapter, we've been painting a picture of the broken, fragile, unusable, and even the competently miserable coming to the end of their striving and growing into maturity in a community of grace. God's goal for us is never just about healing, safety, rest, or even receiving love, as astounding as those gifts are. His goal is that we be released into the dreams we've not been able to shake all of our lives. As our key element concludes, "Communities of grace and trust open the door to gaining permission to share truth among fellow believers and the unbelieving world." Such communities prepare you for the unspeakable days of release, because in this community you are in the process not of becoming someone who is essentially different, but of maturing into the saint God has already made you to be.

FOR REFLECTION AND DISCUSSION

1. Reflect on the various communities you have been a part of during your life. Where have you experienced an environment of grace and truth? What was it that engendered grace and truth in those environments? What communities have you experienced damage in? What was it about those communities that caused damage?

2. How does the way Jesus sees you and others affect the expectation of what it means to be formed in Christ?

3. If you had to write a prayer that indicated who you are now in Jesus and who you will be in the coming fullness of the kingdom, what would you say? What differences should there be between our destiny in Christ and our present experience of it?

4. How does a community of grace help people trapped in sin to move toward holiness?

5. What do you see as the greatest challenge of forming and cultivating your ministry into a community of grace and truth? If it is, in truth, a community where Jesus dwells, why would some people prefer individuality and autonomy?

FOR FURTHER READING

Alcorn, Randy. *The Grace and Truth Paradox: Responding with Christlike Balance.* Sisters, OR: Multnomah, 2003. (This is a very accessible book on the grace and truth dialogue.)

Demarest, Bruce, and James R. Beck. *The Human Person in Theology and Psychology: A Biblical Anthropology for the Twenty-first Century.* Grand Rapids, MI: Kregal, 2005.

Thrall, Bill, Bruce McNicol, and John Lynch. *TrueFaced: Trust God and Others with Who You Really Are.* Colorado Springs, CO: NavPress, 2004.

Thrall, Bill, Bruce McNicol, and Ken McElrath. *The Ascent of a Leader: How Ordinary Relationships Develop Extraordinary Character and Influence.* San Francisco: Jossey-Bass, 1999.

Chapter 3

THE
TRANSFORMATIONAL
PROCESS

Keith J. Matthews

ELEMENT 3: Spiritual formation into Christlikeness involves an intentional public, personal, and communal commitment to living as Jesus' disciples who are being transformed into His image in all aspects of our lives as we learn to obey His commands.

Description: Discipleship to Jesus Christ is a transformational process that begins with regenerated life as a person becomes Jesus' disciple, identifies with the community of faith, and engages in a purposeful pattern of life in which he or she learns to obey all that He commanded (see Titus 3:3-7). Transformation continues as the disciple intentionally pursues being conformed to Jesus' image, which is carried out in our everyday world of personal, public, community, and family life (see 2 Corinthians 3:17-18; Ephesians 5:21–6:9). As we align our lives with Jesus' example and commit ourselves to the purposeful pattern of life in which we learn to obey all that He commanded, all aspects of our lives are brought into conformity to Christ (see Matthew 28:20; Romans 8:29).

✿ ✿ ✿

THE SUMMER OF '72

I can still remember with great clarity the summer I became a follower of Jesus. In Southern California, in the early 1970s, the Jesus movement was in full swing. Although I was a disinterested young church attendee (pulled along by my parents!), I had no real understanding of engaging in a relationship with God (presenting the gospel clearly was not a part of my particular liberal mainline congregation). It took an unchurched friend of mine who had come to Christ to make me think more deeply about Jesus and His message. I just couldn't deny the change in my good friend. At the beginning of the summer, he decided to live with his dad for a few months (he was from a divorced family), and he returned at the end of the summer with a whole new demeanor and outlook on life. Something clearly had taken hold of him in a profound and life-changing way. And how I wanted what he seemed to possess! He was filled with a visible sense of joy and peace, a hunger for Scripture, and, most notably, a passion for Jesus. At first, I was suspect: What can this unchurched friend tell me about Jesus? After all, I was the churchgoer! Yet, as time went by, I could tell that his experience was more than a passing fad in his life. This Jesus really did change my friend! So, what was I to do? How was I to connect with this person named Jesus Christ?

The pattern for becoming a Christian in those days seemed so simple and clear. "Accept Jesus. Read the Bible. And go to church." Or, (A)ccept Christ. (B)elieve He died for you. And (C)ommit your life to Jesus. This would get me started. And it did! My life *really* changed that summer of 1972. I, too, could say, as the popular bumper sticker, "I'm a Christian who is not perfect, just forgiven." I truly experienced a joy and peace that was powerful and exhilarating. Forgiveness was mine and an eternity with Christ as well!

And yet I can say at age fifty, my Christian life has not necessarily been an upward, linear path toward heaven. Over the past thirty-six years since my decision to follow Jesus, I've experienced many highs, numerous lows, a few setbacks, some blind alleys, defeats as well as victories, pain and progress, some unexpected detours, and, more often than not, more questions than I've had answers for.

The decision to follow Jesus led me into the vocation of pastoral ministry for more than twenty years, where I had the privilege to witness countless individuals follow Christ and enter the same kind of spiritual journey. In the lives of many, the vibrancy of following Jesus still remains intact, yet for others, for numerous reasons, the will to stay on the path with Christ has been lost. Now, as a professor teaching the next generation of pastors about the importance of their calling, I have real concerns about the simplistic formula found in a "conversion-centered gospel" appeal, which is so prevalent in the evangelical church today.

At this vantage point in my life, I face some key questions that need reviewing. Perhaps the most crucial one is: What does it really mean to be a follower of Jesus in the complex world in which we now live? And is the gospel just about forgiveness, so I can go to heaven? Or is it really about something bigger? Is transformation into Christlikeness possible in this life? If so, how does it really work? How can I tell if I'm making progress? What is my role in the growth process? And what about God's role? What's the church's role? These questions seem so relevant today, but they weren't even on the radar screen in the seventies. The primary goal back then was evangelism, because supposedly we were in the "Last Days" (this central teaching pervaded everything!). We needed to get people saved since the world was coming to an end and Jesus was coming back. We needed to make Christians quickly. Time was of the essence; Christ was returning soooooooooooooon! Discussions on discipleship or spiritual formation were few and far between. That was a secondary issue to our conversion-centered gospel. People needed to be saved! Certainly, this made sense . . . back then! But what does it mean for us now? That's what we are trying to understand in this chapter.

So, here's the million-dollar question: Does a conversion-centered gospel approach really produce a lifelong transformed disciple of Jesus? The statistical answer is "No!" at least not according to the pollsters. According to Gallup polls, it has been said that up to 40 percent of Americans have had a "born-again" experience, yet the transformative aspects of what that means in "real life," such as marriage and divorce or personal ethics and morality, reveal no discernable difference between Christians and the rest of the population. *But* before we run too quickly to our indictments, let's take a closer look at what might be missing in a conversion-centered gospel.

THE MODERN GOSPEL: CONVERTS VERSUS DISCIPLES

As has been said in chapter 1, the gospel Jesus preached is the gospel of the kingdom of God, offering the present availability and access to a life in God *now*! This invitation has always been in view from the beginning of time, but now it's made accessible *to all* in the person and message of Jesus Himself. This gospel of the kingdom *is* the gospel. Yet, as others in this book point out, it seems to me that we have substituted a reduced gospel that focuses solely on "forgiveness of sins and the assurance of heaven" as our present gospel appeal. But here's the most obvious problem: This conversion-centered approach to the gospel has for many people been interpreted as a finish line or an ending, instead of a starting line or new beginning. This understanding has *huge* implications for how we live life now! If being forgiven and now having heaven assured is what it means to become a Christian, anything I do from there on is an add-on. "Why talk to me about discipleship? Why do I need that? I've been forgiven. I'm already going to heaven. What more do I need to do?" But without foreseeing the consequences, this conversion-centered gospel has created a two-tiered reality for those in the evangelical church. Most people see themselves as Christians at the point of conversion, but the call to be a disciple is for many a second-level option, often reserved for the more serious Christian and notably absent from the conversion-centered gospel appeal.

Now to be fair, over the years there have always been options to help people grow in Christ. Numerous parachurch books and study guides on discipleship have been used to help many. But frankly, most of these Bible studies are about increasing knowledge of Scripture or focusing on "right beliefs" about Jesus—a worthy endeavor, but not necessarily enabling what it means to be a disciple/apprentice of Jesus.

Scripture clearly states that the entry-level follower of Jesus is called a disciple. More than 265 times the common reference to those who follow Jesus were said to be His disciples (*mathetes*) or better understood as students, apprentices, or learners. It is telling that the word *Christian* is used less than four times in the New Testament and is mostly a descriptive term used by others. As time went on, the term *Christian* became embraced by the community of faith, worn as a badge of honor for being called "little Christs."

Dallas Willard stated,

> The New Testament is a book about disciples, by disciples, and for disciples of Jesus Christ.
>
> But the point is not merely verbal. What is more important is that the kind of life we see in the earliest church is that of a special type of person. All of the assurances and benefits offered to humankind in the gospel evidently presuppose such a life and do not make realistic sense apart from it. The disciple of Jesus is not the deluxe or heavy-duty model of the Christian—especially padded, textured, streamlined, and empowered for the fast lane on the straight and narrow way. He stands on the pages of the New Testament as the first level of basic transportation in the Kingdom of God.[1]

Another problem with the conversion-centered gospel is that it has no missional appeal, meaning it doesn't propel me beyond myself. Because the conversion-centered gospel is a private individual transaction, once the prayer is said, it is complete. There is no appeal to enter into a new kind of life whereby we take on God's agenda for the world, is at the heart of the real gospel. Therefore a conversion-centered gospel is a thoroughly passive gospel. Years ago, I was a new Christian being "saved," focused solely on being rescued from my sin so I could go to heaven when I died. Yet never was I told that I was also "saved" for a purpose, to become a part of God's redemptive purposes in the world, that my salvation mattered now, and that becoming a disciple of Jesus was my process in learning from Him how to affect the redemption of the community around me as well as the world. It is no wonder the evangelical Christian world with its conversion-centered gospel has by and large produced passive masses of Christians instead of transformational, missional disciples.

When I think about the good news of Jesus, two approaches in the form of questions come to mind. There are two contrasting questions that form our shift today from making converts to making disciples. Question 1: In a conversion-centered gospel one might ask, "If you were to die tonight, would you go to heaven?" This question focuses on a crisis *event* to enact salvation. Question 2: In a disciple-centered gospel one might ask, "If you knew you were going to live forever, what kind of person would you like to become?" This second question focuses on a *process* of growing toward Christlikeness.

One question is just concerned with getting us into heaven, while the other is concerned with who I am right now. If we get the disciple-making piece right, the heaven piece is secure—not the other way around.

Illustrated below is a chart of the contrast in "Making Disciples THEN and NOW."[2]

Comparison:
Making Disciples THEN with (Most) Discipleship NOW

World of Making Disciples (THEN)	Western Discipleship (NOW)
Hebrew way—doing, action	Hellenistic way—thinking, words, ideas
More concrete	More abstract
Integrated context is understood	Most context is missing

About integration and synthesis—keeping things together	About analysis, categorization, and labels—breaking things apart
"Believe" is a verb	"Belief" is a creed—consenting to a series of propositions
Emphasis on consistent behavior	Much more of an emphasis on ideas
Community more important than the individual—sacrifice personal rights for the benefit of the community	Individual more important than the community—sacrifice community harmony for sake of personal interests
Concerned with right doing	Concerned with right thinking
Willingly submissive to rabbi's authority	Submissive to no one except myself
Submit to rabbi's interpretation	Create my own interpretation of the text
Willing to wrestle with the text for long periods of time	Preference for quick, simplistic answers through short encounters with the text
Focus on developing discernment	Lack of critical-thinking skills
Memorized Scriptures	Widespread biblical illiteracy
Live life in community	Functional lone rangers
Live integrated, holistic lives	Live in dichotomized spheres (sacred/secular, faith/work)
Desire to be a disciple	Often content to just "believe" in Jesus
Total surrender to their rabbi's interpretive authority for living	Partial, elective surrender to Jesus' authority as convenient
Nothing is hidden or off-limits to rabbinic scrutiny	Much of our lives are hidden from others
Life-issue oriented	Conceptually oriented
Dialogue intensive	Information-transfer intensive
Focused on men	Seems more women are being discipled today than men

This chart paints a startling contrast between what discipleship meant in Jesus' day and what it is in our current culture. It is no wonder people are lacking a sense of purposeful growth and dynamic faith in Christ when they don't even understand what it means to be a disciple. Now let's look at another gospel of our times and see if it produces disciples of Jesus.

THE POSTMODERN GOSPEL: GLOBAL ACTIVISTS VERSUS DISCIPLES

While the modern conversion-centered gospel has the result of making the gospel "smaller," the postmodern global-centered gospel makes it too big! This gospel rightly reacts to the modern individualistic conversion-centered gospel, which essentially focuses on me—my sin, my need for heaven . . . me . . . me . . . me.

The postmodern gospel, on the other hand, as espoused in missional or emergent churches, speaks powerfully about extending Jesus' kingdom among the masses of poor and disenfranchised people, among corrupt political structures and dehumanizing and fracturing societies, as well as healing the damaged environment of the global planet. This "big" gospel comes from a *missio Dei* theology proclaimed in the writings of people such as Lesslie Newbigin and Darrell Guder and rooted in scriptural passages like 2 Corinthians 5:19: "that God was reconciling the world to himself in Christ" and that we, too, are ministers of this reconciliation. Yet, just as a conversion-centered gospel produces passive followers of Christ, so too this activistic gospel tends to do the same. Here's why: Perhaps you are a young mom with two or three children, or a young man with a fifty-hour-a-week job, and you hear that the good news of Jesus requires you to change the world, serve the poor, help with the needs in the Sudan, and clean up the environment. You feel the need to respond. And while these issues are certainly important and deserve your efforts, the massive weight and complexity of these problems seem to crush your limited abilities to effect change. They often render men and women today powerless and passive. In effect, this postmodern gospel can be seen as too big.

In general, neither the modern nor the postmodern gospel tends to

make disciples/apprentices of Jesus, and this often leads to passi
what's the answer? The key is well-intentioned, strategic effort in following Christ. So, let's make clear what an intentional commitment to live
as a disciple of Jesus looks like for the ordinary person in the ordinary
and mundane experiences of life. The gospel must work here if it is to
work at all.

INTENTIONALITY AND SPIRITUAL FORMATION

While it is true that being born again is truly the work of God alone,
our growth in kingdom life depends significantly on our own active
participation with Christ through His grace. Dallas Willard gave us this
key truth: "God is not opposed to effort but to *earning*."[3] In other words,
we must engage in well-directed effort if we are to grow. Our growth
into Christlikess does not occur through osmosis. Of course, when we
talk about effort, we are not saying to grit your teeth and just act more
Christian or to use your own will and determination to form yourself
into behaving in a manner more acceptable to God. No! That is the way
of failure, guilt, and discouragement!

What must be understood about intentionality is that the work
of transformation is God's work in us, but we are not passive in the
process. The apostle Paul knew full well this synergistic participation
between God and us. In Philippians 2:12-13, Paul said, "Continue to
work out your salvation with fear and trembling, for it is God who works
in you to will and to act according to his good purpose." Again, in
Colossians 1:29, he said, "To this end I labor, struggling with all his
energy, which so powerfully works in me." Both of these verses affirm
the action of humanity and the action of God working simultaneously.
This is not about works righteousness but about wisdom-filled living.
Dallas Willard has a wonderful little saying that goes like this: "While
it is true that apart from Christ we can do nothing, it is also true, that
if we do nothing it will be apart from Christ." So, this idea of effort and
intentionality is a primary issue if we are to become transformed disciples of Jesus. "Becoming Christlike never occurs without intense and
well-informed action on our part," Willard said.[4]

One of the reasons some have rejected or been skeptical about our efforts in the transformation process is that they appear to minimize or eliminate the role of grace. But this argument simply misunderstands God's grace. More properly understood, grace is God's action in our lives, helping us to accomplish what we are incapable of on our own. Therefore, all our efforts are fueled by God's grace! Titus 2:11-14 echoes this truth:

> For the grace of God that brings salvation has appeared to all men. It teaches us to say "No" to ungodliness and worldly passions, and to live self-controlled, upright and godly lives in this present age, while we wait for the blessed hope — the glorious appearing of our great God and Savior, Jesus Christ, who gave himself for us to redeem us from all wickedness and to purify for himself a people that are his very own, eager to do what is good.

The grace that saves us becomes the grace that teaches us, said Paul in his letter to Titus. Clearly, grace empowers effort! Thus, grace in very real terms becomes the daily fuel for living a holy, transformed life, yet not without our effort. The New Testament gives us some clarity as to what this effort looks like. Jesus Himself used a word that embodies the call to effort or intentionality: repentance (*metanoeo*). This word is possibly the least understood and most maligned of any terms found in the Scriptures. It has often been assigned an affective quality, such as "feeling bad," "sorry," or "sad," but those terms really miss the point of Jesus' invitation. First of all, this word *repentance* is something God leaves for us to do. He will not make us repent! This action, and it *is* an action — of the mind first and the will to follow — looks like this in the context of Jesus' statement: "The kingdom of God has come near; repent, and believe in the good news" (Mark 1:15, NRSV). A paraphrase might sound like this: "Hey, everyone, the kingdom of God is in your very midst, so rethink your way of thinking about reality and take action in accordance with this invitation."

In his wonderful book *A Long Obedience in the Same Direction*, Eugene Peterson amplified our understanding of repentance:

> Repentance is not an emotion. It is not feeling sorry for your sins. It is a decision. It is deciding that you have been wrong in supposing that you could manage your own life and be your own god; it is deciding that you were wrong in thinking you had, or could get, the strength, education and training to make it on your own; it is deciding that you have been told a pack of lies about yourself and your neighbors and your world. And it is deciding that God in Jesus Christ is telling you the truth. Repentance is a realization that what God wants from you and what you want from God are not going to be achieved by doing the same old things, thinking the same old thoughts. Repentance is a decision to follow Jesus Christ and become his pilgrim in the path of peace.
>
> Repentance is the most practical of all words and the most practical of all acts. It is a feet-on-the-ground kind of word.[5]

Countless Christians throughout the ages have misunderstood this word *repentance*, putting it in the category of "feeling bad" for our sin, not knowing that this response to Christ's invitation is the doorway to life, freedom, and power to become a disciple of Jesus. As Peterson said, "[It] is the most practical of all words and the most practical of all acts." Although the root of repentance is intensely practical and primarily volitional, it also has an affective quality based in its vision. This vision is related to one's view of Christ, primarily of His goodness, love, sufficiency, and power—"God's kindness leads you toward repentance" (Romans 2:4). This vision considers deeply the offices of Christ as Lord, Savior, Teacher, and Friend. This reality grounds the disciples' confidence in Paul's powerful claim in Colossians 2:3 that the mystery of God is found in Christ, "in whom are hidden all the treasures of wisdom and knowledge." It is this kind of vision that fuels our repentance and propels us into the kingdom life that Jesus Himself is offering to us.

How sad it is when our vision of God is distorted, making Him out to be a distant taskmaster, concerned primarily with our sinfulness. Oh, how this must grieve Jesus. Our vision of Christ is the key to empowering intention, which leads us toward discipleship and the formation of Christlike character. Let's now examine the importance of discipleship.

DISCIPLESHIP AS CHRISTLIKE CHARACTER FORMATION

Dallas Willard pointed out two things that reveal the intimate tie between the gospel and the disciple: "Does the gospel we preach have a natural tendency to produce disciples or just consumers of religious goods and services? . . . What you present as gospel will determine what you present as discipleship."[6] Clearly, these two statements press us to reflect deeply on our current message about what it means to follow Jesus. If the true gospel is a discipleship-centered approach versus a conversion-centered one, then the announcement of Jesus—"The time is fulfilled, and the kingdom of God has come near; repent, and believe in the good news"—now has important data for us to ponder, especially when we consider Jesus then calling Peter and Andrew with a classic rabbinic statement, "Come, follow me . . . and I will make you fishers of men" (Matthew 4:19).

You see, this life in the kingdom, under the direct rule of God through Jesus, can only be realized if we become disciples, students, or apprentices, whereby we learn from Jesus how to live our lives in character and action, as He would live our lives if He were us. This is what it means to be a disciple. This understanding that Jesus is our Rabbi or Teacher is critical for our lifelong growth. He is more than just a Savior who saves us from our sins. He is also our daily Teacher, helping us to traverse this new life in His kingdom, which, as newborns (i.e., "born again"), we must now learn how to take on His character. So it is that discipleship to Jesus is about our transformation into His likeness, becoming like Him in character and action. In Jesus' day, students would be attached to a rabbi or teacher in order to become like him in character and action. Yet we must understand that this character trans-formation cannot and will not be done quickly, by osmosis, or through passive reception; it is formed through *time* and *experience*. This is why we must say to new disciples, "Now that you have made a decision to 'trust Jesus,' it is the *beginning* of your lifelong process of transforma-tion." Their conversion is not the end but a wonderful new start, with Jesus leading and guiding them along the way. Jesus is not only our Savior and Redeemer from sin and death, but *now*, more importantly, He is our Teacher, who will apprentice us in living life in the kingdom in our daily existence. This idea of apprenticeship is a foreign concept in our Western model of learning.

Apprenticeship is experiential learning, not just book knowledge. I can still remember my youth pastor, who was a plumber by profession, apprenticing me in the plumbing trade during my high school years. No, he didn't hand me a book to read explaining the basics of elemen-tary plumbing, but he took me with him to job sites, first asking me to watch, listen, and ask questions. Then after a few months I was given some tasks to perform that were critical to my learning. Those early tasks were simply "doing what he did," learning as his apprentice. I learned things that a book could never teach me, just by watching and learning from my expert teacher. It wasn't long before I was working alongside him, then working on my own.

This is the standard apprenticeship model that Jesus employed with His disciples. Matthew 10 gives us a portrait of the disciples' first test. Jesus sent them out two by two, asking them to do what He did and then to come back and report what happened. This same risen Jesus does the same with us today, yet we often miss the invitation.

If we humbly embrace this position as a disciple, learner, or appren-tice of Jesus, we must then arrange our lives in such a way that He is able to mold us and teach us. Next, we must learn the training tools for this type of discipleship.

DISCIPLINES ARE FOR DISCIPLES

Arranging our lives for spiritual growth is a challenging process for all Christ followers to schedule. We all live at different paces of life, within differing family situations and dynamics, on jobs with varying hours and expectations, and so on. Yet we alone have the responsibility to place ourselves before Jesus because no one will do this for us. While God molds and transforms us through the daily events of life, through trials and tribulations as well as the ongoing work of the Holy Spirit within us, there is a unique transformative action that only we can initiate. Those actions are classically called "spiritual disciplines."

In 1 Timothy 4 the apostle Paul was giving fatherly and ministry advice to his son in the faith, Timothy, and he used an odd phrase to admonish Timothy about his life. He said, "Train yourself to be godly. For physical training is of some value, but godliness has value for all things, holding promise for both the present life and the life to come" (verses 7-8).

This imagery is familiar when applied to physical training, but training or exercising toward godliness is a baffling thought for many Christians to understand. What does it mean? What does a "spiritual workout" look like? This imagery is certainly beyond what I was given as a new Christian. The only spiritual training I was instructed in was a "quiet time." It was quite simple; I was told to seek God every day through the reading of Scripture, basically reading a chapter or two each day, and to pray for God's direction, guidance, and protection. This was my personal time, outside of going to church and meeting with other Christians. If this was a part of my pattern of life, I was told that I would grow and mature as a Christian. This was good advice and helpful, and I did grow. But like any religious activity, it also had pitfalls. It wasn't long before my quiet time turned into legalism and then superstition, in which I relied on the activity itself to be my righteousness with God. When I missed my quiet time, I would feel as if I was failing God or that God might not be happy with me for my lack of devotion. I've come to learn that the correct practice of spiritual disciplines, exercises, or habits is that they are more related to wisdom than to righteousness, meaning that they don't earn any "brownie points" with God. In other words, I don't earn God's favor or blessing through the doing of a discipline. They are simply means to an end. The end: spending time before God in a particular practice, whereby I can learn to be like Him in character and action.

Before I talk about the different types of spiritual disciplines, let me clarify what a discipline is and explain the approach most often taken by Christians to live more like Jesus. A discipline is an activity within our power that enables us to accomplish what we cannot do by direct effort. For example, if I want to become skilled in a particular endeavor, such as becoming a good musician, say at playing the piano, I would never begin by trying to play a difficult musical arrangement. I don't have the knowledge or skill yet. My direct effort fails me at this point, but I can take on certain activities, such as learning scales, keystroke drills, and other helpful training exercises, that will enable me with time to play the very music I am striving to master. These disciplines are the activities within my power that enable me to achieve a skill (actually playing the music!) that could not be achieved by my initial direct effort. It must be noted that disciplines in this context are wonderful efforts that bring about accomplishments and transformation that would never occur without their use. Just think for a moment about a successful venture undertaken in your life, and see if it didn't involve some persistent disciplines to achieve its success. Literally, all the great accomplishments people make as musicians and athletes or in academics or vocational expertise come through a life of practiced discipline.

Shifting this example to the spiritual life, one can make application in this way. If we are to embody the character of Jesus, cultivating actions of love, patience, kindness, and peace, there are time-tested spiritual disciplines that, if entered into by the grace of God, can produce marked change. This is what Paul meant when he said, "Train yourself to be godly." This training is contrasted with the current WWJD (What Would Jesus Do?) approach to Christlikeness, which is essentially a "trying" model (trying versus training) of Christlikeness. Vast numbers of Christians live with guilt, failure, and futility as they practice daily this "trying" model of change, trying to be more loving, patient, or joyful or trying not to be angry, lust-filled, or greedy. Certainly we have to want to be different—we want to live and reflect Christ with our actions—but our direct efforts often fail, producing frustration and discouragement. Our trying harder seems only to drive these impulses even deeper. That is the futility of a "trying" approach to change. We must embrace a "training" approach to match our unique life situation. We can see clearly how effective this approach is when we look at many "twelve-step" programs. Those who are successful "working the program" know clearly their inner challenges and have deeply embraced individual and community disciplines, which are practiced with clarity and urgency. Many who do this experience deep transformation, but it is not through passivity or just trying harder. It has been said that the twelve steps are not just helpful statements to tell you how to live, but intentional principles on how to stay alive.

Let's look at some basic disciplines that might be used to make your intentions a reality. There are two basic categories[7] of spiritual disciplines: (1) disciplines of abstinence and (2) disciplines of engagement. In pursuing the first category, we "abstain" from something in order to place ourselves before God. With the second category, we "engage" in something in order to place ourselves before God. Here are some examples: Solitude is a primary spiritual discipline, a discipline of abstinence. When we practice solitude, we are abstaining from interaction with people, work, activity, and the like. We are literally practicing aloneness, allowing nothing but the voices inside our heads to capture our attention. Henri Nouwen described the discipline of solitude as "the furnace of transformation." He explained more fully the depths of this discipline:

> Let me try to describe in more detail the struggle as well as the encounter that takes place in this solitude.
>
> In solitude I get rid of my scaffolding: no friends to talk with, no telephone calls to make, no meetings to attend, no

music to entertain, no books to distract, just me — naked, vulnerable, weak, sinful, deprived, broken — nothing. It is in this nothingness that I have to face in my solitude, a nothingness so dreadful that everything in me wants to run to my friends, my work, and my distractions so that I can forget my nothingness and make myself believe that I am worth something. But that is not all. As soon as I decide to stay in my solitude, confusing ideas, disturbing images, wild fantasies, and weird associations jump about in my mind like monkeys in a banana tree. Anger and greed begin to show their ugly faces. I give long, hostile speeches to my enemies and dream lustful dreams in which I am wealthy, influential, and very attractive — or poor, ugly, and in need of immediate consolation. Thus I try again to run from the dark abyss of my nothingness and restore my false self in all its vainglory.

The task is to persevere in my solitude, to stay in my cell until all my seductive visitors get tired of pounding on my door and leave me alone.[8]

The beauty of the discipline of solitude that Nouwen so powerfully described is that it gives us a chance to see ourselves before God in such a way that forgiveness, repentance, renewal, and hope can then be restored within our being. It is in solitude that these insights can be seen, engaged, and renewed by the grace of God. Another primary discipline that is engaged in when practicing solitude is silence. In silence we eliminate distractions, such as music, television, and radio, and unhook from the patterns that constantly scream at us. It is in silence that we learn to hear the voice of Christ.

Another discipline of abstinence is fasting, the voluntary practice of withholding food or physical nourishment in order to receive nourishment from God Himself. This practice is often used hand in hand with a discipline of engagement, which is prayer. Prayer is the activity of asking and receiving from God through a conversational activity.

Let me focus for a moment on two key disciplines of engagement.

The discipline of study, for instance, is critical for engaging our minds on the things of God, most prominently the Scriptures, in order that we might learn more of God and His ways. Confession is another discipline of engagement in which we share with another our pain, sin, temptations, or thoughts in order to live more freely in God and receive His redemption. These are but a few of the timeless spiritual disciplines practiced in the church since the time of Christ. They are classic because they are time-tested by Christ followers in every age.

DISCIPLESHIP IN COMMUNITY

In our time especially, there is great temptation to think that one can walk this journey of discipleship alone, just "Jesus and me." This kind of "lone ranger" Christianity is a common path for many people for a variety of reasons. But this is a great deception and dangerous error, one that is reinforced by the hyperindividualism of our present-day culture.

Community is not just a contemporary buzzword or cool idea. It is grounded in the Trinitarian nature of the Godhead, the three in one (see chapter 8). God Himself exists in a loving community of Father, Son, and Holy Spirit. And we are created in the image of God. So humanity is uniquely a communal creation. We find our deepest understanding of ourselves through the interaction and mirroring we receive from one another. This mirroring is first and foremost received in our biological families, as well as spiritually through the body of Christ, the church, which is ideally represented in a local gathering. There have been numerous studies of children that prove the need for this type of community. Clearly, children who grow up in isolation, without any touch or affirmation from others, suffer great developmental damage to their souls, and they often develop behavioral and social disorders. So it is with humans in general. God designed us this way, and Jesus deeply understood this piece of our personal formation. Jesus' method of calling to Himself a community of twelve disciples was more than just His personal method for passing on His teaching. This community formation was deeply ingrained in the classic rabbinic model of training in Jesus' day.

One can't help but be amazed at the diverse and shocking variety of personalities and backgrounds that Jesus brought together in His collection of disciples, yet these were the ones who turned the world upside-down. Their diversity of backgrounds, personalities, and influences combined to make them a powerful witness to the people around them. Remember Jesus' word to them: "As I have loved you, so you must love one another. By this all men will know that you are my disciples, if you love one another" (John 13:34-35).

Even the apostle Paul, who was uniquely called by Jesus, submitted to the community of other disciples in Jerusalem. Although he experienced a private calling, he knew that this calling was to be carried out within a community of fellow disciples. Other Christian leaders make this point. Watchman Nee wrote,

Alone I cannot serve the Lord effectively, and he will spare no pains to teach me this. He will bring things to an end, allowing doors to close and leaving me ineffectively knocking my head against a wall, until I realize I need the help of the body of Christ as well as the Lord.[9]

In *The Community of the King* Howard Snyder wrote,

Once we see that the church is to be God's agent of redemption of His world, we can understand why the New Testament writers were so persistent and emphatic about the need for believers to be reconciled, to put away all bitterness and slander, to forgive one another, and to walk as Christ loved us. In the Epistles we find the repeated emphasis on restoring or maintaining authentic Christian community. Until the Kingdom of God can be demonstrated in our relationships of love with one another, we have nothing to say to an unbelieving and broken world.[10]

These are powerfully instructive words for us to hear. Authentic community, then, is the primary transforming vehicle in which Jesus

_____ is revealed and glorified in the world today — not just in our words, but primarily in our actions. The words of St. Francis were never more true, "Preach always and if necessary use words!"

While the practice of spiritual disciplines relies on our own efforts, fueled by God's grace, we practice them among people who know us deeply, flaws and all, yet love us unconditionally. Their role is not only to mirror God's grace to us but to mirror back to us our own lives. We learn from others about our own internal attitudes and actions, which are all too visible to others but we are often blind to. Through others, we learn how to love those who rub us the wrong way, hurt us, and even become our enemies. Yes, this is the only way to learn how to "bless those who curse you" and "love your enemies" (Luke 6:27-28), as Jesus said. There is much joy as well as tears along the way, both sadness and laughter. We were created for community and will spend eternity in community, joyfully working together for the living God.

JOYFUL OBEDIENCE FOR THE GOOD OF THE WORLD

As we have seen in this chapter, the goal and appeal of the conversion-centered gospel is to get individuals saved in order that they could go to heaven when they die. This appeal gives no awareness that God has an agenda in calling humanity back to Himself. Yes, God does want to save individuals, but He also has a plan to redeem the world, and we are invited to be in on this plan. Not only is obedience the highest form of worship, but it is also the primary means to changing the world.

When we look at Jesus' calling of Peter and Andrew in Matthew 4, His words have an agenda beyond just their salvation: "Follow me, and I will make you fish for people" (verse 19, NRSV). Following Jesus was less about them and more about reaching others. In the Great Commission Jesus said, "Go and *make* disciples . . . teaching them to *obey* everything I have commanded" (Matthew 28:19-20, emphasis added). A big part of being a disciple, then, is learning to obey all that He commanded.

Imagine playing football for a coach with great knowledge and experience for producing winning teams. He invites you and others to play for him, but instead of listening to the coach's game plan of how to become a winning team, you decide you will just create your own plays. Imagine further that all of the others players are calling their own plays as well. You can well assess the kind of team this might become, all because they didn't trust, obey, and implement the coach's game plan. God has a game plan, too, and our calling is not just about our salvation but becoming part of a team that finds its joy in implementing His agenda.

As you can see, following Jesus is more than passively waiting for the next life to change us. We are invited to join a plan that has been going on since before the foundations of the world. Yes, God is in the salvation business, but not as an end in itself. Eternal life, which is a present possession, begins when we become disciples of Jesus and enter His kingdom. Through this discipleship process, we will learn from Him how to live this life from above and reflect His likeness in character and action. Thus we will fulfill His agenda for the redemption of the world and bring Him glory and honor. This is the great adventure of intentionally following Jesus!

FOR REFLECTION AND DISCUSSION

1. Too often we see the work of transformation as secondary to the gospel and a distraction from our "true" calling to evangelism. How have you seen this play out in your ministry context?

2. Why does intention matter so much in the outcomes of a ministry? Spend a few minutes identifying the intentions underlying your current ministry practices.

3. What terms would you use to describe formation so that it is an extension of the grace of the gospel? What terms have you heard used that make it appear secondary or a works-based approach versus a life of grace, the difference between effort and earning?

4. Can the spiritual disciplines become an impediment to formation?

How do you invite people into the life of the disciplines so that they become life-giving and integrated into life, rather than additional tasks to check off one's to-do list?

5. In what ways can the communities that you are involved with and ministering in become formational and invitational to the full life of the gospel and its forming work?

FOR FURTHER READING

Brother Lawrence. *The Practice of the Presence of God*. New York: Bantam, Dell, Doubleday, 1996.

Foster, Richard. *Celebration of Discipline*. New York: Harper Collins, 1978.

Nouwen, Henri. *The Way of the Heart*. New York: Ballantine/Random House, 1981.

Ortberg, John. *The Life You've Always Wanted: Spiritual Disciplines for Ordinary People*. Grand Rapids, MI: Zondervan, 1997.

Willard, Dallas. *The Spirit of the Disciplines*. San Francisco: HarperOne, 1991.

Chapter Four

SPIRITUAL FORMATION FROM THE INSIDE OUT

Bill Hull

ELEMENT 4: Spiritual formation is a lifelong pursuit of being conformed to the image of Christ from the inside out and not a matter of external activity alone.

Description: Spiritual formation involves a radical internal change in which the spiritual heart directs the transformation of the entire person to reflect Jesus Christ (see Matthew 5:20; 15:18-20; Romans 6:17-19). This means developing congruency between inward transformation and external activity so that the entire person is obedient to Jesus (see Galatians 4:19; Romans 6:12-14; Ephesians 4:22-24). This kind of obedience intends to please God, not humans. Scripture extols effort but opposes forms of legalism that earn favor with God (see Matthew 6:1-18). Inside-out transformation is a lifelong process; while the outer person decays, renewal of the inner person continues throughout one's lifetime (see 2 Corinthians 4:16-18). This lifelong process requires tools and assistance in accomplishing holistic transformation into the image of Christ through every phase of life.

Jesus is the inside man. He lives in us because that is where transformation begins. But that is not where it ends. Change always shows up in the way we relate to others. This chapter is about the process of change, how it isn't a short-term experience but continues all of our lives. Its basis is the development of a spiritual heart that fosters a life of uncomplicated obedience. It is not a passive life but one of sustained effort, and it requires tools, structure, and discipline. It is also a life of suffering. For all of us, suffering is the human condition; for the Christian, it comes with following Christ. Most of all, this life calls for living in community with others. For transformation into the image of Christ to have meaning, it must seek to serve and love others. The big "so what?" of life is that in order to make a difference, we need to be different.

A young person who also is a new Christian often has a vision of his or her religious future. But often that vision is inaccurate. For example, a young Christian man often looks at older Christian men and assumes that sexual temptation will be easy to handle given a few more Bible studies and training in resistance. A prayer life will become as natural as eating or sleeping, and the desire for material things will be brought into submission. There is within the breast of most of us the idyllic hope that spiritual growth is intense for an initial period, and then the mature disciple begins to coast or float above the fray. Angelic choirs sing as the faithful follower—undistracted by thoughts of malice or a thirst for power—naturally serves Christ all his or her days. But life simply takes these naive impressions and shatters them on the hard rocks of reality.

The experienced follower of Jesus knows that his or her spiritual formation is a lifelong experience. Life continues to surprise those who live it. That is fundamental to spiritual formation, which is the focus of this chapter.

SPIRITUAL FORMATION IS LIFELONG

A recent experience forcefully confirmed for me that formation is lifelong. I had just spent four days meeting with writers, pastors, and Christian leaders in the TACT group. It is always an intense time, so

when I boarded my flight home, I didn't want to talk. I needed ~~ ~~ ~~
My seatmate was already settled into 21A, a book in hand, earphones
ready to listen to music after clearing ten thousand feet. I had my iPod
and a book. It looked good, like we could ignore each other. I made the
mistake of saying hello; he nodded his head and looked away—yes,
another good sign. He's not one of those irritating chatterboxes. There
were thunderstorms in the area; the pilot explained why our flight would
be thirty minutes longer as we would need to go around the storms.
This created some unexpected conversation between us. That is when he
asked me a question: "So, what have you been doing in Minneapolis?"
How do you explain that you have been meeting with some of the best
thinkers in the land twice a year for five years and have tried to define
what the problem is with the church. This was a challenge. I had to
condense all the nuance, debates, writing, praying, and discussions into
a simple statement: "Well, we have been wondering if there is a problem
with the church." He laughed, "I grew up a Lutheran in Iowa; I know
there is a problem!" Then he surprised me. "What did you find out?" It
took us ten meetings to define the problem I was supposed to condense
into a simple statement. This was my test: Could I tell him simply? I
drew a breath, "The problem is that many of us have been taught and
believe that we can become a Christian but not a disciple of Jesus." He
understood what I meant. "You mean, say you believe but don't act like
you believe." It almost took my breath away. He really got it. "What is
the solution?" he asked.

If there is anything harder than diagnosis, it is prognosis. I answered,
"The solution is to rearrange our lives around the practices of Jesus so we
will become authentic followers." Then he wanted to know how we were
going to go about implementing the solution. He had now gone further
in ten minutes than our group had in five years. In years past I would
have whipped out my trusty Four Spiritual Laws tract and proceeded
to win him to Christ. But God had been doing so much in me that I
wanted simply to step into the doorway my seatmate offered. I heard
myself saying something that I would have never allowed myself to say
before: "I have spent a lot of my life trying to make things happen and

trying to get the people around me to do what they didn't want to do or didn't have the character to do. I've decided to stop trying to change the world. I've even stopped trying to change the church. People seem to get so angry. I have decided to focus on changing me. I've hit a lot of walls in my life and have hurt a lot of people. I'm finished with that. I just want people to be attracted to Christ because of who I am and what I have to say and the way I say it."

He turned away from me and looked out the window. He became very quiet. I saw his face tighten, his skin redden, and his shoulders slump, and he swallowed hard. He began to cry. Then he began to weep. I didn't know what to do, so I quietly waited. We began to discuss the many walls he had hit, and he found new hope that day in the gospel. It was a gospel that came to him with humility and authenticity. I do believe that young man had not heard the spirit of the gospel until then. And it was because of my own personal ongoing transformation. Our transformation becomes the vehicle through which we deliver the gospel. If it is fresh and current, then it will punch through the wall(s) between people and knock down the barriers and defenses that the Enemy constructs to keep it from those who need it.

Apart from my own experience, there are two things that explain why spiritual formation is a long-term process. The first is the natural need for it, given the length and changing conditions of human life. The very idea of becoming like Christ is strictly impossible in that no mortal is called to become a deity. But we will put on immortality, and we will become like Him in the resurrection (see 1 Corinthians 15:51-58). The "becoming like Christ" called for here is the degree to which a mortal filled with God's Spirit can become like Christ in character and conduct. One only needs to read the fruit of the Spirit to realize that the pursuit of such character is a lifelong process (see Galatians 5:22-23). Events and circumstances become the fuel for the serious disciple's transformation. A young man gets married and learns that sexual temptation is about more than being sexually satisfied. It is also about ego, power, adventure, and conquest. He learns that having what one needs is not enough; there is always a better job, a bigger house, and the latest electronic toy.

C. S. Lewis put it so well describing the human condition: "But a proud man will take your girl from you, not because he wants her, but just to prove to himself that he is a better man than you."[1] The dark side of immaterial nature never improves. It lurks beneath the restraint of proper behavior and social inhibition but, when properly stimulated, strikes without warning.

And then there are the children. They give rise to some of the most commendable emotions; parents have moments when they will do anything for their offspring. Then, of course, these same lovely souls bring out some of life's darkest and most evil thoughts. Children are beaten and left in trash bins; they are neglected and abused in the most horrifying ways. Thankfully, most people don't abuse or hurt their children, but raising them can reveal just how much we need to become like Christ. About the time the children are raised, life surprises many of us with enlarged prostates, diabetes, aching backs, and breast cancer. Our married children divorce and move back home with children that need day care. Resentment, disappointment, and many negative emotions that we believed were gone return with a rage. The senior years provide great highs and even greater lows. As Art Linkletter said, "Getting old isn't for sissies." What becomes so powerfully true is that all events and circumstances form us in Christ. And that formation takes place throughout life; it cannot be done alone. Any person of wisdom understands how much spiritual community is fundamental to being formed into Christ and not malformed into a life of sadness.[2]

There is a second element regarding the need for the lifelong nature of formation. It is the "need for speed" malady of the culture. The most common question asked by the consumers of culture is, "When can I get that?" It is only natural in a world of shopping on the Internet and next-day delivery that people would expect their spiritual formation right now. A very common question to any plan for spiritual formation among church members is, "How can we speed this up?" The consumer culture in which we live is a world of consumption, assertiveness, speed, and fame. Impatience is the most accepted sin in Western culture. We are an impetuous people.

This impatience is not only accepted in the church but is considered a positive quality among church leaders. It is the fifth gospel, the gospel of progress. Everything must be faster and bigger. Impatience is presented as a sign of holy dissatisfaction that drives leaders to take the church to the next level — that is, to grow the church bigger. Every year must bring net growth with new and exciting programs to keep consumer Christians with short attention spans interested. The problem with impatience is that it short-circuits the forming of Christ in persons. With a consumer mentality, there is no basis to enter into a life of submission and humility. According to the consumer mentality, activity, including church, is in orbit around the individual. The mania for success trains people to think in terms of programs and gives them a short-term view of personal development. They begin to believe that if they can get a handle on this character flaw of uncontrolled anger in the next two months, it will be taken care of. If it doesn't work, then they need to find a better teacher, church, curriculum, husband, wife, or workplace. Changing my circumstances will change me.

The formation of character into the person of Christ can't be hurried. It is slow work, and it can get very messy. People fail, delay, make mistakes, resist, and are afraid. It is slow work, so it can't be hurried; but it is an urgent work, so it cannot be delayed. In America, slow and urgent are not compatible; they cancel each other out. In the kingdom, patience and urgency are yoked together. The culture is contemptuous of patience. It is the first thing that gets thrown overboard in a storm. The storm is the mania for numbers — the lust to build a big ministry, a great law practice, a lucrative business — so we can feel affirmed. Then we can have the resources we desire in a time frame we have planned. When this happens, it creates an artificial pressure cooker. If we don't meet expectations, we have failed. Then we must work harder or find a better plan. The hurried and the impatient life are based on pride and a fear of failure. Pride demands success that others will notice. Fear of failure is rooted in artificial goals and the restlessness found in an unsatisfied soul (see Psalm 23:1).

At seventy, John Wesley wrote, "Though I am always in haste, I am never in a hurry."[3] One can work hard and be at rest in spirit. One can be focused and ambitious yet not controlled by cultural demands; there can be a freedom from the toxic nature of both secular and religious culture. When spiritual formation is understood as a journey through life in which God works in and through us in His time, the pressure is off (see Philippians 2:13).

SPIRITUAL FORMATION'S PURPOSE IS TO TAKE ON THE IMAGE OF CHRIST

There are many kinds of discipleship and spiritual formation. Karl Marx had disciples, as did Elvis Presley and Mother Teresa. These disciples longed to be like their leaders, so they took on their beliefs, attitudes, and in some cases mannerisms. In each case, however, the disciples were limited in their ability to become like their hero. The limitation might be the inability to grasp the teaching of Marx, to imitate the anatomical wonder of Presley's swivel hips, or the courage of Mother Teresa. The distinctive of Christian spiritual formation is that every disciple, from the most gifted to the ordinary, is called to imitate Christ and to become like Him (see 1 Corinthians 11:1; 2 Corinthians 3:18; 4:16-18). And the beauty of it is that He provides the power to make significant progress in that direction.

Everyone reading these lines has a pretty good idea what is meant by the image of Christ. Most would immediately think of the gospel stories of how Jesus lived, worked, and died. And that would be exactly where to begin. The second most common thought would be the fruit of the Spirit: "love, joy, peace, patience, kindness, goodness, faithfulness, gentleness and self-control" (Galatians 5:22-23). Again this is right on regarding Christ's character qualities. But there is one other aspect I believe to be central. Incarnation is God with flesh on. Jesus explained God to us, but, even more crucially, He was God with us (see John 1:1-18). I recall E. Stanley Jones quipping, "If God isn't like Jesus, He ought to be." That was his way of saying that Jesus is God and He is very attractive to us. We don't need to swoon under the stars at night and imagine what God is like when we already know. I might add the caveat that though we know what the God-Man is like, the entire Godhead is a more expansive contemplation. But we are not called to be like the Father or the Holy Spirit; we are called to be conformed to the image of Christ (see Romans 8:29-30). If we think of how Jesus lived and died amid His creation, we can grasp what it means to be like Him. I think it should also be said that Jesus is the exact image of God; He has the very character of God (see Hebrews 1:3). To sum it up, think of it this way: Conformity to the image of Christ is to believe as Jesus believed, live as He lived, love as He loved, minister as He ministered, and lead as He led. You can find all that is important in those dimensions.

SPIRITUAL FORMATION IS RADICAL AND INTERNAL, BUT NOT INTERNAL ALONE

Dare we ask which comes first, the "chicken or egg"? Is character transformation more being than doing? More internal or external? Actors address this issue when they practice their craft. Most of them have a philosophy of character development as "inside out" or "outside in." Some begin inside with how the script describes the character and then build an internal emotional structure that is the basis for the character's speech and action in the text. Others start on the outside with the character's clothes, voice, facial expressions, even special makeup with prosthetics. For example, in the film *Rain Man*, Dustin Hoffman worked inside out, while in *Tootsie*—where he dressed as and portrayed a woman—he worked outside in. It is fair to conclude that actors may have a primary bent, but actually they work both inside out and outside in with every character.

Isn't it much the same with followers of Jesus? God works both "inside out" and "outside in." He works inside out through prayer, Bible reading, and the practice of most spiritual disciplines. Yet every action requires the cooperation of the body. External elements are vital. Jesus told those who liked to pray for public display to find a prayer closet. The placement of the body in a place of solitude is both an internal decision

and an external action. The impulse to place *being* before *doi* ᵤ
insist on the internal to the exclusion of the external—should be resisted
because this presents a false choice. Christians, like actors, have a prefer-
ence, but we don't really live that way. God works outside in when we
serve or fit into a prescribed external regime such as church worship (i.e.,
clerical robes, choir robes, monks' or nuns' attire, and religious school
uniforms that all have religious significance). These external actions are
rooted in an internal intention that gives them meaning.

It Does Begin Inside

Transformation begins in that part of the immaterial nature called the
mind. This is definitive because it comes from a direct statement of fact.
"Do not be conformed to this world *but be transformed by the renewal of
your mind,* that you may prove what is the will of God, what is good and
acceptable and perfect" (Romans 12:2, rsv, emphasis added).

The first part of that exhortation puts the priority on change, and
it locates the starting point as the mind. The second part speaks to the
effect of a changed person on those around him or her. God places in
each believer a visceral hunger for Him along with a desire to please.
There does seem to be a starting point and a procedure to the process
of transformation. It is important to ask why a person would want to
change his or her mind, to put on the mind of Christ (see 1 Corinthians
2:16). There is a desire that comes from a regenerated person—all things
have become new, including the desire to please God and to prove His
perfect will (see 2 Corinthians 5:17). The Holy Spirit causes the human
spirit to desire to submit to God's will: "Therefore, my beloved, as you
have always obeyed, so now, not only as in my presence but much more
in my absence, work out your own salvation with fear and trembling;
for *God is at work in you,* both *to will* and *to work* for his good pleasure"
(Philippians 2:12-13, rsv, emphasis added).

Christian spiritual formation is distinctive from other forms of spiritual formation because it begins and ends with Christ. When a person
is "in Christ," he or she possesses the desire and the capacity to change.
God is at work "in you," and He gives the disciple the will to submit to

a pattern of life that leads to character transformation. God is willing us to a certain kind of work that agrees with His good pleasure, what pleases Him. This is the beauty of submitting to the direction of God; He wills certain desires in us that then we can act on. It frees us from trying to do and accomplish everything that should be done. We participate in the part of His kingdom that He has planned for us to work in.

Dallas Willard made an important distinction between discipleship and spiritual formation that can help us here. He said that discipleship is the decision to follow Jesus, to be His apprentice. This is about positioning, making oneself available. Spiritual formation is the direct action of the Holy Spirit upon the inner person.[4] Once a person is "in Christ," God is at work to will and to work all good things. That is the starting point; the next part is how the mind gets renewed.

The Necessity of the Word of God
The apostle Paul encouraged Timothy with this promise: "All scripture is inspired by God and profitable for teaching, for reproof, for correction, and for training in righteousness, that the man of God may be complete, equipped for every good work" (2 Timothy 3:16-17, RSV). Scripture has always been the primary source of knowing God's identity, what kind of being He is, the nature of His plan for the world, for us, and for eternity. God gave man language, spoken and written, to communicate His thoughts to us. At one time it was only spoken or oral tradition. Over time it became a written document we know as the Old Testament. By the time Paul wrote the above words to Timothy, the young pastor was reading a letter that neither he nor Paul thought would have been included in Holy Writ. The New Testament was a growing portfolio of letters and histories with the mission to explain what happened with Jesus and to correct excesses and mistakes of those who were then following Jesus. So when Paul said "scripture," he was referring to that body of written truth recognized by the believing community as from God. That believing community by AD 397 had decided that the twenty-seven books of the New Testament were authoritative and were part of God's written word.

Whatever the Word of God was then, we know what it is now. It is the basis for completeness[5] of a disciple. That completeness is more than skill; a process that includes being taught, reproved, corrected, and trained brings about the completeness.[6] That process of transformation is from the Spirit. It can be painful and frustrating, and it starts with God's Word acting on our minds. The Scriptures tell us what is right; when we go astray, it shows us that it is wrong, puts us back on the right path, and then encourages us to train, to make the new ideas that have renewed our minds our habit and, therefore, our character. The Word of God is necessary because it uses the vehicle of language to make God's thoughts our thoughts. We can believe what Jesus believed; we can see the world the way He saw it; and we can even feel it the way He felt it.

The Word of God also does something in our spiritual formation that even the most clever psychologist or spiritual guru cannot accomplish. God uses it to reveal secrets, things even secret to us about ourselves. It can reveal to us motivations, both selfish and spiritual. And as the following passage says, "Before him no creature is hidden, but all are open and laid bare to the eyes of him with whom we have to do" (Hebrews 4:13, RSV).

When we read Scripture with our hearts open to the Holy Spirit, nothing is hidden. God lays us open; His eyes see perfectly into our inner person. When we submit to the message of His Word, we are not just engaging in a religious rite; we are engaged in an intimate dialogue with God Himself. That is why the more familiar Hebrews 4:12 speaks of the precise nature of God's Word: "For the word of God is living and active, sharper than any two-edged sword, piercing to the division of soul and spirit, of joints and marrow, and discerning the thoughts and intentions of the heart" (RSV).

There is no other path to Christian spiritual transformation than through meaningful interaction with the Word of God. Many Christians have tried to change without its penetrating analysis, wisdom, and comfort but have failed. The nature of Scripture is to address the internal first, but it does not detach thought from behavior. It does not allow abstract theory to sit alone on a high place separated from life and simply ponder doing what is right. It does not permit one to continue to lie or steal while the immaterial nature ponders a change in behavior. It assumes a direct and immediate link between thought and action. In fact, the immediate right action is the best tonic for creating in a person a strengthened motivation. As Cain's counselor, God asked Cain concerning his depressed emotional state, "Why are you so angry? . . . Why do you look so dejected? You will be accepted if you do what is right. But if you refuse to do what is right, then watch out! Sin is crouching at the door, eager to control you. But you must subdue it and be its master" (Genesis 4:6-7, NLT).

What pleased or did not please Cain, what he was willing or not willing to do implies the kind of character he possessed. To use a contemporary phrase, God was telling Cain that he needed to be reprogrammed—that he was of a certain character, but a new one could be formed. Cain could be reformed, transformed, changed. He could become the kind of person who would desire to do right and would experience pleasure when he did. In Cain's case—as well as almost always in Scripture—God's words were spoken for us as well. The Word of God becomes our counselor, for it alone can discern with precision what changes are to be made in us. Spiritual formation begins within, and its primary tool is to take a God-given desire to change and work to reform a person's mind with God's thoughts. A renewed mind fueled by a Holy Spirit–birthed desire creates new actions, which become habits, and habits make our character.

SPIRITUAL FORMATION INCLUDES THE DEVELOPMENT OF THE SPIRITUAL HEART

A great deal of discussion and thought about spiritual motivation and performance totters back and forth between internal/external, motive/action, heart/head. To sum it up, most people innately sense that the healthiest form of spirituality is to have a heart to please God and from that heart of passion to respond in obedience. The flip side, however, is the fear that if we depend on feelings, passions, or emotions, very often we will sin, giving in to the powerful self-interest that gibbers deep within one's loins. We need to take sin seriously. As Reinhold Niebuhr taught Elton Trueblood, "Sin is the precise sense of self-centeredness and the struggle for power."[7] This daily struggle is at the heart of every decision. There is no doubt danger and possibility for disaster when we depend too much on passion or desire. But less passion does not mean less sin; it does not mean more obedience. We are better to cast our lot with C. S. Lewis, who addressed the human tendency to play it safe with God:

> Indeed, if we consider the unblushing promises of reward and the staggering nature of the rewards promised in the Gospels, it would seem that Our Lord finds our desires not too strong, but too weak. We are half-hearted creatures, fooling about with drink and sex and ambition when infinite joy is offered us, like an ignorant child who wants to go on making mud pies in a slum because he cannot imagine what is meant by the offer of a holiday at the sea. We are far too easily pleased.[8]

The spiritual heart can be strengthened, its passions made greater. Can we imagine that by engaging God in the way He recommends in Scripture, we can have a passionate spiritual heart that directs our transformation? That it would keep the internal and external in balance? That it would bring congruency to all of life? It is crucial to understand that one does not arrive at such a state by wishing or hoping. So many have been taught and have experienced spiritual growth as one dream piled upon another dream followed by disappointment. Who hasn't attended a retreat or special event that led to a passionate desire to change, to experience the fullness of God? At the close of such experiences, the renewed passion gives rise to fist pumping and cheerleading. There is a natural desire that for the good feeling, the powerful emotion, to continue, we must not let it waft and wane away. But the truth is that these emotions—as powerful as they have been—will naturally diffuse into the tissue of everyday life. The desire to no longer be abusive to others is only the beginning of the process.

Yet there is a way out of "New Year's resolution" spirituality. *The radical and refreshing truth is that we can become the kinds of persons who naturally do what Jesus would do.* We must take the emotional power present in us and redirect its energy into rearranging our lives around the practices of Jesus. This will make it possible for us to form a spiritual heart or character.

What Is the Spiritual Heart?

Before Sigmund Freud and Carl Jung invented psychoanalysis and excavated the soul, reducing it to primal or mystical motives, there was Franz Delitzsch (1813–1890). Dr. Delitzsch was a renowned Hebrew scholar and commentator. His volume *A System of Biblical Psychology*, published in 1855, remains the most thorough work on the immaterial nature of man. His treatment of what the Bible calls the "heart" is exhaustive. Delitzsch wrote, "The heart is the innermost centre of the natural condition of man, in which the threefold life of man blends together."[9] That threefold part of man is mind, spirit, and body. He continued, "[Heart] denotes also the middle or centre of other natural things. The heart is the centre of the bodily life, it is the reservoir of the entire life-power."[10] A few of the ways the heart is described are as follows:

> The heart is the seat of love and of hatred. . . . It knows or per-ceives; it understands; it deliberates; it reflects; and estimates. The heart is set or directed . . . it is turned away from, or inclined towards . . . [things can be] written on . . . the heart; one knows in his heart if he is conscious to himself . . . the heart is the storehouse of all that is heard and experienced. . . . Because it is the birth-place of the thoughts, the heart is, moreover, the birth-place of words. Words are brought forth from the heart.[11]

It is clear that rarely does the Bible refer to the physical organ of the heart. The heart is a metaphor for the immaterial nature of a person. One of the best known statements from Paul is found in Ephesians 1:17-18:

The God of our Lord Jesus Christ, the Father of glory, may give you a spirit of wisdom and of revelation in the knowledge of him, *having the eyes of your hearts enlightened,* that you may know what is the hope to which he has called you, what are the riches of his glorious inheritance in the saints. (RSV, emphasis added)

The heart can see, feel, know, reflect, and be turned toward God or away from Him. The most basic way we can describe the internal nature of spiritual formation is to say, "I want to please God with all my heart." Spiritual formation is the development of a heart for God. That spiritual heart directs the transformation of the entire person to reflect Jesus Christ. It denotes a passion and warmth of relationship, one that is current and alive, one in which there is communication — honest interchange including disappointment, disagreement, forgiveness, and reconciliation.

One would naturally ask, "What about the will, the spirit, feelings, conscience, the mind, and the other biblical descriptions of the inner person?" Yes, we could follow any of these dimensions of the immaterial nature, but we believe that "spiritual heart" captures them all and does so in the more central concept of heart.

Training the Intention of the Heart

The Bible is clear that Christ being formed in us involves a process that is gradual and lifelong. A regenerate heart desires to be at one with God and to please Him (see Philippians 3:7-16; Matthew 22:37). Some would call the condition of the spiritual heart *character.* Much of the discussion of why Christians do not live according to their beliefs is done around the label of character. But I would like to present it as a deeper issue, that being the intention of the heart.

William Law's *A Serious Call to a Devout and Holy Life* has changed many lives because of its razor-sharp dissection of the heart's intention. So powerful was this work, published in 1728, that it changed the lives of such spiritual greats as Samuel Johnson and John Wesley. It has had a powerful effect on contemporary thought leaders such as Dallas Willard and Richard Foster. Law's premise concerning intention is as simple as it is startling. Law asked why it is that so many professing Christians strangely live contrary to the principles in which they say they believe. He applied this question to the problem of Christian men swearing in their public life but not in their religious life. Law wrote, "Now the reason for common swearing is this; it is because men have not so much as the intention to please God in all their actions."[12]

The reason people continue to swear, Law believed, is that they never fully intend not to. Their heart's intent is to hold back, to reserve a part of their lives that they could continue to control. It is very common that we find ourselves in a constant negotiation with God about who is in charge. But a holy and devout life calls for surrender, not negotiation. All of us must go into training in order to gradually grow out of the grip of our own corrupted hearts and to create the strength of our spiritual hearts (see 1 Corinthians 9:24-27). The Bible makes it clear that the heart cannot be fully trusted:

> *The human heart is the most deceitful of all things,*
> *and desperately wicked.*
> *Who really knows how bad it is?*
> *But I, the LORD, search all hearts*
> *and examine secret motives.*
> *I give all people their due rewards,*
> *according to what their actions deserve.* (Jeremiah 17:9-10,
> NLT)

One does wonder, *How can we have a new heart, one that God has put in us, but at the same time have the kind of deceptive heart that Jeremiah describes?* It has never been said better outside the Bible than was described by Aleksandr Solzhenitsyn, that "the line dividing good and evil cuts through the heart of every human being."[13]

Can a person's intention change or be changed from a power outside of itself? The answer must be yes or there is no need to continue this exercise. Returning to Paul's letter to the Ephesians, he prayed that, "having the eyes of your heart enlightened" (1:18, RSV), the heart can see and will see more as God sees. There is more to know, and through full intention of the will, the heart will be transformed. We will see life transformed through experience, good and bad. We will start seeing life more as God sees it. It is surprising how these changes take place. It is what we call the common or ordinary life.

The Common Life
We have a natural tendency to separate the religious life from the common life. The religious life is attending church services, observing special religious holidays, keeping Advent calendars, and trying not to eat dessert during Lent. The religious life is also daily devotions, going on Christian missions trips, attending a Bible study, helping the poor, and many good things called "Christian." All these activities have intrinsic value, but they still may leave the common life untouched. The common life is how we treat our spouse and children, the way we drive our cars, and the media we take in. It is what is going on "under the hood." How does a Christian business leader treat his employees? Is he a man of his word? Can he be trusted? It is necessary for the disciple of Christ to bring the whole of his life under the direction of his leader. A person may be very attentive to his or her religious life but ruled by worry, anger, pride, and sensuality in his or her common life. William Law gave us an eighteenth-century view of this problem:

> It is very possible for a man that lives by cheating, to be very punctual in paying for what he buys; but then every one is assured that he does not do so out of any principle of true honesty. In like manner it is very possible for a man that is proud of his estate, ambitious in his views, or vain of his learning, to disregard his dress and person in such a manner as a truly humble man would do; but to suppose that he does so out of true principle of religious humility, is full as absurd as to suppose that a cheat pays for what he buys out of a principle of religious honesty.[14]

The real power to affect others is found in the transformation of our inner lives and how it affects the common parts of our experiences. So many times we think we have been transformed because our lives have been free from murder, theft, and adultery. How sad that we have accepted a limited definition of transformation as the exercise of our religious duties and the absence of public sin that will embarrass.

This is what happens when we find a level of religious experience that will allow us to hold on to the core of our flesh, which is to maintain control of our lives. What this leaves out is the pursuit of God, the joys of surrender, the fullness of heart that is so passionate for God that it directs and governs our attitudes and decisions. When it comes to attitude, William Law once again spoke powerfully about the subject of death:

> When we consider death as a misery, we only think of it as a miserable separation from the enjoyments of this life. We seldom mourn over an old man what dies rich, but we lament the young, that are taken away in the progress of their fortune. You yourselves look upon me with pity, not that I am going unprepared to meet the Judge of the quick and dead, but that I am to leave a prosperous trade in the flower of my life. This is the wisdom of our human thoughts. And yet what folly of the silliest children is so great as this?[15]

The great nineteenth-century English preacher Charles Spurgeon was being given a tour of a very expensive home. As the owner was extolling the Italian marble floors and the Kenyan wood-paneled walls, Spurgeon observed, "These are the things that make it hard to die." Spurgeon was simply voicing the human tendency to hold on to this life because of a flawed perspective about the next life.

The heart that has a surrendered intentionality toward God is one that again is described eloquently by William Law:

And it is so far from being impossible now, that if we can find any Christians that *sincerely intend to please God in all their actions, as the best and happiest thing in the world*, whether they be young or old, single or married, men or women, if they have but this intention, *it will be impossible for them to do otherwise.* This one principle will infallibly carry them to this height of love, and *they will find themselves unable to stop short of it.*[16] (emphasis added)

Four things about this statement are riveting. First, notice that true followers of Christ have the sincere *intention* to please God "in all their actions." The focus is on the common life, who we really are, not just the public religious persona that we hope to project. Next, we allow God to dig down deep inside us and get at the deepest reasons we do what we do. Further, we are inspired to pursue sincere intention "as the best and happiest thing in the world." This is at the core of the development of the spiritual heart. The spiritual heart must believe in this "best and happiest" for the intention to govern and direct our lives. For our intention is not sincere until we believe that pleasing God is the happiest thing about being human and that we are not missing anything when we do abstain from sin and pursue pleasing God. A man has won over lust when he believes that he is not missing anything of value by not lusting. We stop lying when we don't miss the advantage or the benefits of lying. Finally, what potentially fills us with glee in this quote by William Law is the confidence that "this one principle will infallibly carry them to this height of love." It's the thought that we would find ourselves unable to do otherwise than please God; in fact, we would not be able to stop ourselves. This is because we are being directed by a sincerely intended heart that is inclined to please God.

Spiritual Formation Finds Its Purpose in Uncomplicated Obedience

Dallas Willard wrote, "Obedience is the only sound objective of a Christian spirituality."[17] Any Christian spirituality that does not lead to uncomplicated obedience is our enemy. Dietrich Bonhoeffer said any other theory of spirituality should have a stake driven through its heart; kill it before it kills the church. Faith is only real in obedience. If faith is only pondering doing what God said, it is not faith. It may be a highly nuanced philosophy that animates the minds of those looking for reasons not to bow the knee to God, but essentially it is useless, something to be thrown into the trash bin of history. That is the blunt end of all theories of spiritual formation: If they don't lead to obedience, then they are worse than rejection of Christ. They are delusionary because they teach those who seek to obey that obedience is complex and optional.

We have learned thus far that what really matters is what we are like on the inside. That is the place where discipleship takes hold and where the only possible foundation for uncomplicated obedience is laid. Jesus made it uncomplicated:

> I have loved you even as the Father has loved me. Remain in my love. When you obey my commandments, you remain in my love, just as I obey my Father's commandments and remain in his love. . . .
>
> Those who accept my commandments and obey them are the ones who love me. And because they love me, my Father will love them. And I will love them and reveal myself to each of them. (John 15:9-10; 14:21, NLT)

We have seen that the spiritual heart is the director of one's life. The spiritual heart is developed and trained in the context of a love relationship. It is the place from which we tell God, our spouse, our friends, and our family that we love them with all our heart. Jesus modeled this for us in the way He related to His Father: He desired to please His Father; He pled with His Father in times of trouble and stress; He poured out His heart to His Father from Gethsemane and the Place of the Skull (see John 5:19-23; 17:1-5; Matthew 26:38-44; 27:46; Luke 23:34,46). He is teaching us a passion of relationship, that loving someone is the desire to please that person, to do things that benefit him or her, to deny self in order to help others. Obedience is uncomplicated when someone who has given his life for you asks for your help; your first impulse is to say "yes." John 3:16 says, "For God loved the world so much that he gave his one and only Son, so that everyone who believes in him will not perish but have eternal life" (NLT).

My life, then, is an answer. God spoke, God acted . . . now, what is my answer? I answer with my life, with my obedience. It's not complicated. I don't hesitate. Just as we teach our children: Obey the first time, every time.

The Complicated Heart

We all know that spiritual conflict lives in us all the days of our earthly lives (see Galatians 5:17-26). What John Wesley and William Law meant by "perfect" is not the meaning of the contemporary word. When we say *perfect*, we refer to something that is clearly unattainable. But Wesley and Law meant *maturity*, and they made allowances for what they called ignorance and weakness. However, they thought a person making progress toward Christlikeness would do so with a heart fully intent on pleasing God. Spiritual warfare is present in a person of vibrant faith, but that is different from a complicated heart. The apostle James described it for us:

> If you need wisdom, ask our generous God, and he will give it to you. He will not rebuke you for asking. But when you ask him, be sure that your faith is in God alone. Do not waver, for a person with divided loyalty is as unsettled as a wave of the sea that is blown and tossed by the wind. Such people should not expect to receive anything from the Lord. Their loyalty is divided between God and the world, and they are unstable in everything they do. (1:5-8, NLT)

Divided loyalty is an apt description. The complicated heart describes a person who has made a decision without full intention. We see it often: One person can't decide if she should marry; a man can't decide whether to take a new job. People wobble around. When uncommitted, a person's spiritual heart will make him unstable: one day he loves, the next day he hates. That person can't seem to get anywhere with God because he wants the benefits of faith and trust without fully believing and trusting. It is the age-old problem of wanting to hold on to control of one's life. Jesus told us the journey to freedom is to relinquish control: "If you try to hang on to your life, you will lose it. But if you give up your life for my sake, you will save it" (Luke 9:24, NLT).

The question we must now answer is: What does a person do in order to get from complexity to an uncomplicated obedience? In other words, how do we develop a spiritual heart?

SPIRITUAL FORMATION REQUIRES SUSTAINED EFFORT

Effort in the spiritual life is good. The Scriptures extol its benefits (see 1 Corinthians 9:24-27; Galatians 6:7-9; Colossians 1:28-29; 1 Timothy 4:7; Hebrews 5:14). In Dallas Willard's often-repeated words, "God is not opposed to effort but to *earning*."[18] God's grace is a gift and is not for sale or given to the hardest worker. But grace gives one the endowment of power and resources to give a full effort (see Ephesians 2:8-10). The mystical relationship of grace and effort is given credence by Paul's autobiographical teaching:

So we tell others about Christ, warning everyone and teaching everyone with all the wisdom God has given us. We want to present them to God, perfect in their relationship to Christ. That's why I work and struggle so hard, depending on Christ's mighty power that works within me. (Colossians 1:28-29, NLT)

Paul worked hard; he struggled — but it was with God's power that he did so. That is the divine dance we do every day. We join hands with Jesus; He leads and we follow. Part of the full intention that creates an uncomplicated spiritual heart is to take action employing the tools

God has given us. Those tools are commonly known as spiritual disciplines. Their usefulness in forming Christ in us is essential. Many people have employed these tools without ever hearing the term "spiritual disciplines." A person with a heart for God might even do them without thinking of them as discipline. But for the record, they are normally understood to be the following: Bible reading, meditating on Scripture, Scripture memorization, prayer, worship, evangelism, service, stewardship, fasting, silence, solitude, journaling, submission, and frugality.[19] Dallas Willard spoke to the power of these practices: "[The spiritual disciplines] are essential to the deliverance of human beings from the concrete power of sin."[20]

So there is the answer to our question, "What does a person do in order to get from complexity to an uncomplicated obedience?" The spiritual heart can be trained by employing these God-given tools. It also is critical at this point to say that the only reason we have to practice them is that Jesus practiced them. The objective is to have Christ formed in us; therefore, we rearrange our practices around His practices. It should also be noted that Jesus didn't practice them in a legalistic way. He was not uptight about them; they flowed out of His natural life. They were the things He did based on His nature. There are numerous ways to explain this, but we have chosen a simple approach.

Desire as the Fuel for Intent
Change begins with the regenerate heart (spiritually reborn), for only the regenerate heart has the capacity for transformation into Christlikeness. When new life is resident in a person, it gives him or her both the desire and intention to be like Christ. This is why we insist that Christian spiritual formation is unique. It is that part of us that yearns for a closer relationship with God. Paul described the source of that longing:

> He died for everyone so that those who receive his new life will no longer live for themselves. Instead, they will live for Christ, who died and was raised for them.
>
> So we have stopped evaluating others from a human point

of view. At one time we thought of Christ merely from a human point of view. How differently we know him now! This means that anyone who belongs to Christ has become a new person. The old life is gone; a new life has begun! (2 Corinthians 5:15-17, NLT)

Faith as Action

Desire and intention prove they are real in action. Dietrich Bonhoeffer was fond of saying, "Only the obedient believe and only those who believe are obedient. . . . Faith is only real in obedience."[21] Faith is not faith unless it acts. This is what the apostle James clearly taught (see James 2:14-16). Jesus said that faith is following Him and answering the call to ministry (see Luke 9:23-27). If a person has a desire to be kind to a difficult person, then faith is to take specific actions of kindness toward that person. The faith of the Western church has often been reduced to intellectual agreement and divorced from action. That is the kind of faith that does not transform because it is not faith at all. A person's immaterial nature or spiritual heart is transformed by acting in faith on its desire.

Desire is the beginning, and one right act prompted by that desire can make a difference in a person's life and for those touched by that action. A single act of forgiveness can restore a life; a generous gift can turn a life around. But there is more to be done to turn these good actions into one's character.

Discipline for Godliness

The continued actions of faith based on desire or intention will eventually become a habit of the heart. This will require discipline, the kind of discipline that most of us do not have. The good news, however, is that God knows this and has a solution. These disciplines are to be practiced in community, in relationship with others of kindred spirit and intent. When Paul exhorted Timothy, "Discipline yourself for the purpose of godliness" (1 Timothy 4:7, NASB), he was not advocating a singular effort, but one joined to the community. One of the joys of life together in

Christ is helping one another keep our commitments to God. Everyone knows how hard it is to break bad habits and make new ones. That is the reason God has given us the gift of spiritual friends. I like to think of them as love and support.

But only a humble person will submit herself to others and see her character developed in community. One of the many reasons God is opposed to the proud is that pride blocks one's growth and transformation (see 1 Peter 5:5-6). When people are living in a spiritual community with helpful relationships, they will discover their hearts being transformed. Their hearts for God will grow stronger and more passionate. This change will happen during the great variety of circumstances of life with all its joys and sorrows. We're strengthened through all our proactive missional efforts and the necessary highs and lows that come with knowing and working with others. And undergirding the whole journey is the intentional effort of practicing the disciplines that God says will help us.

Tools and Structure

There is an idyllic belief among some spiritual-formation advocates that programs, curriculums, and structure will not be needed if we will only spend more time in prayer and reflecting on Scripture. The wish for programs, formulas, and study guides to go away comes from the desire to find authenticity. We want something real not programmed, life-changing not religious.

You may be among the growing number of those disenchanted with the superficiality of filling in blanks on pages but not dealing with the deeper issues of the soul. The truth is, we need guidance, and primarily that means a person or group must become part of our lives. The irony is that we will usually meet most of these people in a church meeting or some other organized group. We will often join a small group that is structured around written materials; it has a stated purpose and meets on a regular basis. We meet people who become friends and provide the love and support we need to keep our promises to God.

Every group of people lives by covenant, written or unwritten, with an understanding of who they are and what they want. The best research indicates that we learn and grow best in an environment that fosters trust, where people feel safe. When people gain trust and lower their defenses, they will be eager to follow a plan or a course of action that will lead them to Christlikeness. When these elements are present in the faith community, good tools really work. Various tools may comprise a group's curriculum, which is a word of Latin origin simply meaning "race course."

Character — The Spiritual Heart

Character transformation will be a result of the process we have been discussing. Christian character is the unconflicted spiritual heart that has a passionate intent to serve God and is trained to do so. We can get at this passionate intent by making a helpful distinction in words: the difference between *trying* and *training*. The life of transformation takes time, and the word *trying* communicates effort that is in a hurry and has a deadline. *Training*, however, indicates a process and leaves room for patience. It gives our lives the space for unexpected events, setbacks, mistakes, and — let's face it — stupidity. Like an athlete who is preparing for a major event that is months or years away, you can take the long view because life is a journey. All the time, the spiritual heart directs this effort with passion and discipline.

IN SPIRITUAL FORMATION, WE ARE
ALWAYS BEGINNERS

A few days ago I was having lunch with a close friend, someone I respect greatly and to whom I listen carefully when he speaks. He had just returned from his brother's funeral, and the subject turned to death. My friend commented, "We Christians are woefully unprepared to die." He went on to explain that we do pretty well at the end, but what precedes the end is a struggle to let go of earthly treasure. It seems we don't have much interest in joining God in eternal bliss.

I'm claustrophobic, and the idea of being in one of those boxes under the ground gives me the willies. When I had to have an MRI a month before my meeting with my friend, I couldn't get in the tube. I returned two days later with Valium and my wife to hold my hand. Of course, my theological mind knows I won't be in that box—but my body will, and I tend to cling to my decaying container. When my friend mentioned how woefully unprepared we are to die, I knew that meant me.

The story that follows is illustrative of a truth: We are always beginners at spiritual formation. Let me tell you why I happened to need an MRI. A few weeks earlier, I was on a ministry trip—teaching discipleship and spiritual formation—in Tajikistan. Just before I left Los Angeles, my doctor discovered I had a hernia. So on this ministry trip, I began to wonder with growing alarm, *What is a sixty-one-year-old man doing ten thousand miles from home with a hernia that hurts and could burst?* If it did rupture and I was not operated on within twelve hours, I would die. One night in a hotel near the airport in Dushanbe, Tajikistan, I lay in a cold bed trying to get some rest between flights on Tajik Air. I trembled in the bed, praying—given my location—the "Jesus Prayer" of the Eastern Orthodox Church: "Lord Jesus Christ, Son of God, have mercy on me."

Still gripped by fear, I quoted, "Do not be anxious about anything, but in everything, by prayer and petition, with thanksgiving, present your requests to God. And the peace of God, which transcends all understanding, will guard your hearts and your minds in Christ Jesus" (Philippians 4:6-7). I wanted it to work; after all, I wrote a book on the subject of anxiety in 1987—before the enlarged prostate, the colon polyps, heart arrhythmia, a numb foot, and now the hernia. I prayed and tried to remember my "five steps to freedom from anxiety," but I continued to shake in fear. I castigated myself for being so stupid in making the trip. I had a primal urge to try to catch the next flight out of that forsaken land. And who would blame me? Most people wouldn't make such a trip in the first place. Just then I heard the roar of jet engines as the lone plane out of the country for the next three days disappeared into the early-morning sky. I moaned, gritted my teeth, and stuffed my face into the pillow.

The next few days, I faithfully taught four hours a day. And I can tell you that a hernia and public speaking are not friends. The pain got worse as the days went by, and so did my anxiety. By sheer force of will, I made my presentations and fulfilled my mission. But I must say I didn't enjoy it, and I couldn't wait to get out there. It felt so good to lift off from the barren terrain of that former Soviet satellite state and fly toward Istanbul. Imagine: Somehow I thought I was safer and more protected by God when I was headed home. What a foolish man I had become!

I was on airplanes for the next twenty out of thirty hours until I returned home. I felt better in Istanbul, even better in New York, and absolutely giddy when we touched down at LAX. I thought, *I will get this hernia fixed in the next week or so and get on with my life.*

But it wasn't that simple. I scheduled the surgery, but then I developed some problems in my right leg. Because of the long flight, I feared that I had a blood clot and was in danger of immediate disaster — death! Doctors go on vacation; tests are hard to get when you are not president of the United States. I went to the emergency room near my home and was tested for clots. The tests proved negative. A few days later, I was back at the same ER with the same complaint, but now I had a new swelling behind my right knee. They wouldn't repeat the test because they had complete confidence in the first test. But they X-rayed me in various places. They also did a CT scan of my pelvis. The surgeon who ordered the CT scan called me while I was in the ER. With great confidence he lectured me that I did not have a blood clot. After more tests, the ER doctor came into my cubical and lectured me as well: "There is no evidence that you have what you think."

But no one could tell me what I did have. My doctor had his own issues; his wife was having brain surgery, so he had taken a few days off. Finally, I decided I needed to take charge of my own health care, so I went to Urgent Care. This doctor thought I might indeed have a clot, so they administered blood thinners via a needle in my abdomen. They gave me two days of shots until the report came back on the test: no clots.

I went home very happy but still skeptical. I couldn't sleep without a pill; my ability to focus had become an obsession. Medicine, after all, is the process of elimination until a diagnosis is made. I went back to my doctor; he ran more tests, rechecked me, and sent me home. That night I had pains in my leg, and they seemed to be getting worse. I was on the verge of going to the ER once more, but I thought they would throw me out.

The next day, I walked into my doctor's office. I had no appointment; in fact, I found him on his lunch break. He looked at me and said, "You look sick, toxic." He was stumped. We spent about an hour doing a few more checks, and he invited a colleague in to examine me. I think they were just trying to convince me that I was not in peril. My doctor finally closed his office door and sat down on one of those little stools on wheels that doctors use for examinations. I didn't realize how bad I looked, but I had lost twelve pounds and was in misery. I couldn't seem to get an answer as to why I had the problems I had. My doctor told me to put off the hernia surgery until I was feeling better.

I took a deep breath. It seemed like it was my turn to confess. Confession is good for the soul, especially when it is true. I told him I thought I was the product of more than thirty days of anxiety, stress, and not knowing what to do. I hate loose ends, and this was a serious loose end. I couldn't — by my best efforts — make the solution happen fast enough. I couldn't control it. I might have to cancel my ministry schedule, which accounts for a good share of my income. And to add insult to injury, my back had seized up on me, and I was in pain.

My doctor is a very funny person and very smart. He is experienced and has seen almost everything. He began to tell me about his wife's brain surgery and his journey of faith. He shared some of his life experience that was very honest and moving. We talked about prayer and the spiritual side of the equation. Science and faith are friends, we agreed, but where is the balance? Doctors are instruments; they can set broken bones, but God heals the bones. Finally, my doctor rolled his stool over to my side of the room, grabbed me by the knees, and said, "Well, Reverend Hull, it is time to believe."

I left his office and got into my car. I began to cry. It was the first time that I had been able to release the tension. People had been praying for me, and God had sent one of His chosen, my Jewish doctor, who is on his own journey of faith. I was so embarrassed and ashamed for my lack of faith. I had to ask myself, *Why, after all the prayer, Bible reading, retreats, seminars, years of writing books and helping people all over the world, could I be so weak?* I taught that if we practice the spiritual disciplines, then over time we will naturally begin to do the same things Jesus did. We will take on His character, and we will develop the capacity to do His will—in other words, to obey.

But now I would like to point out that Jesus Himself sweat great drops of blood when He realized His own death was near. His Father never truly forsook Him but in some way allowed Jesus to experience the same things that so many of us do. In the end, it is always a "not my will, but yours be done" conclusion (Luke 22:42). I told my home Bible study group this story, and I cried and sobbed, only able to get it all out with assurances from my wife that I could do it. They seemed to understand it better than I did. My formation in Christ is like most others, I told them, except that I am a licensed professional with theological degrees and have written a pile of books. I said I wanted to issue an immediate apology to all of the people whom I was impatient with when they couldn't believe God in some difficult situation.

I confess I am still in this process. I still am not sure what is going on, and, yes, there is still the hernia. But I have found a new degree of peace and rest. It isn't perfect, and I still will move forward with diagnosis. When I cried and confessed with my group, I was able to say, "Okay, Lord, my days are in Your hands. I can't control or add one day, one hour, one second more to my life through worry. But I think this struggle needs to be addressed. I have spent more than forty years focused on being a disciple and making other disciples. People who know about my life's work might call me the 'discipleship man.' So why should a weak man like me have a task like mine? Why should anyone listen to me?"

My only answer is that God has called me to it, and the urge won't go away. It could be that my story in some way will help you in your own struggle not to obey yourself but to obey God. John Calvin said it so well: The ruin of a man is to obey himself. When I obey myself, I end up losing fifteen pounds because I can't eat; I have dark circles under my eyes; I spend hours in emergency rooms taking test after test. Then I talk about it endlessly to my wife, and I slip an Ambien under my tongue every night to get some sleep. It sounds more like the kind of life Lucifer planned for me: to steal my faith, to kill my body, and to destroy my joy, for "the thief's purpose is to steal and kill and destroy" (John 10:10, NLT).

When you look in the mirror and see the light gone from your eyes, when you stop laughing, listening to music, or thinking about a positive future, then let John Calvin's words penetrate because you see a ruined man's reflection. And let the words of Jesus restore your hope: "My purpose is to give them a rich and satisfying life" (John 10:10, NLT).

FOR REFLECTION AND DISCUSSION

1. Why do you think we tend to focus on outside-in orientations of formational ministries as opposed to inside-out? How would you communicate to people the value of the inside-out approach?

2. Given that most people are not focused on spiritual formation as a lifelong process, how do you ensure that when you call people to formation, they do not become weary and heavy laden?

3. What is the relationship between external activities and being formed into the image of Christ? How would you communicate the necessity of external activity without losing sight of the role of the internal work? And vice versa, what steps would you make in your context to ensure your community does not become strictly inward focused?

4. How would you describe what it means to be formed into the image of Christ, to have the heart of God? How can you make this idea meaningful to avoid it becoming a vague concept without usefulness in real-life transformation?

5. In what ways does your ministry context encourage obedience out of pure effort? In what ways does it encourage obedience out of the

spiritual heart? Can people tell the difference in the motivations and outcomes?

FOR FURTHER READING

Law, William. *A Serious Call to a Devout and Holy Life*. London: Richard Clay and Sons, 1906.

Palmer, Parker J. *Let Your Life Speak: Listening for the Voice of Vocation*. San Francisco: Jossey-Bass, 2000.

Peterson, Eugene H. *The Jesus Way: A Conversation on the Ways That Jesus Is the Way*. Grand Rapids, MI: Eerdmans, 2007.

Willard, Dallas. *The Great Omission: Reclaiming Jesus' Essential Teachings on Discipleship*. San Francisco: HarperOne, 2006. (See especially chapter 6, "Spiritual Formation in Christ Is for Whole Life and the Whole Person.")

Chapter Five

WHOLE-LIFE
TRANSFORMATION

Keith Meyer

ELEMENT 5: Spiritual formation is a continual process of transforming the whole person, including the healing of woundedness and rebellion, by the power of God, not to be confused with mere technique or program.

Description: People have been created in the image and likeness of God. The Fall marred every part of that image and likeness and brought struggle and corruption into our experience so that we are deeply rebellious, alienated from God and one another, troubled, wounded, and our souls are in ruin.

The journey of the human life is a process of experiencing lifelong changes in our relationships, our physical maturation, our sufferings, and our goals, desires, and hopes. The Bible's primary metaphors for spiritual development likewise focus on long-duration concepts of growth: training for a race, wandering in the wilderness, and healing of woundedness and rebellion. In contrast to this, our culture's primary metaphors are those of quick fixes based on proper techniques, tools, and programs. Against this the Scriptures point us to the lifelong goal of transformation into the likeness of Christ using in the process techniques, programs, and life circumstances.

❧ ❧ ❧

DAD, ARE YOU HOME YET?

In what seems like a few lifetimes ago in my ministry career, one day I came home early from the piles of work on my desk in the church office to fulfill a promise to myself and my wife to spend some "quality time" with my six-year-old son, Kyle. Quality time for Kyle sometimes meant watching cartoons together, and today that was just what I needed—some vegetative TV watching. I plopped myself down next to him in his cartoon reverie.

And then I noticed that I was really tired. Not just tired physically—I was tired of ministry and the kind of life that it seemed to require of me. I was preaching, teaching, and creating programs about living the Christian life and the way to get to heaven, but I was living in what seemed like a kind of hell on earth.

My wife and I were having arguments about how I was spending my time. Too many nights out each week, long hours, and preoccupation with ministry were not her idea of the kind of marriage and family life she signed up for when she said, "I do." I had grown up as a "PK" (pastor's kid) in an evangelical culture where time spent in church or in ministry activities often edged out time at home. I was now modeling to my family what I had been shown as the right way to serve the church and God.

Looking back on it now, I can see that I was pursuing a twisted idea of "success"—not in the secular forms I regularly preached against but in the sanctified activism and workaholism sometimes called professional ministry. A growing church—as in higher attendance at services, more and more programs, and bigger budgets and buildings—was the mark of a successful ministry in the clergy circles I ran with at that time. I was not alone in this pursuit. Even at denominational conferences,

more often than not the conversation would soon turn to compa— —
church-attendance figures or building programs. A subtle form of ambition seemed just below the surface of our desire to grow our ministries.

Although uneasy with the practice, I often found myself comparing
my age and the size of my congregation with my father's at the same
age. At age thirty my father had one thousand at worship; I had five
hundred. I lost, both at ministry and family. So on that day with Kyle at
my side vegging on cartoons, I was surprised by his breaking the drone
of the TV to ask me a question.

Without even looking at me he asked, "Dad, are you home yet?"

His question hit me as strange and surprising. Home yet? What did
he mean? Hadn't I been sitting there with him for at least twenty minutes watching his favorite cartoon? I didn't quite know how to answer
his question. It troubled me and reminded me of my wife's complaints of
how absent or distant I had been to her. The life I was living with God,
myself, my family, my church, and the world around me was coming
into clear focus, and it was deformed and driven, spinning out of control, and split into a million directions fueled by a million good intentions, with me at the center. Was there another way to live? Was there a
way home to a life that I whiffed in the Scriptures but really didn't think
possible in real life?

A JOURNEY HOME FROM INCOMPLETE TO WHOLE-LIFE TRANSFORMATION

Kyle's question awakened me to some gaping holes in the fabric of my
life. It began a process of measuring the distance between who I was
and who I wanted to be and, further, between what ministry was and
what it should be. About this time, a friend suggested I read a book that
addressed my questions. In Dallas Willard's *The Spirit of the Disciplines*
I read that life in Christ is more than just being forgiven of our sins; it
is having power over sin. Christ's commandments, which call us to a life
not ruled by anger, contempt, worry, or lust, were meant to be obeyed
so that we could live like Jesus. And freedom from these sinful attitudes

and behaviors could actually become the atmosphere of our lives rather than occasional whiffs of life found only in the afterlife. He also claimed that the process of becoming like Jesus was not to be "as a pose or by a constant and grinding effort, but with the ease and power he had," which he called the "easy yoke."[1]

Dallas Willard not only thought change was possible; he said it might even be easier on the soul and body than disobedience. Almost everyone I knew was faking it, grinding it out, taking it all for granted—or had given up entirely. I started out without any noble idea of becoming a "saint"; I just wanted to get my family back. Kyle's question helped me become aware of how far I was from the kind of life Dallas Willard claimed that Christ offered—and that I now longed for—but getting there would raise more questions. However, with a hopeful heart I set out to find my way toward true transformation.

THE TRANSFORMATION GAP: GOING TO HEAVEN WITHOUT LIFE HERE AND NOW

How could I be so sure of being "saved" and "born again" and on the way to my home in heaven—but so far away from home in my real life? My first step toward whole-life transformation was to acknowledge that I didn't have a vision for what transformation meant for my whole life—my life on earth and not just when I got to heaven. Today's reduced version of the gospel (see chapter 1) called for repentance for only a brief time at conversion and placed almost any other significant life change in the future—so far, in fact, that it was beyond our reach in this life. Many people view the call to live up to what the Scriptures present as the normal or mature Christian life as "works salvation" or "perfectionism." But I longed for the possibility of a different kind of life *now*, not just later in heaven. I had a personal relationship with Jesus and was assured of being with Him when I died, but that didn't seem to help me in my relationships at home. Nor did it help other people at my church.

Like that of most of my congregation, my conversion had brought an initial spurt of change, but then I settled down into basically the same life as any non-Christian if measured by my experience of anger, rage, worry, pride, and self-centeredness. Sure, I wasn't partying hard, but neither were most of those I knew who didn't claim to be Christians. The same was true for others of my brand of born-again, supposedly life-changing Christianity. What was supposed to be the difference in us? Was it only our being forgiven? I was leading people to accept Christ and doing many good things for others, but something was missing. While I preached on loving your enemies, I too often lived in contempt of anyone at church who got in the way of my ministry goals (as did many of our leaders and members), and now that included my own wife!

This led to a reexamination of what I had experienced as "the abundant life" and what it is called in the Bible. I came to the conclusion that there was indeed a difference between the life Jesus called us to in the Scriptures—and that Jesus and Paul exemplified—and my expectations for life in Christ. As I attempted to live differently and call others to this in my ministry, I became aware that most people don't believe the life modeled by Jesus and Paul is possible today. At best, it is only possible for a few star athletes. But generally that life was for Bible-sized heroes who no longer exist. However, to my surprise, I found in my study of church history that this kind of deep and radical life change is not only possible but was expected of believers as recently as the late 1800s; without it one might seriously wonder if you were saved.

Richard Lovelace has identified a gap or hole in current evangelical theology and experience, what he called the "sanctification gap."[2] It is the missing element of *life change* or transformation that is called for in the Scriptures. It happens in the time between our conversion and our death, and it has been missing for the last hundred years since the great revivals. Lovelace made the point that historically revivals or awakenings in the church resulted in radical change of life for individuals and for the society they lived in. We see the difference clearly when we study the stories of Christians living before the sanctification gap.

The hymn "Amazing Grace" is now the theme and part of the soundtrack of a Hollywood film about the life of William Wilberforce, the English evangelical who led parliament in a twenty-year fight for the abolition of slavery in England. It cost Wilberforce his health and his wealth. The self-proclaimed former "wretch" and slave trader John Newton, who wrote the hymn of testimony, is featured in this film recounting the changed lives of these men and their powerful influence on their world and culture.

One of the books that brought John Newton to faith and a radically new life in Christ was the fourteenth-century classic on formation titled *The Imitation of Christ* by Thomas à Kempis. This book clearly calls for transformation of life as the sign of genuine conversion, and its message has been second only to the Bible in popularity. It addresses tangible changes in behavior, from forgiving enemies to keeping the tongue from slander and gossip.

The author (or authors—many scholars believe *The Imitation of Christ* to be a compilation of a couple of generations of community wisdom) clearly expected change of life for those who claim to know Christ. Specifically, the book calls into question the genuineness of knowledge of God that can articulate theological concepts like the Trinity but shows little evidence of Trinitarian life and love. It is no wonder that it had an effect on Newton's conversion and change in character, occupation, and worldview.

James Lawson's *Deeper Experiences of Famous Christians* documents the stories of those who lived in the time before the appearance of the sanctification gap. These stories share life journeys into powerful formation in the life of Christ by using the spiritual disciplines over time to shape apprentices of Jesus. Today, books calling for and expecting significant change in believers are rare. Some writers have even admitted that significant progress in obedience in this life is not possible. There is a growing acceptance of the sanctification gap (or we could call it a "transformation gap") as being not only our real experience but even normal. Grace settles our eternal destiny, but we will have to wait for it to do much more for us until we get to heaven. Our life on earth becomes more of a waiting room than an adventure or journey with God.

One of the greatest difficulties in ministry is that now even pastors and leaders—not just those they minister to—no longer expect significant life change beyond that at conversion. The kind of life Jesus presented in the Sermon on the Mount is not seen as possible. Many have given up on a life free of worry, lust, anger, contempt, gossip, and greed. As the bumper sticker says, "Christians aren't perfect, just forgiven." Perfecting or progressing in holiness is not expected in this life, despite the many Scriptures that claim this life is the only perfecting place we can expect.

Dallas Willard had captured my imagination, and I began to get a vision of what life in Christ is supposed to be. I, along with others on this same journey, have begun to put on Christ's "easy yoke," believing that change is possible. Over time, we have found this vision to take hold in us and in those who have been influenced by our lives, many without our even saying a word. They just saw a difference in me, for example, starting with my wife and kids and my friends and workmates.

Although I feel that I have barely begun to progress and don't live up to what I now know, I actually have learned to put away an anger that used to quickly turn into a cold and calculated rage. I'm learning to love my enemies, to live without contempt, to live more at peace than in worry and fear, to let go of my need to control, to trust more in God and others. Though I still fail to live fully and freely in this new place—and I have lots of ground to cover in many areas of my life—there is no doubt that I am being changed and cannot go back to the way I lived before. In fact, I have found that loving an enemy and leaving my life in God's hands are less work and easier than being bound up in contempt and control. I am beginning to know the truth of the "easy yoke" and 1 John 5:3, that God's commands are not burdensome; in fact, they are enjoyable!

THE EVANGELICAL DOUBLE LIFE: A SPIRITUAL OR CHURCH LIFE ALONGSIDE YOUR REAL LIFE

How could I have become so inattentive to my wife and son in my real life while believing I was paying attention to God in my spiritual life—regular devotions and service to God's kingdom? Besides being something here and

...., ..ot just in heaven, I also came to see that I kept transformation in only one part of my life—my spiritual life. This resulted in my living a double life, with my real life unaffected by my spiritual life. I had my devotions and considered myself to have a good spiritual life. I knew and studied the Scriptures as well as any pastor I knew. I even memorized verses. I was very busy with Christian service and rather proud of how much I was doing for God and our church. But I didn't understand why my professional and devotional life didn't have much to do with how I treated my wife and son. As I grew in my new journey, I became aware that my "real life" and my "spiritual life" were two different categories in my head and that I was living a "double life." I had even been promoting this same split life in my preaching without being aware of it. I had been asking people to attend to their spiritual lives, which meant having their devotions and going to church. This involved attending preaching and worship services, participating in programs, and serving at church. Were their real lives as untouched as mine? Did they notice that too? I began to realize that when someone asks, "How is your spiritual life?" he usually means, "Have you been practicing spiritual disciplines and been involved with church?" He's not asking about the spirit or quality of your relationships or your character.

I began to see that all of life is spiritual. To split off religious activities as my spiritual life betrayed the fact that I didn't consider the rest of my life as needing transformation. A person's whole life, in all its dimensions, needs to be transformed, and it must be more than just church activity or practicing some disciplines simply laid alongside the unchanged reality of that person's life. This includes all areas of a person's life, including mind (thoughts, feelings), body, spirit (heart, will), and social relationships. In *Renovation of the Heart,* Dallas Willard explained, "When successful, spiritual formation (or, really, *re*formation) unites the divided heart and life of the individual. That person can then bring remarkable harmony into the groups where he or she participates."[3]

My anger, control, rage, lust, people pleasing, worry, and fear—and my general drivenness—was split off from God's touch. And that contributed to my lack of harmony with others. At best, I confessed these patterns and asked forgiveness for my guilt, only to fall into these same sin habits over and over in what Dallas Willard called "sin management."[4] But I never thought repentance and real change or mortification of these sins was possible.

Much advice on spiritual growth and Christian living in evangelical circles unwittingly teaches a form of the double life — the assumption that the disciplines and church activity make up the spiritual life and that somehow just doing your devotions will change your real life. How is it we believe that one or two hours on a Sunday morning can bring significant change to our lives? Most remedies for sin boil down to lack of church attendance or failure to maintain a devotional life. We believe that church programming, small groups and Bible studies, missions trips, and service at church are the ways to bring change to our real lives. But they often remain untouched.

Willow Creek Community Church in South Barrington, Illinois, has done a courageous self-study called Reveal, which analyzed its church and six others to determine whether their programs were actually producing life change. Their conclusion from the reports of their own people is that participation in church programming does not effect significant life change beyond conversion. They concluded that teaching on the practice of the disciplines alone is not enough. There needs to be deep community in coaching and mentoring relationships with those more experienced in the Christian life so that people are trained in how the disciplines result in life change. In the foreword to the Reveal study, Bill Hybels, the megachurch's flagship pastor, tells of his pain in hearing from his top leaders that the research they had done on three decades of Willow Creek church activities revealed to them that Willow Creek had not done as well as they had thought in making fully devoted followers of Jesus. He shared that "when I heard these results, the pain of knowing was almost unbearable. Upon reflection, I realized that the pain of not knowing could be catastrophic."[5] This kind of courageous evaluation and honesty is needed across the board in evangelical ministry if we are to reconcile our spiritual lives with our real lives.

Most of the best-selling books by Christian authors on the Christian life reflect well-intentioned attempts at filling the transformation gap but actually contribute to a fragmented or double life by giving more head knowledge or formulas that don't bring life change. They have been used to help bring many to a conversion experience and to church, but they fall short of a vision and means for deep character building and kingdom life. We can dive into programs that incorporate spiritual practices into our lives, yet if these practices don't result in life change — if there is no solid instruction on how to actually change habits of anger, rage, lust, contempt, and control — we may simply redouble our religious activity. Without a vision for a new kind of life and the means to appropriate that life, our best intentions will just produce more of what we already have.

Others have tried to fill the transformation gap with versions of the "health and wealth gospel." This kind of teaching concentrates on the promise of "faith" for kingdom success. But it looks suspiciously like the American dream, not the dream of the kingdom of God or an eternal kind of life now. There simply are no shortcuts and no promises of worldly success or avoidance of suffering in the gospel of the kingdom. Paul said that in this life we should be content with food and clothing and expect to suffer loss for Christ. He said these kinds of sufferings actually are the program God has ordained for our growth in character. They are the way to real life.

My own chase after a successful ministry, my own kingdom-sized dream as measured by increasing attendance and programs, began to betray the kind of harried, driven, empty culture I was leading. I began to realize why so many successful ministers fall so hard. At first, when I would occasionally hear of a leader who had fallen off a pile of hard-won success to have an affair or self-destruct in some other way, I didn't put it together as I do now that he was not finding ministry all that fulfilling. Now I notice that many actually justified their behavior as what they felt they needed to do to find some relief since they were so depleted from ministry. Instead of church boards wondering what might be wrong with the whole system, including them, they simply either tolerated the sinner with cheap forgiveness or kept going on in the same way. Or they would scapegoat the fallen, going on to find another superstar who could fill the house. The show must go on! But the show began to come to a halt for me. And the stop sign that slowed me down surprised me when it showed up in a simple question from my son: "Are you home yet?"

Although I didn't fall hard through a sexual affair, my son's question exposed an affair I had been in with "success in ministry." But all these contradictions really hit home when my wife asked me to read a book about dysfunctional families, and it showed that my evangelical upbringing might be plagued with issues of performance, control, people pleasing, and ambition. When I saw it in me, I began to see where it was in my church, too. The gossip and power grabs, the pull to please powerful people, the need to have my way, and the fear that I wouldn't ever have as large a church as my father looked as broken and unhealthy as the church reflected in the well-known stastistics from Gallup and Barna. It was a documented loss of character in those who claim to be born again to a new kind of life. These were not counted as sins but as life as normal in church. I could no longer hide behind the mask of success in numbers. And that led me to an even deeper journey below the surface of my life to some issues that were hidden to me.

MINISTRY MASKS: SYSTEMS OF AMBITION, CONTROL, PERFORMANCE, AND PEOPLE PLEASING

How could I be so effective in church-growth methods and managing the church but so stunted in my own relational life? And if my family and I were in this condition, what was the true shape of the lives of the people so busy working out my ministry plan? Part of my journey involved facing my own brokenness and rebellion in my family system and in the church. My wife's journey included facing family-of-origin issues — some family secrets and dysfunctions that she began to work through with the help of a twelve-step group. We read a book by John and Linda Friel titled *Adult Children: The Secrets of Dysfunctional Families*, and we both took a test in the first chapter of the book that measured one's experience of family dysfunction. To my surprise, my family of upstanding evangelical professional workers scored even more dysfunctional than my wife's family, which my family considered kind of "messed up"!

The book explains that dysfunction comes in both "obvious" and "subtle" packages in family life. I found out that even though my family didn't have the obvious dysfunctions that typical twelve-step groups deal with, we had the subtle issues of performance, people pleasing, control, and ambition, which may even be rewarded in certain ways and are often rewarded in church cultures. I found that there were many like me in both professional and lay ministry. We were "performers" who pleased the "consumers" but missed most of the sheep who needed more than our religious goods and services offered in the dream of organizational success.

Once I had come to see that my real life was in need of transformation here and now and that my spiritual life was not the same as my religious activities, I recognized some areas of woundedness that lay below the surface of my life. These issues needed to be addressed if my real life was to be transformed rather than just dressed up in another form of the double life, only now called "spiritual formation." Without addressing these wounded areas, performers will turn an invitation to transformation into another opportunity to churn out different behaviors without a change of heart and life.

As I began to face these issues in my life, my marriage, and my own family as well as our extended families, I found the same issues in the systems of my church. This was especially true for my leaders but also for many in the congregation. There were those who looked good yet had the subtle issues that I did. Most of them were in church leadership—the church's performers. We wore our performance as masks of a false identity, hiding from our real selves but not knowing the kind of grace that would allow us to put these masks away and find our worth and identity in Christ rather than success. I began to make the connection to an ungodly ambition that was illustrated by my comparison of attendance figures as a measure of ministry success. I began to see how this ambition influenced many church ministry plans and was the cause of our drivenness.

Our church also had plenty of those with obvious problems like sex, alcohol, or drug addictions, but they didn't seem as bad as those in our church who were habitual gossips or control freaks with nasty tempers. And workaholism didn't even count as a problem, especially if you were the pastor. My ambition, which fueled so much of my frenzied activity, was a problem hidden to me until I began to question the direction of my life.

Kent Carlson, pastor of Oak Hills Community Church in Folsom, California, has said that when you "combine the dry wood of the average consumer Christian with the high octane jet fuel of pastoral ambition, you get an unholy fire" that masks systems of power and control in church leadership circles.[6] In her book *Counseling Adult Children of Alcoholics* Sandra Wilson has identified unhealthy patterns in church leadership and what she calls "unhelped helpers."

> These pastors, counselors, and others have never faced their own childhood struggles and scars from childhood experiences in dysfunctional families. They are less than helpful helpers because of their own misbeliefs, inaccurate identities, disrespectful relating patterns, and distorted God concepts.[7]

She said that it is "essential for Christian helpers to be honest about their needs for wise counsel and/or professional therapy once they have recognized their own brokenness."[8] If these broken areas of one's life are not identified and dealt with, they lie just below the surface and are powerful influences but go undetected in attempts to control others and perform to their expectations.

My identity reflected a woundedness that was unhealed and unrecognized. I felt the shame of this woundedness without knowing how it drove my obsession with attendance numbers of my church compared with my father's or those of other pastors I knew. Instead of being a ministry based on an identity informed by what God had done for me in Christ, my identity was tied up with what I did for God and how effective it was in terms of how many wanted my ministry. Although

I knew something was wrong, I thought I was the problem, and I attempted to rid myself of what I now know is shame by increasing my performance. But there was always someone or some church that was doing better. My identity was also tied up in how well I performed in my spiritual life. Doing my devotions and working for the church were legalistic measures of how spiritual I was, regardless of what my real life was like.

Through counseling and spiritual direction, I came to see that my true identity was not in the masks I put on to perform at church but in Christ and His grace. The moment of truth came when God helped me to take off my mask and begin to see myself through His eyes instead of my own and those of everyone else. Now the disciplines are not ways to prove my spirituality but ways to immerse myself in God's grace and His love for me. With issues of identity settled, ministry is now oriented around the needs of others instead of my need for affirmation. The disciplines become ways of moving into the new life Christ has for me rather than ways to perform or please others and God.

Without this healing of below-the-surface issues and the cultivation of safe environments of grace, the pursuit of the disciplines and transformation will actually be harmful and contribute to more performance-based and hypocritical communities. When my wife and I began our healing, we attended twelve-step groups like Adult Children of Alcoholics. We often remarked that the acceptance and support we experienced at these groups were what we thought should be the atmosphere of every church community. The church we now attend and serve is known as such a place of grace and safety. Being real, authentic, and vulnerable with one another is a stated value of our community.

Issues stay buried below the surface in environments filled with performance. Communities of grace must be cultivated where there is safety and trust for people to risk revealing their needs below the surface (see chapter 2). An increased call for transformation and use of the disciplines without grace-based communities will not just frustrate people with below-the-surface issues of life; it may actually do further damage and add to the hypocrisy and dysfunction in our communities.

At the least, it will result in accomplishing a shallow spiritual-formation makeover, covering up the unresolved problems in one's life and community. Care must be taken to deal not only with the obvious issues of chemical and sexual addictions and other dysfunctions that are seen as shameful by the community; we must also deal with the subtle issues of workaholism, performance, ambition, and people pleasing, which are often rewarded and disguised as evidence of spirituality.

EXAMINING MINISTRY METAPHORS: DOING BIG BUSINESS OR MAKING APPRENTICES OF JESUS

How did I get to the place where I was so off task, caring more about my church's "institutional extension and survival" and measuring success in business terms of attendance, buildings, and cash rather than in becoming and making mature disciples of Jesus? After leaving my former church to take a yearlong break from ministry and to work on my life and find some healing, I reentered ministry to become executive pastor of a church that was much larger than my previous one, with three thousand in attendance. I was drawn to this church due to its unique "recovery" spirituality and my hunger for a kind of church that wasn't just about big business.

Most of our staff and lay leaders, including the senior pastor, set out on this journey of formation together. We noticed that the programs we were successfully promoting were not only weak in transforming people but were taking us off task from our own formation. Our church had reached the capacity of our facilities and was at the point where churches usually add more services or go to multisites. We knew we had a choice to make with our limited time and energy. Would we pursue our own individual and corporate transformation as a community of disciples, or would we spend our lives on attracting and managing bigger crowds?

I knew pastors who ran from service to service or from one multisite to another in the effort to accommodate bigger crowds. We wanted no part of that. We didn't want to put on as many Christmas services as we could possibly manage, huffing and puffing in exhaustion while trying to communicate the peace of Jesus. The business metaphor that controlled most churches promoted the organization more than the transformation of people. We began our own corporate journey home to becoming a transforming community, but we needed some new metaphors for what we were doing.

As I began to get at my below-the-surface issues and found healing, I was able to take a more careful look at my ministry philosophy and the controlling metaphors behind it. Darrell Guder, in his book *Missional Church*, has concluded that the effect of our primary metaphors of managers and program technicians rather than leaders who model and foster disciple-making communities has co-opted the mission of the church. These metaphors presume that churches act more like businesses that produce religious goods and services. He has made the observation that many well-intentioned pastors and leaders of Christian organizations in the West have made as their priority "institutional extension and survival" as influenced by modernist perspectives of the church-growth movement.[9] The growth of the organization becomes the mission rather than the spiritual growth of the people. And regardless of a church's size, this business metaphor shapes the expectations of congregations to prefer pastors who act more as managers and CEOs of entrepreneurial corporations than of churches. Guder's challenge is to find new metaphors for leadership and ministry in order to enter into whole-life transformation.

In a journal for church leaders, a prominent evangelical megachurch pastor who is looked upon as a model for others was asked what he read to keep him sharp in ministry. His answer and his reasons are telling for understanding how the metaphors of formation have changed. After sharing that he almost exclusively reads secular business books as his preparation for ministry, he explained that he has traded his metaphor for leading from that of the pastor or shepherd of a flock of people to that of chief executive officer of an organization. He sees "pastor" as more appropriate for when churches were smaller and the pastor was a counselor for people's life problems. As churches are now growing larger and need to offer a variety of programs and services to meet people's needs, they require more and more management of paid and lay staff as well as technical leadership expertise in organizational design, just like any large growing business.

His understanding of pastoring as being therapeutic counseling and not the formation of disciples explains why he has abandoned it for the CEO metaphor. His near-exclusive reliance on business books reveals a presumption that organizational improvement will mean fulfilling the church's mission. He presented a good picture of how far we have moved away from the biblical and formationally powerful metaphor of pastoring as "care of souls" for growth into the character of Christ. But pastoring in the Bible is not about therapeutic counseling or organizational success. It is cooperating with the Chief Shepherd as under-shepherds in the formation of apprentices of Jesus, guiding them into "paths of righteousness for his name's sake" (Psalm 23:3) and not for the sake of the organization's growth.

Large and growing church enterprises abound, and they often package their programming success in conferences for other churches, presuming that you can bottle the success of technique and management and transfer it like a business plan to other churches. One conference I attended was promoting the latest business practices for adoption by churches. There was a discussion of "McDonaldizing" church activities to find a one-size-fits-all program that we could put everyone through quickly and then, once people are so "equipped," employ them in service to the church's activities and mission of growth. When I questioned whether this would produce mature disciples—and some in the group became interested in discussing my topic—the facilitator confidently redirected the group back to McChurch, asserting that we can take for granted that we are making disciples. With the results of studies like Willow Creek's Reveal, more and more leaders are no longer taking for granted that we are getting the job done with our present practices, even with best business practices.

Seldom is a church program given more than the one- or two-year life span before it is scrapped for something else if it doesn't bring numerical growth. Significant life change is expected by the end of the worship service—or at least at the end of forty days of intensive programming. Churches are grown in a marketing "minute" with advertising blitzes that create a critical mass of a minimum number of attendees in hopes of breaking the two hundred–, five hundred–, eight hundred–, one thousand–, and finally three thousand–people attendance barriers resulting in a very large church. Pastorates become stepping stones to larger ministries where the pastor's gifts can reach more people. While there is nothing wrong with the CEO or business model, it cannot become our primary metaphor for ministry. The dangers of focusing too much on it must be addressed.

The Bible offers several metaphors for our consideration. Paul's athletic metaphors for the spiritual life involve intense and extensive training and competition for three sports: long-distance running, wrestling, and prizefighting. These all presume a different approach than the assembly-line manufacturing and consumption aspects of big business. Paul urged us to train for godliness (see 1 Timothy 4:7-8) and called Timothy to be an example of what a trained spiritual athlete would look like. These metaphors are more organic than organizational and presume coaching, one-on-one relationships, and intensive and individualized training in learning life skills. What come to mind are the programs of a great football team or a high school wrestling or track team where coaches teach and conduct practices to form habits of living.

Other metaphors are those from agriculture, the military, and travel. Through his letter to Timothy, Paul called the individual to be like the good farmer or soldier who is faithful over time, who isn't shipwrecked on the journey toward home. These metaphors are connected to life's duration and even include pain, deserts, and dark nights of the individual and corporate soul. They fly in the face of the quick fixes offered in church programming, self-help sermons, and motivational worship experiences each week. Being more organic than organizational, the metaphors require a different kind of order for our communities and leadership training. The metaphor for a pastor who has the "cure of souls" is that of a trainer or coach offering patient preparation for the game or a farmer working through long seasons of plowing, sowing, watering, and finally harvesting. Or they are military commanders with recruits in battle, wounded to tend, and ground to occupy. They are pioneers with whole communities weathering mountains, valleys, and deserts on a long journey of migration.

Another set of powerful biblical metaphors for formation are those of modeling, apprenticeship, or mimicry, which call for the kind of close life-to-life relationship that Paul had with Timothy. Paul was able to say to Timothy, "You . . . know all about my teaching, my way of life, my . . . sufferings" (2 Timothy 3:10-11), because Timothy had simply been with Paul for long periods of time in all aspects of his life, and Timothy was able to catch formation more than even being taught it.

David Fitch, author of *The Great Giveaway: Reclaiming the Mission of Church from Big Business, Parachurch Organizations, Psychotherapy, Consumer Capitalism, and Other Modern Maladies*, has raised the question whether our business metaphor and church-growth methods reflect a loss of the church's mission to form disciples. He wondered if the typical success story of a church going from one hundred to one thousand in one year is not just undesirable but even wrong. His point is that the people who start that church often trade away meaningful relationships and transformative interactions for the business of servicing a larger and larger organization. Although his bias is for small congregations, his point bears merit that the larger a church grows, the harder it is to stay true to the mission of forming disciples and creating a transforming community that engages the world.

Hand in hand with this business model of ministry is the growth of consumer Christianity, which flips the church's mission from forming servants for service in the kingdom of God to managing and designing an organization that serves the needs of consumers of religious goods and services, called "programs." Many of the messages in our churches are also short self-help quick fixes that give the formula for being a good parent or having a good marriage. I referred earlier to the multitude of conferences offering to sell packages of proven programs. And yet studies of these teaching churches show that "using discipleship curriculum developed by any of the large, highly regarded churches" doesn't work for making disciples.[10] The many Bible studies and small-group programs contribute to more Bible knowledge without change of life. The fact is that we cannot mass-produce disciples. That is only done in communities where there are models of organic life-to-life relationships. There is no substitute for what the Spirit of God does as people living in the real world become missionally engaged with the least and the lost as a part of their everyday lives.

I am one of the pastors of a very large church, but one that has redirected everything it does to making mature disciples of Jesus. I still read business books like *Built to Last* and *The Wisdom of Teams* because part of what I do has a business aspect, and I find most of these authors to be very helpful. The best of them, such as Jim Collins and Patrick Lencioni, have much to say that fits with sound spiritual practices. But, ultimately, they don't help with what I am supposed to have as my bottom line. Our church is a large and complex organization and a significant business endeavor, but that is not the controlling metaphor for our leadership.

In contrast to the business metaphor, Darrell Guder has suggested the metaphor of the kind of leadership found in religious orders. He called for designers of formation cultures in communities. He challenged our current models that train and employ the core members and leaders to pull off consumer programs that attract greater numbers, then employ these new members just to attract a larger crowd, presuming that disciples are somehow being made. Guder suggested that churches have a different strategy for the core leadership: to help them in their formation and to cultivate missional communities of formation. These become models of formation for the congregation. So instead of concentrating on using the core to build larger crowds, the core concentrates on those wanting to live in formation. They, in turn, invite others in the congregation into that formational journey.

This strategy is confirmed in the Reveal study. Reveal showed that many of Willow Creek's top leaders were considering leaving the church due to dissatisfaction with serving in the church's programmatic approach and its organizational focus on more numbers in programs. They preferred to be in coaching situations where the disciplines were not just studied in isolation but were part of a mentoring relationship resulting in life change.

Dallas Willard has often said that when leaders enter into apprenticeship with Jesus, their ministries may not look much different from the old way. We will need similar kinds of programming. The difference is in how and why we are programming. Is it to build the organization in a driven way that depletes those who minister? Or is it to create an environment that is life giving and restful?

THE WAY HOME TO WHOLE-LIFE TRANSFORMATION: A PLACE TO START

Dad, Will You Ride with Me?

I had the privilege of accompanying my son, Kyle (now twenty-five), as he qualified for his Professional Golf Association player's ability test. As part of becoming a golf pro, he had to play two rounds of eighteen holes on one day within a certain number of strokes. He played well and passed, a feat few accomplish as most have to try again and again. I arrived with Kyle at the event, surprised to find none of the other pros with a partner like me—and certainly not their dads! I asked him why he had asked me to ride along. He told me something I will never forget; it probably didn't mean as much to him as it did to me, in light of his question so many years ago. In explaining what my presence meant to him on that special day, he said, "Dad, you calm me down." Immediately my mind flashed to that day so many years before when Kyle's question had stopped me in my tracks, calling me away from a driven preoccupation with success in ministry that was pulling me out of his life. That question helped steer me to a different kind of life with God, my family, and others—a kind of life that others will want and will follow because it leads to home, to God, and to each other. It was a kind of life that I was able to model to Kyle in a way that touched him and caused him to want my influence.

Paul's Question: Are You an Example for Others?

Another question has captured my attention in the way that Kyle's did. It comes from Paul's frequent call in his letters for people to follow him as he followed Christ. Kyle's question awakened me to my example and how far it was from that of Paul or Christ. I used to think that Paul's question was not for me. It seemed impossible — not just for me, but for most of us. I now see that the gospel of the kingdom asks Paul's question of all of us.

As I started living this new life, my wife began to notice the changes. She asked me about my spiritual director and found one for herself. I didn't push what I had found on our staff. But they, too, began to ask about the changes they had seen in my life and wanted to know how that was happening. I began to take retreats to care for my soul and learned to spend time in silence and solitude in order to hear God's voice and submit to His work of formation in me. This has led to our staff asking to join me in a retreat of quiet and solitude. Called "Wasting Time with God and Each Other," it has become the high point of our year and has powerfully transformed the lives of our leaders. I learned that the best teaching we can do comes from our own lives as we journey with Jesus.

Dallas Willard asked if the kind of life we lead as leaders is the kind of life that others would want. Bill Thrall and Bruce McNicol asked that same question a little differently: "Are we the kind of leaders others would *want* to follow rather than *have* to follow?" I have a saying too: "Your ministry is your life and your life is your ministry." Character is not just a qualification for ministry; it *is* our ministry. Our ministry plan is mainly the lives of our people, and that starts with staff—and staff starts with me.

For years I had read the words of Paul in 1 Corinthians 11:1, "Follow my example, as I follow the example of Christ," and viewed it as a call for the superspiritual and not for ordinary people or leaders. I thought you had to be almost perfect to say that. I know now that anyone who is intentionally following Jesus and has asked Him to be his or her teacher in life can say those words and expect to say them to others as intentional examples to imitate. The first point of our ministry plan was intentional modeling as apprentices of Jesus. Paul called his readers to follow his example as he followed Christ.

When you ask most believers if they can say this along with Paul, they balk and say they would have to be perfect. Somewhere along the way we have lost the view of salvation as a life we could actually imitate and live. Paul's letters challenge us to be living examples of Christ's life. He not only thought it possible, he saw it as the only way for salvation to be passed on. And as he crossed life's finish line, he knew His Teacher was alive and well and would continue to give his followers instruction.

Our lives—and the example we pass on to others—are the most powerful "program" we can work on in ministry. Paul told Timothy, "Watch your life and doctrine closely. Persevere in them, because if you do, you will save both yourself and your hearers" (1 Timothy 4:16). Of course, we are all trying to "uncatch and unlearn" certain bad things that we received into our lives without asking for them, from family, parents, peers, schoolteachers, church workers, and others who had formative influences on us. But we are also grateful for all those things that we learned and caught that shaped us for good. The power of an exemplary life is probably the most important teaching of Jesus, Paul, and the other writers of the New Testament as well as the early church fathers. Imitation and mimicry abound in their writings and testimonies. There is a passed-down living tradition of *life* that we are missing.

But as it says in Hebrews 13, we can remember those who preached the Word of God to us and consider the outcome of their lives. If that is absent or not alive to us now, we need not be discouraged. "Jesus Christ is the same yesterday and today and forever" (verse 8). He is the only great religious teacher of life who is alive today and giving moment-by-moment instruction to those who ask Him for it. And when two or more are asking, Jesus shows up and holds class in powerful formational and missional community!

In his first letter to Timothy, Paul described what a transformed life looks like. It contains a message that I find mostly ignored, except for the verses about preaching and teaching. Paul's main concern was that Timothy had a life that taught and exemplified his oral teaching; without that, his teaching was just words.

> Command and teach these things . . . set an *example* [τυποσ] for the believers in speech, in life, in love, in faith and in purity. . . . Be diligent in these matters; give yourself wholly to them, so that everyone may see your progress. Watch your life and doctrine closely. Persevere in them, because if you do, you will save both yourself and your hearers. (1 Timothy 4:11-12,15-16, emphasis added)

The Greek word τυποσ (*tupos*) has four different meanings. First, it can mean "to mark from pressure or to strike" or "to leave a mark." You might call to mind the popular expression "That'll a leave a mark." Second, it means making a "copy" or an "icon" and is used to describe the similar look of a child's facial features to a parent. Third, it means "a pattern or form of life" or "a common way of life." Fourth, it means something like a "type" or similar kind.

Paul's use of this word implies that there is a process that is "life on life" in such a way that one is marked or becomes different, and (as in the verses above) we begin to look like Jesus. Paul was concerned with calling individuals into his life to be marked by him as he was marked by Jesus' life.

The word *tupos* is also used for a corporate example. Paul called communities to become patterns that were marked as well. The church in Thessalonica, after seeing and following Paul and his workers' examples, became an example as a whole community. Paul said their example became a message that rang out across the whole nation. Is it possible that even today we could see a nation or nations affected by the power of a few leaders with vision, means, and intention to be transformed by Christ? Are there groups of leaders today like those in John Wesley's holy club and the resulting classes and societies that contributed to the great revivals of England and New England—groups that produced changes in culture that are still with us today in hospitals and educational institutions?

Kyle's question—"Dad, are you home yet?"—continues to be on my mind, but now it is a spiritual discipline that calls me back home to the life that is, more and more, making a home in me, my family, and my church. Are you—are we—on our way home yet to the easy yoke of obedience and abundant life that is available in Jesus?

FOR REFLECTION AND DISCUSSION

1. In your ministry context where is the transformation gap present? Is the assumption that there is a gap central to ministry or accidental?
2. What would you communicate as the expectations for formation in this life and what things will be deferred to the next life? How can you communicate the latter without diluting the blessings of the former and the calling to move into the blessings of formation available in this life?
3. Do you believe that there is an inherent trade-off between ministry expansion and ministry depth? Does your ministry context, and, in particular, those in leadership with you, experience tension between these two?
4. What steps would need to take place in your ministry in order to eliminate the distinction between the spiritual life and the rest of life? What resistance would the people to whom you minister have regarding the movement toward whole-life formation?
5. What ministry masks are you currently wearing? How invested are you in those masks? What elements of your true identity are those masks hiding from the people in your ministry contexts? How would taking those masks off provide an example to those around you?

FOR FURTHER READING

Barton, Ruth Haley. *Strengthening the Soul of Your Leadership: Seeking God in the Crucible of Ministry.* Downers Grove, IL: InterVarsity, 2008.

Guder, Darrell L. *The Continuing Conversion of the Church.* Grand Rapids, MI: Eerdmans, 2000.

Lovelace, Richard. *Dynamics of Spiritual Life: An Evangelical Theology of Renewal.* Downers Grove, IL: InterVarsity Academic, 1979.

Willard, Dallas. *Renovation of the Heart: Putting on the Character of Christ.* Colorado Springs, CO: NavPress, 2002.

Chapter Six

FORMED THROUGH
SUFFERING

Peggy Reynoso

ELEMENT 6: Spiritual formation occurs when God, in His grace, invades the destructiveness of suffering that results from the fall of man and uses the pain of suffering for His redemptive purposes in His people. There is also a unique suffering that shapes the formation of believers as they enter into the call to love a lost world and the inevitable suffering that results from that love.

Description: For the follower of Jesus, no suffering is without meaning in our formation in Christ. All humanity suffers as a result of the Fall, but in the believer's journey of following Jesus, suffering takes on formational meaning when God, in His grace, enters into the pain of suffering to comfort and shape us into the image of Christ. Beyond suffering that is common to all men, followers of Jesus Christ are called to a particular kind of suffering as they embrace and live out God's love in the world and experience the inevitable suffering that results from that love (see John 15:18-20). This unique suffering opens the door to enter into the fellowship of Christ's sufferings, and we fill up what is lacking in Christ's suffering (see Colossians 1:24).

❧ ❧ ❧

Spiritual formation often occurs in the refining crucible of suffering. Our inmost selves are revealed in affliction, and as we learn to commit ourselves more deeply to the redemptive purposes of God, we grow in our capacity to exercise faith, hope, and love in the midst of troubles and trials. God uses adversity to shape our souls—and thus to spread the aroma of Christ.

God calls us to participate with Him in the process of our spiritual formation, but we do not initiate some of the most life-changing experiences in our journey. They are unexpectedly thrust upon us in the form of failure, loss, injury, illness, pain, exploitation, and unfulfilled desires. These painful experiences can shake our foundations and expose our deepest longings and weaknesses. Because suffering affects us deeply, it can also be profoundly transformative, giving us opportunities for knowing our inmost selves, deepening our experience of intimacy with God, and growing in Christlikeness.

In a book on spiritual transformation, you might think that the chapter on suffering would tell you what good things suffering and loss can be, but the misfortunes, illnesses, deprivation, and cruelty that cause our pain are still intrinsically bad, despite how God may use them for good. While we have the great promise of Romans 8:28 that God may redeem suffering by bringing good out of it for those who love Him, it is not what we want, nor should want, and it is not what God wants or originally intended.

Our experience of suffering must be linked to our theology of suffering so that we do not offer easy answers to the problem of pain. Our unrealized longings ground us in the strange muddle of divine love, truth, and grace and the forces of sin that form the believer's reality in living out the kingdom of God on earth. They remind us that we are human, that we cannot know all that we are desperate to understand, and that we desperately need God. As we grapple with doubts and questions that arise out of our own suffering, we are changed in the process and are given an opportunity to incarnate the gospel for our generation. As others witness our struggles and faith in adversity and see God's sustaining grace bringing light to dark, painful places in our lives, they receive hope that God can be trusted in their own broken lives.

Suffering brings us face-to-face with the painful question of why a good and powerful God would allow bad things to happen to beings he professes to love. Like Jacob, great men and women of God have wrestled with God over the questions that arise out of suffering, and in the end they come away with few answers but a greater reassurance of God's goodness and promises. Our failure to fully grasp the "Why?" question does not change the fact that God Himself has lifted the veil sufficiently for us to see—and experience—some reassuring truths about suffering, some of which are found in surprising places.

THE REALITY OF SIN

In our technological age, a train wreck in China appears on our computer and television screens within minutes of the accident. The evening news brings images of an earthquake's destruction in Ecuador, a drive-by shooting on the South Side, and a teen's fatal auto accident. Even though we have become accustomed to a daily diet of disaster, pain, and loss, this disorder does not feel natural. When our turn to face tragedy comes and the dreaded knock wakes us in the middle of the night, when test results indicate advanced cancer, when chronic pain once again denies us desperately needed rest, our spirit bows under the weight of suffering and rebounds in protest. It doesn't seem right, and it doesn't seem fair.

The experiences that cause our suffering feel unnatural because, directly or indirectly, they are a result of sin. When God warned Adam in Genesis 2 that if they ate of the tree of the knowledge of good and evil they would, as the NIV puts it, "surely die" (verse 17), in the Hebrew there is a repeat of the word for death, and some scholars prefer the translation "dying you will die." Sin does not result in a single act of death and misery; it brings repeated death and suffering to a world that was created good.

Sin is not only an individual act or predisposition, it is also a force in our world. In Romans Paul spoke of sin as an active agent. He told us that sin entered the world through Adam, bringing death with it to reign on earth (see 5:12-14), calling sin a slave master who controls those who obey it (see 6:12-18). He spoke of sin seizing the opportunity to condemn us through the law (see 7:8), of sin living and working in us to make us do what we don't want to do (see 7:14-20). The consequences of sin in our world are not always a result of an individual's sinful choice. When sin entered the world through Adam, it took on a life of its own.

The wages of sin, in all of its forms, is death, in all of its manifestations, and though Jesus paid the price of death for us, not all of sin's consequences are erased by pardon.[1] Believers and unbelievers alike live with powerful effects of sin in our world, most of which are not direct results of our personal choices, and the wounds of our world will not be completely healed until Jesus returns. We err when we look to suffering to reveal whether God is just or unjust because what it best exposes is the destructive nature of sin. The pain that results from sin's fallout is the suffering common to all humans, and it originates from three primary sources: (1) human choice, (2) creation in bondage, and (3) powers and principalities.

Human Choice: When Sinful Decisions Cause Suffering

"To err is human," Alexander Pope's famous words remind us, and most of our errors originate from a perspective warped by sin. This is the inner-heart disease that Augustine called *homo incurvatus in se* (to be turned in on ourselves). We turn away from God and our fellow man to an inward focus on ourselves. Whether we view Adam and Eve's sin as a fall from perfection or as a failure to attain that for which they were created, from the time they ate the forbidden fruit there are ways in which all humans are marked by sin — most notably, that from birth our perception of reality is skewed by mistrust and self-centeredness. Like sheep that have gone astray, each of us has turned to our own way (see Isaiah 53:6), and the consequences have been ones that we — and Adam and Eve — never imagined.

We are idol worshippers when we choose to go our own way, placing our trust not in God but in ourselves and the objects of our desires. In our self-reliance we make choices that harm us and others. Incompetence and rebellion lead to foolish decisions, risk taking, and overindulgence, which in turn cause accidents, injury, disease, death, and suffering. Intentional and malicious harm that humans inflict on one another causes a world of grief, pain, and injustice. Choices that spring from ignorance, neglect, and indifference passively but effectively hurt individuals and people groups, sometimes perpetuating unjust systems on entire nations of people. Deliberately inflicted pain has a special sting because the wounding is personal. In slights or attacks on our character, our person, or our loved ones, we have been targeted and disrespected. Our wounds require not only physical, spiritual, and emotional healing but also the healing that only forgiveness can bring.

Not all harmful choices are intentional or sinful. To err is human not only because we sin but also because we have human limitations. Ask any parent whose toddler has drowned; a moment of distraction can result in a lifetime of regret. Sometimes we cannot prevent tragedy simply because our strength and knowledge are not sufficient or we are not in the right place at the right time. Our human limitations remind us that we are not God, that we cannot prevent calamity, that we will give and receive pain in this life. Our limitations have nothing to do with sinful choices but with our nature as finite human beings, reminding us of the only place we can seek absolute strength.

Creation in Bondage: Reaping the Harvest of Sin

All creation suffers hurt, damage, erosion, death, and decay (see Romans 8:20-22) because God linked nature to the consequences of Adam and Eve's sin, refusing to leave us as the only creatures on earth that die and decay. God allowed sin to distort His creation and cause suffering for the redemptive purpose of drawing us back to Him. The impermanent life cycle of decay and violent food chain of death that we know as integral elements of nature are in fact characteristics of a temporary, unnatural state. God put Earth under death's reign in the hope that "the creation itself will be set free from its bondage to decay and will obtain the freedom of the glory of the children of God" (Romans 8:21, NRSV). Meanwhile, until its liberation the natural world suffers pain, and humans suffer with it through the wildness of nature: lightning, earthquakes, tsunamis, floods, droughts, violence of hunter on prey, and the slow degeneration that causes aging and dying.

The outcomes of sin in nature are so obviously beyond our control that we refer to them as "acts of God." When natural forces cause suffering, we recognize that no one but a supernatural being could control nature's power. God may use nature to carry out His plans, but He is not the source of damage and death in our world. The Bible tells us about instances where God uses nature to protect (for example, the parting of the Red Sea so the Israelites could escape from the Egyptian army) or punish (drought in the time of Elijah to remind Israel of God's power), but we should be wisely cautious about viewing natural disasters as punishment from God. What we can be sure of is that they are a consequence of creation's distortion by sin.

Powers and Principalities: The World, the Flesh, and the Devil War Against Us

Until Christ returns, we live in a world in which the darkness of sin and evil corrupts human systems. As God's children we are called to live, as much as possible, as citizens of the new age, redeeming, to the extent we can, the world that C. S. Lewis called "the Dark Planet."[2] This includes guiding others into the redeeming rule of God and extending the influence of God over human structures, institutional forces, and societal influences. Though we tend to think of powers and principalities only as evil spiritual forces, the apostle Paul dealt with the trouble of living in this world through a cluster of terms that included power(s), thrones, authorities, virtues, dominions, and names (see Romans 8:38; 1 Corinthians 15:24; Ephesians 1:21; 3:10; 6:12; Colossians 1:16; 2:10,15). The powers and authorities, in the broader understanding, are "cultural, sociopolitical, economic, and spiritual forces which give structure to the shared human endeavors which make up our world, both the outer and the inner structures of life, both the earthly and the heavenly."[3] Joel

Shuman and Brian Volck, in *Reclaiming the Body*, defined the powers as "the seen and unseen, personal and impersonal institutional forces that provide necessary order, or 'structure,' making possible a common human life."[4]

Life in this world is hard, because of the effects of sin on creation (among them our own corrupted desires of the flesh) and because flawed human systems (the world) and malevolent spiritual beings (the Devil) work against those who seek to live by God's values. Human and spiritual structures come under the influence of damaged and corrupt world systems, insatiable desires of the flesh (i.e., greed), and Satan, who desires to enslave the hearts and souls of men and women. The result is suffering beyond measure. Powers in the form of war, ethnic cleansing, slavery, systemic prejudice, and unjust dominance of the strong over the weak, from the schoolyard bully to Idi Amin, break spirits and bodies by the weight of suffering they impose.

Jesus defeated the powers through His death and resurrection (see Colossians 2:15), and through Him "God was reconciling the world [*kosmos*] to himself in Christ, not counting men's sins against them" (2 Corinthians 5:19). *Kosmos* includes the world of humankind and its order or structure, so we can say that God was in Christ reconciling to Himself not just individuals but people groups with their unifying structures. Though Jesus has triumphed over the powers, their reconciliation to God is being worked out through an ongoing process, just as God's reconciliation with individuals is an unfolding realization of Christ's work on the cross. Christians participate with God in reconciling human systems when we move them toward carrying out the desires of their Creator.

MY STORY

In the last fifteen years our family has experienced grievous losses that have caused us to see suffering in a different light. Soon after we moved back to the United States in 1993 (after twenty years as missionaries in Mexico), my husband was diagnosed with advanced prostate cancer.

His doctor was initially reluctant to treat him, suggesting instead that he make the most of the time he had left. After a year of mourning his impending death and enduring surgeries, radiation treatments, and hormone therapy, we began to hope that God had chosen to heal him. Now, twelve years later, he sees his surgeon twice a year because the doctor can hardly believe the walking miracle that is Paul.

About the time that my husband's health was returning, our oldest son, who was married and living in a nearby city, began to manifest the first signs of severe depression and schizophrenia. He and his wife separated, and he moved back home with us. Over the past nine years we have lived experiences we thought were unimaginable in our family, and daily we grieve how mental illness has severely limited and rearranged his life and ours.

A year after our oldest son's dark journey began, our fifteen-year-old daughter, Paula, began having nausea, dizziness, and vomiting in the night. At first it was episodic, but the attacks became more frequent with each passing month. In the third and fourth years she was violently ill every night and every morning, and sometimes nausea and vertigo kept her bedridden around the clock. Helplessly we watched her suffer as we consulted one doctor after another. Our situation was much like that of the woman with chronic bleeding who reached out to Jesus for healing: "She had suffered a great deal under the care of many doctors and had spent all she had, yet instead of getting better she grew worse" (Mark 5:26).

While we were living with two children in downward spirals of physical and mental illness, another son had recurrent lung collapses; Paul fell out of a tree and shattered his shoulder, never recovering its full use; I was diagnosed with a congenital electrical problem of the heart that required catheterization and ablation; and I lost fine motor skills in my hands, particularly handwriting, from developing dystonia. After five years of stress and anguish, we were worn out physically and emotionally. In desperation, we clung to the God who apparently wasn't there. We talked and wrote openly about our struggles and doubts, as well as our faith and enduring hope. Our letters read like the Psalms, opening with hard truths, progressing to analyzing issues behind our questions, and ending with affirmations of God's goodness and love.

Things went from bad to worse for our daughter. Despite the limitations long-term illness had imposed on her life, she handled her suffering with grace and good humor for three years, entertaining friends and family with stories about her medical misadventures—until the fourth year of her illness, when she became discouraged and depressed. Her doctor put her on medication, but antidepressants sometimes deepen depression in teens, and such was the case with Paula. She began talking about suicide, and many nights I would stay up with her until one or two in the morning. After she went to sleep, I would stay up longer and pray, begging God for her life and recovery. After a change in medication, she began to pull out of the depression, though her vertigo symptoms were unrelenting. In spite of her illness she enrolled in community college and enjoyed being in school again.

A month later, at age nineteen, our daughter was killed in an automobile accident, a passenger in a car whose driver fell asleep at the wheel. Her shockingly sudden death has been the hardest experience of our lives. In the past I had written about suffering, but I couldn't think of this loss as being in the same class as trials and tribulations because it was like comparing a Category 5 hurricane with a summer thunderstorm. Over the last three years my personal experience with suffering has taken on new and dark dimensions.

WHERE IS GOD WHEN WE HURT? THE FELLOWSHIP OF HIS SUFFERINGS

I want to know Christ and the power of his resurrection and the fellowship of sharing in his sufferings, becoming like him in his death, and so, somehow, to attain to the resurrection from the dead.
—Philippians 3:10-11

After our daughter's death, my husband and I entered into an awful fellowship with other bereaved parents. At a seminar on grieving and in chance encounters of daily life, we were drawn as if by a magnet to other parents who had lost children. We also felt instant affinity with those who had suffered other tragedies. A co-worker with a ten-year-old son, who had escaped from a physically abusive marriage only to be destitute and jobless, shared her story with me and then apologized for eliciting my compassion. "I know I have no idea of what you have gone through; nothing compares with losing a child," she said. "Maybe not," I told her, "but you know what it is like to be desperate." Pain is pain, and it is not diminished by comparing it to the pain of others.

The fellowship of suffering joins those who share little else in common. The intimate knowledge of our own pain allows us to enter into the suffering of others and awakens us to the pain of God and the suffering of Christ. This is a measure of what it means to share the sufferings of Christ. We identify more fully with Christ's struggle and sacrifice because we know our own pain. As we identify more with His suffering, our gratitude for His sacrifice is deepened. Just as Jesus' death was a necessary step before His resurrection, so our death to ourselves in suffering allows us to experience more of the power of His resurrection (see Philippians 3:10). Suffering is a prelude to experiencing resurrection.

Our sufferings also bring us into partnership with Christ. "Now I rejoice in my sufferings for your sake, and in my flesh I do my share on behalf of His body, which is the church, in filling up what is lacking in Christ's afflictions" (Colossians 1:24, NASB). Christ's afflictions are not lacking in their atoning sufficiency; they are lacking in that they are not experienced by all people.[5] Jesus did some of His most powerful work through suffering and self-denial, and now He calls us to do the same. His agonizing death on the cross made it possible for us to draw near to God, and God now draws others to Himself through revealing His power and faithfulness in our faith in the midst of suffering.

L. Ann Jervis, in her excellent analysis of suffering in the books of 1 Thessalonians, Philippians, and Romans, said,

> Believers know affliction primarily because [it] is the necessary prelude to . . . the birth of the new age in which God's will is done. And believers, who are essential to God's continuing project of delivering God's creation from evil, will necessarily

partake of suffering, since, as Christ himself demonstrated, deliverance requires suffering.[6]

She continued,

Paul understood the sufferings of Christ to be related positively to the birthing of the new age . . . [choosing] the word [for a woman's birth pangs] to describe both Christ's and believers' suffering. . . . Therefore, while the good news promises eternal life and escape from the wrath to come, it also requires that now believers wait. And, in the waiting is suffering, for we are waiting for the full emergence of the new age. We are in the throes . . . of giving birth. Just as Jesus' suffering contributed to the birth of the new age, so does the suffering of believers.[7]

For those who place their hope in Christ, suffering is life-giving. In Karl Barth's words, "Our suffering is no longer a passive, dangerous, poisonous, destructive tribulation . . . but is transformed into a tribulation . . . which [is] creative, fruitful, powerful, promising."[8] Sometimes we get to see how our hardships and pain draw ourselves and others to God, giving us glimpses of being part of a far-reaching divine plan. When we do not see how any good could come out of the bad that has befallen us, we have the hope that our suffering will be productive in God's economy, that our affliction will be used as part of God's eternal plan and saving work. While it may be costly, it will be rewarded. Though its cause may be unclear and its purpose unknown, our suffering is not random or senseless because God's work in and through us gives it meaning.

SUFFERING FOR THE CAUSE OF CHRIST

God invites Christians into a type of formational suffering that is not the consequence of illness, accidents, or natural disasters. This pain comes as a result of our commitment to honor Christ and live by the values of His kingdom. It may result as a consequence of forgiving one who has wronged us, continuing to serve someone who has mistreated us, making a choice of integrity in our work, opposing an unjust authority, or simply loving a difficult neighbor. Literally, we pay a price for the sake of the gospel.

Christ has set an example for us in believer-specific suffering. Hebrews 12:2 says that Jesus "endured the cross, scorning its shame" for our sakes, and for the joy that would come after the Resurrection. The writer of Hebrews encouraged us to remember Jesus' sacrifice so that we would not lose heart in our own suffering for the gospel. Peter told the church that it is to this kind of voluntary suffering that God invites us: "To this you were called, because Christ suffered for you, leaving you an example, that you should follow in his steps" (1 Peter 2:21). This is not a masochistic seeking of suffering but a choice to accept the same cost of obedience that Jesus endured. We do not choose suffering, but as we try to live out the values of God's kingdom in a world that does not submit to Him, conflict and suffering inevitably result. This formational suffering is unique to the Christ follower. A young adult who chooses not to party immorally, at the cost of friendships, bears the mark of Jesus and pays a price for the sake of the kingdom. A businesswoman who chooses to do the right thing, at the expense of her career in which she has invested years of training and experience, follows in the footsteps of Jesus.

Even in Christian fellowship, living in community will expose selfishness, ambition, jealousy, dissension, and impurity, presenting us with choices that can result in personal stress and loss. We may actually suffer more for the sake of the gospel within the Christian community than outside of it. When we are defrauded or mistreated, only the Christian carries the obligation to "forgive as the Lord forgave you," over all other virtues to "put on love," and to "as far as it depends on you, live at peace with everyone" (Colossians 3:13-14; Romans 12:18). Acts of love require Christlike sacrifice.

Peter understood that Christians mature when they suffer for doing right: "The God of all grace . . . after you have suffered a little while, will himself restore you and make you strong, firm and steadfast" (1 Peter 5:10; see also 2:19-21; 3:14). Peter implied that one of the reasons we should rejoice in this suffering is because through it we will mature into Christ Jesus, who "suffered for you" (1 Peter 2:21; see also 4:13; 5:10).

Because we know that obeying God and living by kingdom values will cause us to pay a price, sometimes we choose to avoid suffering and settle for less than God has intended for us. In doing so, we miss out on experiencing the powerful reality of Paul's words, "that I may know Him . . . and the fellowship of His sufferings" (Philippians 3:10, NASB). God does not will this kind of suffering on us but urges us to accept what price the gospel may bring us.

Suffering is a discipline we receive, not one we seek, but there is a sense in which the Scriptures enjoin us to choose suffering, and that is in bearing one another's burdens (see Galatians 6:2). As we do the work of Christ, we lift heavy loads for others in many ways, and this verse particularly refers to the oppressive weight of temptation and spiritual failure. We also unburden those in emotional and physical pain by entering into their place of suffering with them, crying with them and carrying their pain in prayer to the Great Comforter. When we choose to enter into the suffering of others, sharing their pain and comforting them with the same comfort we have received from God (see 2 Corinthians 1:3-5), we lift some of the weight of suffering off them. This is a voluntary choice to suffer in the service of Christ.

THE TRINITY SUFFERS WITH US

In all their troubles,
he was troubled, too.
He didn't send someone else to help them.
He did it himself, in person.
Out of his own love and pity
he redeemed them.
He rescued them and carried them along
for a long, long time. — Isaiah 63:9, MSG

Two weeks after my daughter's accident, I was lamenting in prayer over how damaged Paula's body was. She had been an attractive young woman at the apex of her beauty, but in the accident she was thrown from the car and crashed against a concrete barrier. When I first saw her body in the casket, I thought we had walked into the wrong chapel. As I relived the horror of her shattered body with God, His quiet voice spoke inaudibly, "I felt that way, too." I was shocked into silence as I remembered that He, too, was a bereaved parent. But it was hard for me to comprehend that it hurt Him to see His Son's body destroyed. I had always thought that God was above such things. After all, He was the one who made the decision to sacrifice His Son for the good of the world.

I came to see, however, that God the Father's willingness to submit God the Son to the pain and humiliation of the cross means that He suffered along with His Son. Jürgen Moltmann opened his book *The Crucified God* by saying, "The cross is not and cannot be loved," but he described the Trinity's victory out of death and suffering as essential to the beginning (creation) and the end (eschatology) of humankind:

> In the cross of his Son, God took upon himself not only death, so that man might be able to die comforted with the certainty that even death could not separate him from God, but still more, in order to make the crucified Christ the ground of his new creation, in which death itself is swallowed up in the victory of life and there will be "no sorrow, no crying, and no more tears."[9]

In *Spirituality Old and New*, Donald Bloesch described God's role in our lives as ever active and ever working:

> He is not a passionless observer of the human scene but is deeply involved in the human drama, overcoming evil with good. He is not the impassible Absolute of classical theism but being in action. He is not simply the Architect of the universe but its Sustainer and Renewer. He is unchanging in the integrity of his

purposes, but he is not removed from the sufferings of a fallen humanity. . . .

The God of biblical revelation does not lift humanity above sorrow and tribulation but guides humanity in the midst of tribulation.[10]

The triune God shares our suffering and pain, even when He has sent—or at least allowed—tragedy to reach us. In Isaiah we see God causing the affliction of a people group yet grieving with them:

> So I weep, as Jazer weeps,
>   for the vines of Sibmah.
> O Heshbon, O Elealeh,
>   I drench you with tears!
> The shouts of joy over your ripened fruit
>   and over your harvests have been stilled.
> Joy and gladness are taken away from the orchards;
>   no one sings or shouts in the vineyards;
> no one treads out wine at the presses,
>   for I have put an end to the shouting.
> My heart laments for Moab like a harp,
>   my inmost being for Kir Hareseth. (Isaiah 16:9-11)

In 715 BC, the Assyrian army marched through Moab, murdering and plundering. God told us that He sent the oppressors and that He put an end to the Moabites' idolatrous and pleasant lifestyle. While He allowed the Moabites' slaughter and exodus into exile, He suffered and grieved with them. God suffers with His children even when He has chosen to allow our losses. Dietrich Bonhoeffer wrote,

> It is good to learn early enough that suffering and God is not a contradiction, but rather a necessary unity; for me the idea that God himself is suffering has always been one of the most convincing teachings of Christianity. I think God is nearer to

suffering than to happiness and to find God in this way gives peace and rest and a strong and courageous heart.[11]

God the Son, as our head, shares the pain of each member of His body. When Jesus appeared to Saul on the road to Damascus, He didn't ask Saul why he was destroying His church but said, "I am Jesus, whom you are persecuting" (Acts 9:5). When Jesus' body suffers, He who was perfected by suffering suffers with us (see Hebrews 2:10). His life as a human allowed Him to experience what it feels like to obey when everything within is crying out for a less painful way, and He taught us that struggling with choices of obedience is not sinful. He who was without sin resisted to the point of loud cries and tears. Sweat poured off Him as He agonized in prayer hours before His crucifixion. As a result of experiencing every kind of suffering, He feels our pain and intercedes for us as our high priest (see Hebrews 5:7-10).

Scripture also indicates that God the Holy Spirit enters into our suffering when He intercedes for us with groaning too deep for words (see Romans 8:26-27). Paul could have simply said that the Spirit interprets our true desires, but instead he used a Greek word that carries a strong emotive connotation and is elsewhere interpreted "to groan" (of an inward, unexpressed feeling of sorrow), "with grief," or "sighed."[12] Our frustrated desires and heaviness of heart expressed in prayer are carried in empathetic sorrow by the Spirit. God's divinity does not keep Him from sharing our anguish and angst. Though He is above time, He fully enters into our pain, in our moment of time, and grieves with us.

I am very aware of my small place in the universe amid the clamoring needs of our world, whose population as I write today is estimated at 6,771,740,951.[13] When I think about God caring deeply about the needs of the multitude of people on earth, I am not always confident of His focused attention on me. Philip Yancey helped me see God's capacity in another light:

God operates by different rules of time and space. And God's infinite greatness, which we would expect to diminish us, actually makes possible the very closeness that we desire. A God unbound by our rules of time has the ability to invest in every person on earth. God has, quite literally, all the time in the world for each one of us.[14]

God's unlimited capacity allows Him to be a doting parent to each of His children, sharing every grief and delighting in every quirk and accomplishment (see Zephaniah 3:17). He does not remain aloof from our suffering but draws near to us in our anguish, crying with us in the dark nights of our souls.

SUFFERING REDEEMED

And even is our sleep pain that cannot forget, falls drop by drop upon the heart, and in our own despair, against our will, comes wisdom to us by the awful grace of God. —Aeschylus, *Agamemnon*

The Power of the Cross

Subsequent to faith in Christ, all that we live is experienced in Christ, including the troubles of human life. Whatever painful, troubling, or shameful experiences come our way, we walk through them with God's enabling power and presence. This suffering common to man is experienced by the believer as suffering "in Christ." We also experience believer-specific suffering as a result of being Christ followers. We could call this suffering "with Christ," because for His sake we are being called to shoulder the burden of the cross's pain and shame.[15]

Our suffering "in Christ" and "with Christ" comes in the context of the continuing presence of the Cross. Jesus showed us that God's most powerful work on earth is often done through humble submission in pain and sacrifice. The transforming power of the Cross is replicated in our suffering, giving us hope that our inglorious, grinding pain will be transformed into something amazingly good beyond what we can now see. God redeems our hardships so that they have a salvific aspect, bringing good to us and to others. Just as Paul's imprisonment advanced the gospel (see Philippians 1:12), we have hope that our suffering will be used of God to further His work. Our afflictions come to us with the permission of our powerful and loving Father, and He uses them to reveal Himself and to draw others into glorious relationship with Him. Jervis added,

> The cross's presence at the center of his good news means that Paul does not shy away from either the existence or the experience of suffering. . . . [The gospel] . . . does *not* promise its converts transformation into super-humans capable of transcending or avoiding the troubles of human existence, [but rather it calls us to share in God's redeeming work]. This good news is hard. . . . This hard news is also good.[16]

God's Strengths Are Made Perfect in Our Weaknesses

C. S. Lewis wrote that "[God] is not proud. . . . He will have us even though we have shown that we prefer everything else to Him."[17] It is God's persistent, enduring love for us that reassures us He will not sacrifice us to accomplish His plans; that is not to say that He does not use our suffering for His purposes, to bring life out of death. Pain is God's stage for displaying His glory in a fallen world, allowing us to experience and others to observe His power and goodness in our suffering.

Jesus told His disciples that the blind man who came to Him for healing was born blind, not because of his sin or his parents' sin, but to demonstrate the power of God (see John 9:3). Perhaps there is no greater demonstration of God's power than that revealed through faith in the face of great loss and pain. Suffering showcases the work of God in our lives, allowing God to reveal Himself through weakness and great need. In the flesh Christ assumed roles of weakness—baby in the manger, despised Galilean, carpenter of humble station, foot-washing servant—and through His weaknesses He effectively revealed the divine power and character. The exertion of human power and pride are always hindrances to the work of God in our lives. Through suffering we are given an opportunity to let God's glorious person be revealed through our brokenness, when we are most weak and can attribute none of His power to our own efforts. Ephesians 3:10 reminds us that this display of God's grace and power through the members of His church is for an audience of not only human beings but also spiritual ones.

SUFFERING AS DISCIPLINE

The biblical concept of being tested, tempted, tried, and proven is not like passing or failing a test nor is it punishment. It is testing in that it reveals the true nature of our substance, refining us through adversity by burning away all that obscures the purity of our faith.

> In this you greatly rejoice, though now for a little while you may have had to suffer grief in all kinds of trials. These have come so that your faith — of greater worth than gold, which perishes even though refined by fire — may be proved genuine and may result in praise, glory and honor when Jesus Christ is revealed. (1 Peter 1:6-7)

God ordains suffering to help us release our hold on worldly hopes and put our "hope . . . in God" (1 Peter 1:21). The fiery trials are appointed to consume the earthly dependencies and leave only the refined gold of genuine faith (see 1 Peter 1:7). It's the supremacy of God's great faithfulness above all other securities that frees us to "rejoice . . . as [we] are sharing Christ's sufferings" (1 Peter 4:13, NRSV). Therefore, joy in suffering for Christ's sake makes the supremacy of God shine more clearly than all our gratitude for wealth.[18]

Suffering has a clarifying effect on us. It strips us down to the basics, where we have no pretense or fluff, and reveals things in our inner selves that we didn't know were there (or wished weren't there). Suffering sharpens our focus. That clarity of vision changes our worldview, to the extent that Peter could say that he who has suffered physically is "done with sin" (1 Peter 4:1). This is the sense in which suffering is discipline for the believer, not a corrective or punishing discipline but a refining one. God is not punishing us in affliction, but we are called to "endure hardship as discipline" (Hebrews 12:7) because God has allowed it to come to us and is using it to strengthen us. Just as an athlete lifting weights grows in capacity when his body tears muscle and rebuilds it to withstand greater endurance, the process is painful (see Hebrews 12:11) but results in strength of character and the ability to endure in the midst of resistance and stress.

Suffering burns away our deceptions and exposes our desperate need of God, opening a new level of communication with God and with our inner beings, freeing us from what Thomas Merton called "the shadow self." Brennan Manning, in his book *Abba's Child*, responded to this false self Merton described:

> This is the man I want myself to be but who cannot exist, because God does not know anything about him. And to be unknown of God is altogether too much privacy. My false and private self is the one who wants to exist outside the reach of God's will and God's love — outside of reality and outside of life. . . . For most people in the world, there is no greater subjective reality than this false self of theirs, which cannot exist. A life devoted to the cult of this shadow is what is called a life of sin.

Merton's notion of sin focuses not primarily on individual sinful acts but on a fundamental option for a life of pretense. "There can only be two basic loves," wrote Augustine, "the love of God unto the forgetfulness of self, or the love of self unto the forgetfulness and denial of God." The fundamental option arises from the *core* of our being and incarnates itself in the specific choices of daily existence — either for the shadow self ruled by egocentric desires or for the true self hidden with Christ in God.[19]

Pain deconstructs the lives that we have constructed for ourselves. When we accept and enter into suffering, rather than minimizing it or running away from it, our strongest desires are revealed, allowing God to comfort, change, and commune with the naked heart that emerges from our pain. This truth challenges the common belief among Christians that we can only give God glory in the midst of suffering by minimizing our pain while "giving glory to God." Christians have taken a page out of the John Wayne handbook for learning how to handle suffering: Suck it up, tough it through, praise God, and pass the ammunition. But when we soldier on as if the pain were not there, we can hinder its transformative power. It is in lamenting and processing our pain with God that we experience healing and hope in the midst of adversity. Victory in suffering will not always look victorious. It will likely involve an ongoing process of hurting and, at times, questioning God. Triumphant suffering is a journey, not a destination, and we can short-circuit God's transformative work in our hearts by trying to reach the end too quickly.

SUFFERING MATURES OUR FAITH

Distress not only wounds, it also heals our hearts of self-reliance, misplaced security, fears, and complacence. Our journey through suffering can deepen our faith and increase our endurance. Desperate times cause us to reach deep within ourselves to try to make sense of the uncomfortable world into which they have thrown us. As we hurt, question, cry, and grieve through our pain, our hearts go through a process of faith affirmation. Faith is not complete until the heart trusts it, and the heart believes only what it experiences. Suffering offers us the opportunity to live what we believe in the face of adversity.

In her book *Transformed into Fire*, Judith Hougen wrote,

When the intellect engages with a fact, the fact is stored as truth, and belief results. In contrast, the heart believes only what it experiences. . . . We're created to establish belief through two pathways—cognitive and experiential . . . only when both pathways are engaged does belief become complete.[20]

The definition of faith is to believe in what we cannot see (see Hebrews 11:1), but faith is not always belief in what we have not experienced. We cannot see the love of God, yet we have experienced it. When life does not turn out as we desire and we struggle to trust God's plans for us, what gives us faith to trust God in the midst of chaos?

Trust is dependent on our personal interaction with truth. A truth that is learned with accompanied experience (living proof) and emotional engagement (life impact) becomes etched on our hearts. The mind may remember impersonal truth, but the heart will only partially trust it. We sometimes have to obey impersonal truth through an act of the will, which can be an appropriate act of faith. But eventually faith should take us beyond self-discipline and self-control, to the realm of trust. God desires to change not only our minds and our actions but also our hearts. He wants us to obey Him, and He wants us to trust Him from the heart. Suffering allows us to experience our faith in a way that matures it by reaffirming our trust in God through experienced grace.

SUFFERING GIVES AN ETERNAL PERSPECTIVE

It is ironic to me that suffering can actually enhance our faith. "How is it," I asked a friend, "that the most dreadful things that happen to us are those that most increase our trust in God?" Experiences that rock our foundations, or that grind them down, cause us to choose repeatedly whether to trust God. Jervis said, "Both believers and nonbelievers may be blinded to God's trustworthiness and so choose to live in the shadow of our definitions of God and ourselves rather than in the light of faith. In Romans 9–11 Paul describes this wretchedness."[21] As we reject our doubts, one by one, and persevere in trusting God in the midst of affliction, we build inner strength. In future difficulties we are not as easily swayed by fears and doubts because we have faced worse. We don't sweat the little stuff because we have gained a more eternal perspective.

Paul, James, and Peter told us that we can rejoice in our sufferings (see Romans 5:3; James 1:2; 1 Peter 4:1). This is more than stoic endurance of our suffering. This is looking beyond our troubles to the future time when the end product of persevering in affliction is steadfast hope in God, a hope that will not disappoint (see Romans 5:3-5). Only the believer who has faced distress can develop steadfastness, which in turn develops character. A deepened, tested character results in confidence that God will see us through anything, no matter how awful it may be. In the midst of suffering we can be strengthened by the same motivation Jesus had in submitting Himself to the torture and humiliation of the cross, which was looking ahead to the future joy that awaited Him (see Hebrews 12:2). As we go through suffering, we experience the power of God in giving us comfort, joy, and enablement that perhaps we would not have experienced without affliction.

Sometimes we suffer not only as individuals but as a people group. Through slavery and institutionalized racialization, the African American community has a two-hundred-year history of oppression and suffering, which demonstrates both the destructive power of prolonged suffering and the amazing strength of tested faith. The faith-affirming Negro spirituals give testimony to the latter, revealing an enduring hope in the midst of hopeless circumstances and confirming that suffering points us to our true home. A friend who disciples believers in an African American inner-city community of Detroit shared with me that sometimes she feels presumptive in sharing tools of Christian disciplines with the female towers of faith she meets there. The faith of these women is mature because it has been refined not by self-imposed spiritual disciplines but by the rigorous discipline of suffering.

RESPONDING TO GOD IN SUFFERING WITH OUR WHOLE SELVES

In the grief that consumed us in the months after our daughter's death, the friends who comforted us the most were those who shared our grief and pain. I found the same to be true in my relationship with God.

Every night for the first year I would go out and stare at the vastness of the night sky and cry out my pain to God as my questions tore themselves out of me. The immensity of the heavens reminded me that my Creator could handle the enormity of my tragedy, and as I shared my pain with God, my trust in Him was inexplicably deepened.

When we talk about how we should respond in the midst of suffering, the most important truth to remember is that we need to bring our true selves to God. In painful times, this may mean bringing our hurt, anger, and questions. In his book *Prayer: Does It Make Any Difference?*, Philip Yancey told a story about a hospice chaplain who met with a terminal patient in great distress.

The patient was in the last stages of cancer and was feeling very guilty because he had spent the previous night ranting, raving, and swearing at God. The following morning he felt dreadful. He imagined that his chance of eternal life had now been lost forever and that God would never forgive one who had so cursed and abused Him.

The chaplain asked the patient, "What do you think is the opposite of love?" The man replied, "Hate." Very wisely, the chaplain replied, "No, the opposite of love is indifference. You have not been indifferent to God, or you would never have spent the night talking to him, honestly telling him what was in your heart and mind. Do you know the Christian word that describes what you have been doing? The word is 'prayer.' You have spent the night praying."[22]

God is not looking for our "right" responses; He is looking for relationship. When we respond to Him in the midst of suffering, we are giving Him the response He desires.

CORPORATE RESPONSE OF THE BODY OF CHRIST

After the death of our daughter, we leaned heavily on the support of Christian friends who loved us well through acts of service and comforted us by grieving with us. But sometimes members of the body of Christ are uncomfortable with the suffering of others and feel unsure about how to respond to their pain, questions, and messy neediness.

A friend's mother-in-law spent the last three weeks of her life in a hospital, and my friend and his wife stayed with her twenty-four hours a day, sleeping on the floor beside her bed when there was no cot available. Two weeks after his mother-in-law's death, my friend met with a hospital administrator to discuss setting up a payment plan for the sizable hospital bill. The manager asked for some time to consider the case and called back a few days later. He said that the hospital administrators had decided to absorb the cost of my friend's bill because the hospital staff had rarely seen such dedication and faithfulness of care from family members, especially Christian families. He explained that usually Christians would be attentive in the early stages of a health crisis and would pray with great faith for the healing of their loved one. As time passed and no cure came, family and friends would disappear because they were uncomfortable when there was no miracle. The patient's declining health was a spiritual defeat for them.

Our theology of suffering must take into account the reality that suffering is a consequence of sin in the world and that death, in all its forms, will continue to affect Christians, even though sin has been defeated on the Cross. Because we live in the "already but not yet" of the kingdom of God, our victory over sin is best characterized not by escaping misfortune but by caring for sin's victims. When we are in crisis, we sometimes question if God loves us. When other believers withdraw from us, their actions reinforce our doubt. The message we get is: "What is wrong with you that God is sending you all these things?" The body of Christ has the power to embody God's grace and love in the midst of suffering by being the hands and feet of Christ in serving and supporting those who suffer enduring afflictions that do not go away despite our prayers.

LIVING WITH MYSTERY AND PERSEVERING

Suffering highlights our vulnerability and heightens our questions about God. When times are good, our unanswered questions can be answered with a glib "Well, when I get to heaven, I'm going to ask Jesus about that." It's easy to trust when our lives don't depend on it, but when the bottom falls out and all that we hold most dear is being sucked out of the hole, we have to know if God is there for us. Pain drives us to God and humbles us, forcing us to recognize that we have little control over protecting that which is most precious to us and that we cannot know all that we are desperate to know. As we trust Him in our unanswered questions and unrealized desires, we learn to live with mystery.

Suffering is a powerful force, drawing forth our deepest emotions and desires. We cannot be neutral in the midst of anguish. Pain drives us to run either to God or away from Him. Our response to Him in the midst of suffering determines whether we will mature and grow through trials or withdraw from God and turn inward, becoming bitter and self-protective. After our daughter's death, my husband and I understood why so many people self-medicate with drugs and alcohol. Our greatest problem has been to know what to do with the constant pain. By bringing our anguish to God, day after day, we find the strength to keep enduring in hope, though not without struggle. In our painful surrender God transforms the destructive power of suffering into a redemptive force, bringing life out of death and blessing out of pain. Suffering takes place in the context of joy, not in the bleakness of abandonment to suffering. Though we suffer loss and pain, we also receive a grace disguised. We have no choice about receiving the pain, but we can choose what to do with it. At great price, suffering can bring us wisdom, comfort, amplified perspective, core strength, and endurance.

LIFE TO THE FULL

The thief comes only to steal and kill and destroy; I have come that they may have life, and have it to the full. — John 10:10

When people hear about the multiple difficulties life has brought my family, they tend to feel overwhelmed and vaguely guilty because God has spared them major loss. On the other hand, when I hear the stories of those who live years as sex slaves, of children whose families have been slaughtered by roving gangs, of a woman who bears the physical and psychological scars of being tortured and raped every night throughout childhood by her father and her uncle, I wonder if God's grace is big enough for them, if it would be enough for me if I were in their shoes.

I have come to be thankful for all of life, not just the good parts—though not all of the life God has given me is the life I would have chosen. Seeing my son disappear into the abyss of mental illness is a source of great sadness, and living with his mental illness has revealed things I would rather not know about myself. Watching my daughter suffer year after year wore me down, and part of me died with her in that car accident. I didn't want to live those agonizing experiences then, and I don't want to live with them now.

When life is hard, we cannot help but ask if this is the abundant life Jesus came to earth to give us. We will only experience full life in the glorious freedom that awaits us on the new earth and new heaven, but meanwhile, my life has tastes of the rich and bountiful living that He wants to give us, even in the terribly hard things. My instinct is to avoid suffering whenever possible, and when it can't be avoided, to hold my breath until it goes away. But you can hold your breath for only so long, and I had to come up for air a long time ago. As we reject pain avoidance and choose to live fully in the midst of suffering—even if it means feeling more pain—we are opened up to God and experience His power in our pain. In a fallen world, suffering is a key element to living life to the full.

I hear Christians say that God is good (because) "He delivered me from . . . ," (because) "He provided . . . ," (because) "He answered prayer . . . ," (because) "He healed . . . ," (because) "He opened up a parking space . . . " If I followed that same line of reasoning, I couldn't say that God is good. He didn't answer my most heartfelt prayers; He didn't spare my son; and He didn't save my daughter's life. I have found that when God's gifts are not the reason I give Him thanks, I rediscover that God is good.

In affliction, our trust in God is deepened because suffering tests and affirms our faith in His goodness and trustworthiness. In good times, we experience God's goodness in the good things He gives us. In hard times, we experience His goodness through His tenderness, mercy, and loving compassion manifested to us in the midst of suffering. God is not sometimes merciful and sometimes just; He is eternally and infinitely just and merciful and good in all that He is and does. From that reality spring our hope and comfort in suffering.

FOR REFLECTION AND DISCUSSION

1. In reviewing your own life, can you see how you have been formed in the experiences of suffering and disappointments? Honestly, has the formation of these experiences made the pain of the things suffered worthwhile—not good, but vital to whom you have become?
2. What role does forgiveness for those who have caused us harm play in the forming of our lives? Think of those in your life and ministry contexts who have not forgiven the people who have harmed them: Has it limited or halted their formation?
3. How would you speak about suffering in your ministry contexts so as neither to minimize its reality nor to dismiss the importance of its role in our maturing and formation? Have you seen this done well?
4. How do we encourage the sharing of our sufferings in community? In what ways can this be done to create an environment for healing and formation? In what ways can it be done to choke off growth and diminish trust in God?
5. Because for so many, suffering challenges our faith in God, how does the reality of God's suffering with us, and even taking the experience of suffering into the Trinitarian life through Jesus' suffering, encourage your faith and call you onward toward the image of Christ?

FOR FURTHER READING

Jervis, L. Ann. *At the Heart of the Gospel: Suffering in the Earliest Christian Message.* Grand Rapids, MI: Eerdmans, 2007.

Lewis, C. S. *The Problem of Pain*. San Francisco: HarperOne, 2001.

Piper, John, and Justin Taylor, eds. *Suffering and the Sovereignty of God*. Wheaton, IL: Crossway, 2006.

Sittser, Jerry. *A Grace Disguised: How the Soul Grows Through Loss*. Grand Rapids, MI: Zondervan, 1995, 2004.

Yancey, Philip. *Where Is God When It Hurts?* Grand Rapids, MI: Zondervan, 2002.

Chapter Seven

PARTICIPATING IN GOD'S MISSION

Paula Fuller

ELEMENT 7: Spiritual formation in Christ is a process of growing in kingdom living and participating in God's mission. This begins with our personal reconciliation with God and results in an irrepressible manifestation of God's good news. Disciples of the kingdom labor in community for reconciliation with God and one another as a central priority of mission. They also pursue justice and compassion for all people and work to correct institutional sin inherent in human structures.

Description: The kingdom of God is the reality of God's transforming presence, power, and goodness manifested in the community of Jesus' disciples (see Matthew 5:13-16). This community witnesses to the reality of the presence of the kingdom throughout this age (see Ephesians 2:1-21). Spiritual formation is not the end itself but is always pursued through and focused on the advancement of Christ's kingdom. We are God's chosen strategy for the world. The Spirit-energized community of Jesus' disciples is God's agency of reconciliation in this world as it calls all people to be reconciled to each other across divisions of class, gender, race, ethnicity, and nationality as they are reconciled to God (see Matthew 5:24; 9:35-38; 2 Corinthians 5:18-21). Witness comes both through the declaration of the gospel message and through the example of living out the gospel message as a family of faith characterized by humility, purity, accountability, discipline, reconciliation, restoration, and forgiveness (see Matthew 18:1-22). The task is profoundly beyond us, but God's invitation is to take what He gives and return it to Him in simple obedience. As we follow Him in His risky and costly call, we become the aroma of His life to a broken and needy world—and God works a miracle.

❦ ❦ ❦

Evangelical Christians have long understood and valued the role of discipleship for spiritual growth. We view it as an essential element for leadership development and building healthy congregations. However, we have often struggled with the practice of mission as central to our Christian experience. In the early twentieth century, our spiritual forefathers fought with the proponents of theological liberalism regarding their notion of a "social gospel."[1] While liberal theology often had little use for Jesus Christ, on the conservative side of the theological divide, we reduced the gospel to a proclamation about a better world "above." Meanwhile, we often left untouched the lives of people in the here and now, the very lives that the gospel of the kingdom of God was meant to touch and transform. Ray Bakke, a Christian leader who has spent his life developing and living out a theology of the city, summarized the dichotomy between evangelism and social justice this way:

> To bring the gospel and free people from their sins but leave them in bondage to the rest of our Enemy's vices is not the gospel. But likewise, to bring the gospel, release people from bondage to the world, but leave them in bondage to their sins is not the gospel. The gospel of Jesus brings liberation to the whole person.[2]

While most evangelical Christians would affirm missions or out-reach programs as important and near to God's heart (see Matthew 25:31-46; James 1:27), far too many of us struggle with the desire to *engage* in mission due to busyness, apathy, or fear. In many Christian contexts, missions has become a practice that is delegated to a church committee, viewed as an optional activity for those with a particular set of spiritual gifts, or offered as a developmental experience for youth and college students to expose them to poverty and injustice and create an awareness of the world's needs, their privilege, and God's heart for the oppressed. In earlier chapters, we have explored various aspects of the Christian life and the implications for our spiritual formation. In this chapter, we will explore the role of mission in our spiritual formation. We will see how God's mission and our role as agents of His kingdom are essential, not only in God's redeeming work in the world but also in His transformational work in our lives.

WHAT DOES "THY KINGDOM COME" MEAN TO THOSE IN NEED OF GOOD NEWS?

It was September 2005, and the United States was still in shock almost a month after Hurricane Katrina ravaged the Gulf Coast and the levee system failed in New Orleans. Many of us had spent hours with our eyes glued to the nightly news, dumbfounded and reeling from the video footage of New Orleans, the images of the residents, primarily African American, who were clinging to rooftops, wading through the flooded section of the Ninth Ward, and seeking sanctuary in the Houston Astrodome football stadium. Our country wasn't prepared for the convergence of poor city planning, inadequate federal crisis response systems, racially segregated neighborhoods, and economic poverty. The horrific results of this convergence left many of us grasping to under-stand the significance of what was unfolding before our eyes.

I was traveling to a meeting in Colorado Springs, Colorado, in late September where I would be discussing principles of spiritual forma-tion and transformation with the Theological and Cultural Thinkers

(TACT) group. The day before I arrived, I visited a former classmate, a pastor helping with relief efforts for victims of Hurricane Katrina who had been relocated to Denver, Colorado. As we walked through the former military base where almost a thousand people were being temporarily housed, I saw adults and children lining the halls of a central building waiting for assistance. Many were physically present but mentally and spiritually gone, eyes glazed over, staring into space, no doubt struggling with posttraumatic stress disorder. Two volunteers were organizing activities for the children and teenagers, hoping to persuade them to board buses with promises of fun activities and pizza, but many of the children were reluctant to leave their parents. I left the military base several hours later, visibly shaken by my brief exposure to the aftermath of the disaster.

As I slid into my seat at the meeting that evening, I struggled to make the emotional and mental shift from the military base so I could be fully present at the spiritual-formation meeting. I was experiencing a high level of dissonance. I was very aware of the fact that I was the only African American in the room, in fact, the only person of color, and one of two women in a room of thirty or so white men. As we opened the meeting in prayer for our next few days together, images of the victims from Hurricane Katrina began to flash before my eyes. Before I knew it, I was sobbing, quietly at first but with growing intensity. I began to pray aloud, through my tears, asking God to meet us during our time together and also remembering the faces of the people I had seen earlier that day. In that moment, I realized that whatever we produced through our time together had to address the pain, brokenness, and despair of the people I had met that day. If we failed to create a model that was relevant to those who had experienced such severe suffering and displacement, our message would be missing something that was central to the gospel that Jesus preached. However, the people of New Orleans and the displaced residents needed more than a proclamation of the kingdom of God. What they needed was a demonstration of the kingdom of God.

Within the safe, warm confines of my hotel room later that evening, I realized that the victims of Hurricane Katrina weren't the only ones who needed to experience the power of the kingdom of God in that encounter. It was also a critical moment for me *and my understanding of the gospel*. As I engaged, at even the most minimal level, the pain and challenges that those families were experiencing, it was a transforming moment for me in terms of my understanding of what it meant to have the kingdom of God present and available for those who were in need of physical as well as spiritual salvation. It wasn't enough for them to hear that God loved them and had a wonderful plan for their eternal salvation. The majority of the individuals whose lives were devastated by Hurricane Katrina were not questioning whether or not there was a God. They were wondering *why* God had allowed such a devastating set of circumstances to happen. They wondered if God cared about their current condition and what He was going to do about it.

It doesn't take a natural or man-made disaster to create opportunities to taste the pain of the world. That engagement can come in our interactions with family members, friends, and neighbors in our immediate surroundings, just as well as it can with those living across the country or on the other side of the world. Within the Christian church, we have tended to define spiritual growth as disengagement from the world rather than *engagement with* the world. We often measure spiritual growth and formation as an increase in cognitive knowledge about God or religious activities (i.e., greater knowledge of Scripture, a disciplined prayer life, weekly church attendance). In many contexts, discipleship has been redefined as a weekly meeting at Starbucks with a mentor who helps me grow in understanding God and how my spirituality facilitates my personal development. Many pastors and Christian leaders who disciple new believers don't include evangelism or service as part of the growth and maturation process. As a result, our vision of discipleship can look very different from the experiences that Jesus introduced to His disciples. Modern-day disciples of Jesus can confess belief in the right things, but their lives are not congruent with the values and actions of Jesus. And what is more, they don't see how the living out of those values and realities in mission is necessary for them to experience the promises of God.

GOD'S HEART FOR MISSION REVEALED TO US

In the gospel of Luke, when Jesus returned from the wilderness in the power of the Spirit, His first act of public ministry was an announcement of His mission, which He articulated as the fulfillment of a scriptural passage in Isaiah 61 that He read from a scroll in the temple:

> *The Spirit of the Lord is on me,*
>   *because he has anointed me*
>   *to preach good news to the poor.*
> *He has sent me to proclaim freedom for the prisoners*
>   *and recovery of sight for the blind,*
> *to release the oppressed,*
>   *to proclaim the year of the Lord's favor.* (Luke 4:18-19)

This pronouncement and the specific Scripture passage that Jesus quoted are found solely in the gospel of Luke. This gospel account places an emphasis upon the disenfranchised—Gentiles, women, and the poor.[3] He provided unique stories in the biblical narrative that often serve to create hope for the hopeless. The message that Jesus proclaimed in the temple is indeed good news for some, but for others, it is not a familiar message that is connected to our concept of salvation. For many Western Christians, the "gospel" has been reduced to an *individual* transaction based on a set of cognitive declarations where an individual prays "the sinner's prayer"[4] and receives forgiveness from God for personal sins and the gift of eternal life after death. While we, as Christians, embrace the proclamation of the gospel as good news for all, and not specifically for the poor, we don't generally include acts of service or a commitment to address injustice as part of our mandate to carry out Jesus' mission.

The Christian mission has been narrowed by many evangelicals to making disciples and baptism (see Matthew 28:19). Unfortunately, we have not done as good a job teaching those same disciples to "obey everything [Jesus] commanded" (Matthew 28:20). Those who are baptized in the name of the Father, the Son, and the Holy Spirit live with few, if any, Christian mandates between the time of their personal confession of sin and entry into the pearly gates after life on earth is done. This missing element of mission has created a chasm between belief, feeling, and action. Dallas Willard has already laid out how dangerous it is when we preach a gospel that is simply entry into a future heaven and does not touch the person and his or her environment today (chapter 1). The gospel we proclaim is good news for today, as well as good news for eternity. If our commitment to the gospel has nothing to do with bringing good news and practical help to those in need, then we have detached our experience from Jesus' self-professed mission.

Jesus' mission in the gospel of Luke does address the need for forgiveness of sins. In Luke 5, Jesus addressed a paralytic and said, "Friend, your sins are forgiven" (Luke 5:20). However, the Pharisees and teachers of the law sitting in close proximity began *thinking among themselves* that Jesus was blaspheming because only God could forgive sin. Jesus knew their thoughts and asked,

> "Why are you thinking these things in your hearts? Which is easier: to say, 'Your sins are forgiven,' or to say, 'Get up and walk'? But that you may know that the Son of Man has authority on earth to forgive sins. . . ." He said to the paralyzed man, "I tell you, get up, take your mat and go home." (Luke 5:22-24)

Jesus did not overlook the matter of personal forgiveness of sin. In fact, in this instance, He healed the man to *demonstrate* His authority on earth to forgive sins.

ETERNAL LIFE AND THE SIGNIFICANCE OF LOVING MY NEIGHBOR

Our Western paradigm for personal salvation stands in stark contrast to the words of Jesus when He was asked by a legal expert what he must do to inherit eternal life. Jesus asked him what the law required and affirmed that his answer was correct—"'Love the Lord your God with all your heart and with all your soul and with all your strength and with all your mind'; and, 'Love your neighbor as yourself'" (Luke 10:27-28). When asked by the legal expert, who was seeking to justify himself, "Who is my neighbor?" Jesus responded by presenting the parable of the Good Samaritan:

> A man was going down from Jerusalem to Jericho, when he fell into the hands of robbers. They stripped him of his clothes, beat him and went away, leaving him half dead. A priest happened to be going down the same road, and when he saw the man, he passed by on the other side. So too, a Levite, when he came to the place and saw him, passed by on the other side. But a Samaritan, as he traveled, came where the man was; and when he saw him, he took pity on him. He went to him and bandaged his wounds, pouring on oil and wine. Then he put the man on his own donkey, took him to an inn and took care of him. The next day he took out two silver coins and gave them to the innkeeper. "Look after him," he said, "and when I return, I will reimburse you for any extra expense you may have."(Luke 10:30-35)

Our twenty-first-century evangelical understanding tends to equate "eternal life" with "going to heaven when I die." For people in Jesus' day, eternal life was roughly equivalent to living a life in God's kingdom that transcends the current regime of life. Within this context, a person desiring to experience life in God's kingdom had to embrace a way of life that intrinsically tied loving God with loving others, and in this particular story, love for neighbor was expressed by sacrificial action.

Historical background here is important: The Samaritans originated from people whom Esarhaddon (677 BC), an Assyrian king, brought to Samaria from Babylon and other places. These individuals settled and intermarried with the poorest and most uneducated Jews who were left behind when the Israelites were taken into captivity. The newcomers brought with them their pagan religions but also adopted some of the religious practices of the Jews (see 2 Kings 17:24-33). When the

Jews returned from captivity and set about rebuilding the temple, the Samaritans sought to partner with them and were rejected.[5] From this point on, the Jews and Samaritans were enemies. The Samaritans were the people the Jews wanted to avoid and for whom no one thought the good news of God's kingdom should have any implications. By the time of the New Testament, the hatred between Jews and Samaritans had reached its zenith. They had nothing to do with each other (see John 4:9). Furthermore, the Samaritans were viewed as a theologically flawed people who worshipped God apart from the temple (cp. John 4:20). They were not orthodox. In fact, if the Jewish man hadn't been wounded and very likely unconscious, he would not have accepted so much as a cold drink of water from the Samaritan. Given the tensions between the Jews and Samaritans, Jesus was telling a very controversial story.

Jesus was radical in the way He taught about love for one's neighbor and the implications for those who desire to partake of the eternal life that God promises. The ones in the story who appear to be "in" are "out" and the one who is "out" is "in." The priest and the Levite are insiders—those who are closest to following God's law and presumably closest to understanding and receiving eternal life. However, they are really "out" because they fail to perceive the significance of expressing their love for God through an act of kindness to a fellow human being. Proper belief was insufficient. When the priest and Levite saw the wounded man, they crossed to the other side of the road, continuing their busy lives of service for God. They were unaware of how this lack of compassion affected their standing in the eyes of the One they were committed to serve. The Samaritan is the outsider—the one who is furthest away from God and eternal life—but in the eyes of Jesus, he's "in" because he gets it. The Samaritan has every reason to reject this wounded Israelite whose people have vilified his, yet he demonstrates that his affections and care for another person created in God's image are appropriately ordered. He cares for the wounded man, seeking his good, and invests time, money, and energy. He may even risk his own safety. The picture is extraordinary. It is a picture of the condition of the heart. According to the Jewish cultural and theological standards, the

Samaritan man was far away from God's law, but he was actually very close to God's heart in his display of love and mercy.

Jesus chose the Good Samaritan as the hero. The one who is unorthodox according to the law is living in a way that captures the essence of what is important to God. Jesus didn't tell us to be like the priest or the Levite. Jesus declared that it is better to reject religious duty than to neglect a deed of mercy. He pointed to the actions of the Good Samaritan and said, "Go and do likewise" (Luke 10:37). Note that the words of Jesus charge us to "go and do" not "go and believe."

The Challenge of Mission in a Pressure-Filled Society

In the parable, the Good Samaritan comes upon a wounded Jewish man on his way from Jerusalem to Jericho. The road from Jerusalem to Jericho was a steep descent and about seventeen miles long. The route was described as a "rocky thoroughfare lined with caves," which made it an attractive location for robbers.[6] You get the sense that this road was occupied by merchants, robbers, priests, and those working in the temple of God traveling back and forth to their homes. It was a place where folks were routinely robbed and often killed.

Both the priest and Levite in the parable are vocational ministers. Their lives are defined by their religious service to God's people. If anyone understands the law of God, it should be them. If anyone understands the need and importance to serve others, it should be them. However, in this story, they fail to recognize the significance of stopping to care for a wounded and dying man. They do have a slight dilemma. The law is filled with rules that deal with ritual cleanliness (see the numerous passages in Leviticus on cleanliness; see also Numbers 19). From a distance, the man might have appeared to be dead. If they were to touch a dead body, they would be unclean, and it would require a certain set of rituals and a number of days for them to be declared clean and able to serve in the temple. Ritual cleanliness was critical for them to represent the people before God and to reconcile the people to God through the sacrificial system. However, in obeying the religiously defined letter of the law, they ignored the heart of God embedded in the law. They were ceremonially clean yet unclean on the inside, unable to acknowledge the worth of a child of God lying in the road. By contrast, the apparently unclean Samaritan demonstrates compassion and behaves like a true neighbor.

Similar to the priest and the Levite, we also live in a world where it is easy for Christians, who have an understanding and commitment to live in ways that please God, to see someone in need and pass by on the other side. We're busy people. American workers put in more hours than anyone else in the industrialized world.[7] In the 1990s, Harvard economist Juliet Schor showed that "in the last twenty years the amount of time Americans have spent at their jobs has risen steadily."[8] But further, even in our leisure time, we are busy people. In his book *In Praise of Slowness*, Carl Honore reported that "our love of speed, our obsession with doing more and more in less and less time, has gone too far; it has turned into an addiction, a kind of idolatry."[9]

In the process of speeding through our lives, many of us have perfected the ability to avert our eyes and walk quickly past homeless people standing with signs or hands outstretched desiring assistance. We live in areas with elaborate freeway systems that will expedite our travel from suburban areas to our destination, conveniently bypassing less desirable areas of the city where we are likely to encounter those who are in need.

If I can arrange my life so that I keep others who are different at a distance, then I am safe. I can choose to arrange my life so that I am surrounded only by churched people or those who have the same socioeconomic background. However, when I enter into a relationship with someone who is different, I have the opportunity to see life from a new perspective and encounter issues that affect his or her life. His issues have the potential to become my issues. Her issues might even become important to me. In the parable of the Good Samaritan, the Samaritan closes the distance between himself and the wounded Jewish traveler. The Samaritan's proximity to the wounded man causes him to see the man as a real person, as he might see a brother or a friend. His willingness to get involved opened up the possibility for God's transforming power to be at work in the wounded man's life. In the process, there was a miracle of reconciliation in the midst of an ethnically divided social system.

The Filter of Race Shapes Our Understanding of Who We Embrace as Neighbors

Jesus introduced an element of ethnic tension into the parable by selecting a Samaritan as the one who modeled the right action, rather than the priest or the Levite, who were respected members within the Jewish religious community. When Jesus asked the legal scholar, "Which of these three do you think was a neighbor to the man who fell into the hands of the robbers?" (Luke 10:36), the legal expert did not even use the word *Samaritan* in his reply. He identified the neighbor as "the one who had mercy on him" (Luke 10:37). Since Jesus made a point of the ethnic identity of the Samaritan but not the wounded man, we presume that he was a fellow Jew. It would make sense for the priest or the Levite to come to the aid of a fellow Jew. In this instance, the reason they do not stop to attend to the wounded man has nothing to do with ethnicity. Where the ethnic barrier must be overcome in the biblical account is the point where the legal expert and other listeners must identify a Samaritan person as the "neighbor" of the wounded Jewish man. If all Jesus wanted to do was teach His audience that they should be willing to cross ethnic and cultural barriers to demonstrate love for their neighbor, He could have made the wounded person a Samaritan. A Jewish person showing compassion could be the hero. Instead, Jesus made the Samaritan, the person they would never consider worthy of admiration, the honorable person in the parable. In the process, the legal scholar was led to recognize that neighborliness is a matter of active care for those in need, and the parable introduces the idea that a neighbor is not restricted solely to the Jewish people, who were the custodians of correct doctrine.

Through the parable of the Good Samaritan, Jesus enlarged the boundaries of how we define a neighbor and who we embrace as our neighbor. He issued a challenge to that particular audience, and also to us, that the definition of *neighbor* goes beyond the individuals or families that live adjacent to our homes. A neighbor is anyone we come across who is in need of mercy. Second, Jesus challenged us to embrace those we might normally exclude or reject as neighbors. It's relatively easy to trade places with the Levite, priest, or Good Samaritan and ask ourselves what we might do if we were in that person's shoes. How does our experience of the story change if we see ourselves as the wounded man on the side of the road? In this instance, we might be willing to accept assistance from anyone willing to tend to our needs. Imagine if the wounded man was someone who fiercely hated Samaritans. How might his view be changed by the overwhelming generosity displayed by the Good Samaritan who tended to him? How could that one act of sacrificial kindness transform his attitudes and perspectives about Samaritans and his willingness to engage or help someone different from himself in the future? Within the parable, a radical act of love and the willingness to step outside of his comfort zone to interact with someone who was different from himself created the opportunity for the Good Samaritan to dismantle the ethnic filters through which Jewish people saw God and the path to the life God promised.

Eddie Broussard, a senior leader for The Navigators, recounted an experience on a Sunday morning when Navigator leaders were sent out to participate in church experiences in different ethnic communities. Some individuals attended African American megachurches; others visited Hispanic immigrant churches; and still others visited Indian (South Asian) churches. The leaders returned buzzing with excitement and astonishment at what they had experienced. What happened next was telling. The entire group met to share their experiences with each other. As leaders shared, they didn't just share what they saw, they shared how it made them feel. The ethnic minority leaders watched as the community instructed, inspired, and challenged each other through their stories. Through the remainder of the conference Eddie walked past many conversations of leaders in twos and threes talking, praying, and musing on the newly awakened understanding. They had touched the pain and reality of people who had been so distant, and now, as one leader commented, "I'll never be the same." One leader left the event and started a new ministry to Native American men and women at The Navigators U.S. headquarters office.

This group of leaders set in motion an initiative that resulted in The Navigators launching a new fund, the Kairos Fund, that collects 1 percent of all Navigator income for use in ministry to and among ethnic minority Americans. These leaders who accepted the invitation to enter different communities had read all the right books. They had studied the Bible, including the very passages we are examining here. But it was going out and engaging with the lost, the broken, and the disenfranchised that brought about the transformation. It took the knowledge from their heads, connected it with the lives of others, and brought it home to their hearts. The Holy Spirit, working through this mission encounter, revealed things to these leaders about God and themselves that never would have happened without their willingness to engage in mission. Although these leaders were already mature Christians, they were spiritually formed in the midst of the mission experience.

Addressing Injustice in Systems and Structures
Over the centuries, the racial hatred that existed between the Jews and Samaritans became institutionalized and embedded in the social systems, cultural norms, and practices of both ethnic groups. Similar to the racial discord between the Jewish and Samaritan communities, the United States has a legacy of racism and ethnic divisions, and we are still living with that inheritance. America is a great nation built on powerful ideals — the self-evident truth that all people are created equal and granted by their Creator certain inalienable rights including life, liberty, and the pursuit of happiness.[10] Many immigrants came to the United States in pursuit of that dream and found the road to happiness paved with difficulty. The narratives of the early settlers are replete with struggles of poverty, illness, war, and premature death. From its birth, the United States of America has not fully lived up to its ideals. From the very beginning, the ideals of some were achieved at the expense of others. The collective prosperity of our nation was built upon the

genocide of indigenous people, wrongful seizure of their land (in far too many instances), the enslavement of Africans, and oppressive working conditions for Chinese immigrants in the early nineteenth century. As our nation grew, the political leaders enacted laws and exclusionary policies that systematically denied people of color access to citizenship, voting rights, or the means of production. European immigrants would continue to advance at the expense of other ethnic groups.

Although current-day European Americans have not participated in the evils of racism, slavery, and its later iterations, they are nonetheless beneficiaries of those past acts. Similarly, those ethnic groups that have been adversely affected live at an economic disadvantage, and the effects of centuries of an unlevel playing field can be readily seen in comparative statistics for unemployment, net wealth, health care, and so on. Not all of the pain is historical — we need only look to the current generation of indigenous people who are struggling with genocide, those who are victimized by modern-day slavery, and the often inhumane and oppressive conditions immigrants face. According to Michael Emerson and Christian Smith in their book *Divided by Faith*, "Health, life, and even death are racialized."[11]

As the cultural, social, and political systems were formed, the evangelical church was involved in the development and refining of American culture and its ethnic subcultures. During the early Provincial Period (1700–1730), clergymen played an active role in legitimizing slavery and used the gospel as a "force for social control."[12] Theologian Ernst Troeltsch concluded that the "teachings and practice of the church constituted one of the main sanctions for [slavery's] perpetuation."[13] From that time period until now, the church has not been exempt from the racial divisions and tensions within the prevailing culture. In fact, eleven on Sunday morning is still referred to as the most segregated hour in the United States as Christians gather for worship, primarily along racial lines. There are a number of historical and sociological factors that account for the reasons we separate to worship. What is perhaps the most painful aspect about this phenomenon is that we, as the church, are divided even though we live with the truth of the gospel's power to reconcile us to God. God "has committed to us the message of reconciliation" (2 Corinthians 5:19).

In November 2007, I attended a Native American theological conference along with other national leaders from InterVarsity Christian Fellowship's multiethnic ministries department. Our department did not have a dedicated associate director for Native American ministries, and it was the desire of one of our senior leaders that the entire department and some of our Native American staff attend a Native American event so we could immerse ourselves in the culture and realities of Native American people. As we sat through a number of presentations, heard testimonies, and read articles about the historical and present-day atrocities committed against various tribes, I did not have words to articulate the anguish, brokenness, and pain I was experiencing. In that context, I did not feel like a fellow disadvantaged ethnic-minority woman. In that moment, I was attending as the vice president of a prominent parachurch ministry seeking to grow in my understanding of how to minister to Native American college students.

After the conference ended, we held a consultation with the Native American leaders who convened at the conference to seek their insight and counsel on our campus strategy for Native American students. We sat for several hours as they shared about their tribal histories and personal stories. When we began to discuss our ministry goals, one of the leaders asked, "Why are you interested in ministering to Native American students? Do you plan to indoctrinate them into a system that has resulted in the destruction of their people and culture, or are you coming in a way that is restorative?" As I reflected on the history I had heard that day, I realized that many of the perpetrators who had committed injustices against the Native American community were people who said they came in the name of the Lord. What could I say that would communicate that I was bringing a gospel that was actually "good news" for the Native American people?

The story of the Good Samaritan is not a story about systemic injustice. The Good Samaritan did not advocate with the Roman or Jewish officials to create better military surveillance or to recommend a civic policy to reduce crime on the Jericho road; he extended himself to rescue a wounded man who most likely would have died without intervention. This is a story of an individual who demonstrated a willingness to inconvenience himself and give time, effort, and money to care for someone who had been wrongfully treated and left for dead. However, there is a broader message that speaks to the church. We live in a society where many people have been wrongfully treated and are lying wounded and vulnerable on the sidelines of society. Too often, in our busyness, we are like the priest and the Levite, who pass by on the other side of the road. There are those who watch us passing by without stopping to engage in acts of radical love that would bring restoration to those in need. We, as the church, fail to act neighborly. Furthermore, there are those who will not receive the gospel that we are preaching because they fail to see us living lives that intrinsically tie our love for God to love for our fellow brother or sister. They hear what we say, and they ask the question, "Is the gospel that you are preaching really good news?"

MISSION IS MESSY, BUT SO IS TRANSFORMATION

When we open up our lives to the mission of God, it's likely that our lives are not going to be the same. Sometimes God decides that we are to become intimately involved in the heartache and injustice of others through painful events that happen in our families. Eric and Marion Stolte, Navigator staff in Canada, are active volunteers with the Canadian Hemophilia Society (CHS) and the World Federation of Hemophilia (WFH).

In February of 1977 their son, Lyf, was born with hemophilia.[14] During the 1980s, blood that was contaminated with hepatitis C (HepC) and HIV was used as a source for the plasma needed to make FVIII. As a result, many people with hemophilia were infected. Lyf, although spared from HIV infection, did contract HepC. The responsibility for this tragedy rested with the Canadian government, which refused to be held accountable for it.

Eric described their experience as follows:

My wife and I are active volunteers with the Canadian Hemophilia Society. Their mission is to strive to improve the health and quality of life for all people with bleeding disorders and to find a cure. Their vision is a world free from the pain and suffering of bleeding disorders. We volunteer as an expression of Christ in our lives because we believe that He too wants a world free from the pain and suffering brought about by bleeding disorders.

Living through the horrible days of the tainted blood scandal in Canada that infected with HIV/AIDS the innocent lives of thousands of people with bleeding disorders as well as many others who received blood or blood products in the '80s and early '90s was painful. We attended far too many funerals of people who had become dear friends. But as a result of the primarily volunteer efforts of our society, Canada's blood system was recreated without the Red Cross and made systemically much safer. We continue to maintain a diligent vigilance to ensure blood and blood products will remain safe.

Also, while active in the Saskatchewan chapter of the CHS, we entered a "twinning" program through the WFH. Hemophiliacs in Mongolia were struggling to form themselves into a volunteer society and needed help. Like so many others in the developing world, the access to care was negligible. I traveled there with two other volunteer colleagues in 1997 to visit with members of the society and observe firsthand the care available. It was heart-wrenching to meet six-year-old Enjig who had severe hemophilia, knowing that he would probably not see his twentieth birthday. Our efforts lent energy to the Mongolian volunteers to advocate for care with their government. These efforts continue to this day.

It is through this community pain that we have been touched with a greater measure of how Jesus Himself must feel as He lives with all those who suffer injustice through the greed and avarice of others. We've learned more about loving others in pain, certainly a part of spiritual formation, than we would have in any other context in which we would naturally find ourselves. As we remain engaged, we continue to have experiences that form us more into Jesus' own image. We've received so much more than we've given.[15]

We can also engage individuals who, under normal circumstances, might actually see us as the enemy. Greg Paul, director of Sanctuary, a ministry to Toronto's poor and homeless, wrote of a deeply forming experience in caring for a gay man dying of AIDS. Neil had deteriorated to a shell of his former self, without strength or mobility. One day, Greg stopped in on Neil to find him in a panic, struggling with his bedsheets after having soiled himself. Greg picked him up, bathed him, cleaned his bed, dressed him, and placed him back in the bed.

He lay quietly back against the pillows and allowed me to take his feet, one at a time, and tuck them under the covers. Doing so, I noticed that one foot, somehow, had not gotten completely clean. Getting a washcloth, I wiped that foot. As I did so, I was struck by what I can only describe as a powerful revelation, two streams of thought converging, and both seeming to me to be the voice of God.

Cradling his foot in my hands, my mind was filled with the image of Jesus washing the feet of his disciples at the Last Supper, a towel around his waist, determinedly taking the servant's role. I had been meditating on that story from John's gospel just the day before, and now I could almost see Jesus hunched over Peter's foot, his hair hanging forward and obscuring his face, quietly insisting against Peter's protestations that those feet, but only the feet, needed to be washed. *This moment was what my whole time with Neil had been for! This was what it meant to be the presence of Christ.* I had been looking for opportunities to preach, wanting to effect a clear and possibly dramatic conversion. I realized in that moment that my longing for those things was as much or more an indication of my desire to be successful as they were of my passion for Neil's soul. It became clear that being Jesus to Neil, while it certainly included praying for him and announcing the good news to him, was most perfectly summed up by the mundane and even odious task of gently wiping excrement from his foot.

At the same time, I was deeply touched by his profound vulnerability. His foot was bare, and he hadn't even enough strength left in his ruined body to lift it and put it back under the covers. The words of Jesus were ringing in my ears: "I needed clothes and you clothed me, I was sick and you looked after me. . . . Whatever you did for one of the least of these brothers of mine, you did for me." This, too, was the purpose of my time with Neil. For the first time during our whole relationship, I saw Jesus in Neil. I had been seeing him as someone upon whom I could practice my own imitation of Christ, and had missed the Presence right before me. *I recognized that Neil was, at that moment, a physical representation to me of a vulnerable and dying Christ.* Jesus was allowing me to clothe him, and look after him, by caring for his "brother."

After a quiet moment or two, trying to assimilate these powerful impressions, I asked Neil if he would like to pray. "Yes, I'd like that," he whispered. I prayed first. I have no idea what I said. When I was done, I thought Neil might have fallen asleep. But then he spoke, whispered, into the stillness of that room. He didn't address his prayer to anyone, just spoke. And the words he spoke were words of blessing upon me. He knew he was dying, yet he asked nothing for himself; instead, he blessed me! Then he was so quiet and still, I thought again that he might have drifted off. But he spoke once more, without opening his eyes, and his voice this time was clear and surprisingly strong.

"In the name of Jesus."

Apart from saying good-bye, they were the last words I ever

heard him speak. When I visited him again a couple of days later, he was curled up in a tight little ball, unconscious. A week after that, he was gone.[16]

In carrying out Jesus' mission, we may find Him where we least expect to see Him. In many instances, we see ourselves bringing Jesus to those we are serving. It can be a shocking realization to discover that we can see Jesus in those we have come to serve. In the gospel of Matthew, Jesus told of a future day when He would separate those standing before Him into two groups: those who were active in feeding the hungry, giving drink to the thirsty, welcoming the stranger, clothing those who were in need of clothes, caring for the sick, and visiting the prisoner and those who encountered people with the same sets of needs and did nothing. In that moment, the individuals will discover that those who served others were in fact caring for Jesus and those who failed to serve others were likewise not caring for Jesus. One group would receive a reward; the other group would go away to eternal punishment (see Matthew 25:31-46). This Scripture passage can often strike fear or induce guilt in the hearts of the inactive. However, it is helpful to realize that our love for Jesus is practically demonstrated by caring for the least and the lost and the forgotten. We can easily profess love for a God who doesn't need practical help from us in any capacity, but we can test our profession of love for a God that we haven't seen by how we treat our brothers and sisters that we do see. Scripture informs us that anyone who does not love a brother that she sees cannot love God, whom she hasn't seen (see 1 John 4:20). How different might we approach the work of mission and reaching out to others if we could readily see the face of Jesus in their eyes and recognize an opportunity to care for Him in meeting their needs?

TWO ILLUSIONS TO GET PAST IN SPIRITUAL TRANSFORMATION

In order to embrace mission as critical to my spiritual formation, there are two illusions that I must dispose of: the illusion that mission is unnecessary and the illusion that God's kingdom will come quickly when I participate in God's mission. Both illusions are false pictures of reality that distort my perception. One of the first things that can happen when we engage in mission is a feeling of disillusionment. We discover that the filters and lenses we use to make sense of the world and create safe spaces for our personal worlds do not accurately depict life for everyone. In fact, those filters can insulate us from the pain and discomfort of the world. It is the dismantling of those filters and lenses that creates an opportunity for us to feel the pain of others or engage a need so great that only God can meet it.

Disillusionment is an essential corrective on the journey of spiritual formation. Isolation or disengagement often reinforces blind spots that are not exposed until we engage in mission. Yet engagement with reality *dis*illusions us; this is a good thing, because part of transformation is *dis*illusionment. *Dis* means removal, and an *illusion* is a picture of reality that is not true. We constantly construct illusions of reality that we believe are real. It is engagement with God's mission in the real world that debunks the illusions in our belief systems that have debilitating, distorting power in our lives. This process is key to transformation and will happen only as we engage in experiences that carry us beyond the carefully controlled borders of our comfort zones.

When we live with an illusion that we don't have to be engaged in God's mission to grow to maturity, we believe that we can get everything we need for our spiritual development from our personal relationship with God and other Christians. This means that we can grow to complete maturity in Christ without ever joining God in extending His love, grace, and truth to those who are not in the kingdom. Jesus never gave the idea that we could walk in fellowship with Him and not be engaged with Him in mission. He told His disciples, "Follow me . . . and I will make you fishers of men" (Matthew 4:19). He said that He did "not come to call the righteous, but sinners to repentance" (Luke 5:32) and that He came "to seek and to save what was lost" (Luke 19:10). To grow spiritually, we have to be with Christ and have fellowship with Him. If we want to walk with Jesus and have fellowship with Him, we must go with Him, and He is bringing the good news of the kingdom to those who are outside. We must also follow His Word to have fellowship with Him. In His Word we are instructed to "go and make disciples of all nations, baptizing them . . . and teaching them to obey everything I have commanded" (Matthew 28:19-20). As we engage in this ministry, we are not simply obeying God's commands, we are being spiritually formed as we carry out God's mission.

A second false image of reality we face on the path to spiritual transformation is the sense that if God is present, we can expect change to happen quickly. This type of "quick fix" approach reflects a shallow view of reality. Transformational change in the lives of individuals, communities, and societal systems must occur on multiple levels because sin affects multiple levels of human existence. Sin influences our psychological, social, emotional, and intellectual worlds. Sin also takes up residence in systems of education, business, government, law, and health care. Solutions that don't resolve issues on multiple levels do not achieve transformational change because the change does not address the depth of the problem. Change that is transformational and permanent usually takes time. A prominent example of someone who was committed to transformational change and dedicated his life to political reform is William Wilberforce. Wilberforce, a British statesman and reformer, was committed to the abolition of the Atlantic slave trade in Britain. In 1787, he became the chief spokesman for the Society for Effecting the Abolition of the Slave Trade. In 1807, Parliament passed legislation prohibiting the slave trade. He pressed on for the complete abolition of slavery, and the bill abolishing slavery was enacted one month after his death, in 1833.[17] Wilberforce spent his political life fighting a battle in the political system to bring about change, and the result was freedom for millions of people.

How Mission Transforms Us

To be spiritually formed into the image of Christ, we must be willing to engage our neighbors, the ones who are physically present in our neighborhoods and the ones whom God brings across our paths in the course of our daily activities. It is in this engagement that we become like Christ. It's not enough to believe correct theological facts; right beliefs alone will never lead to transformation. Ultimately, spiritual transformation rests on our obedience—our willingness to love God and our neighbors. We live in a world where it is easy to overlook people in need, whether we choose to pass by people on the other side of the street or on the other side of the world who are trapped in situations of poverty and oppression. Given the tremendous amount of need in the world, it can be overwhelming to think of all the billions of people in the world as my neighbors. Fortunately, Jesus does not expect us to meet the needs of every person we encounter. There were times when Jesus healed everyone who came to Him (see Mark 1:32-34) as well as an instance when He went to the pool at Bethesda and Scripture records that He healed only one person (see John 5:1-9). Jesus came to do the work of the Father, and He did only the things that God instructed Him to do.

The Evangelical Covenant Church in Chicago hosts an experience titled Journey to Mosaic, during which participants go on a four-day bus trip that includes stops in Oakland, central California, and Los Angeles. They are paired up with teammates of other ethnicities to examine the historical experiences of African Americans, Hispanic Americans, and Asian Americans. On the bus ride, participants watch videos and engage in discussions of the painful histories and experiences of these three ethnic groups. Participants also spend time interacting with community leaders who are engaging in issues of community organizing and justice. On the final day, the participants visit skid row in Los Angeles and spend time distributing bag lunches and praying for homeless people. The trip is designed to create feelings of dissonance and pain as you encounter the historical and current realities of various ethnic groups. As I watched the videotapes dealing with historical racism and systematic oppression, I began to experience anger. There seemed to be a conspiracy of forces at work—the invisible hand of the marketplace and the covert expressions of institutionalized racism that dismantled the efforts of these groups to organize and accumulate power. My feelings of anger turned to hopelessness as time and time again individuals and ethnic groups were systematically denied access to fair housing loans or rights of citizenship or equality through the court system. On the third night of the trip, I was overwhelmed by mental and spiritual heaviness, and I sought comfort in the Scriptures.

As I turned to Ephesians 6, I was reminded that the battle I was witnessing was not a battle of flesh and blood. Racism is a principality, and the social events that I learned about were examples of spiritual wickedness in high places. Thankfully, Scripture assures us that God has given us weapons of warfare that are strong enough to pull down strongholds (see 2 Corinthians 10:3-4). On the final evening, we headed out into the night to distribute food and minister to the homeless on skid row. I was overwhelmed by the sights and smells, the mentally ill people, and the vulnerable women and children. In a very short time, we had distributed all of our food, but everywhere around us were people in need. As we began talking to individuals, others saw us praying and came over for a conversation and prayer. As I stood there praying and touching people—people who were used to being overlooked and avoided—I was struck afresh by the power and hope of the gospel in an environment that was brimming with hopelessness and despair. In that moment, I realized that on that particular night, the kingdom of God came through my willingness to advance it. While I could and often did pray for God's kingdom to come and His will to be done, on that night I was the hands and feet of the gospel. In that moment, God did something for me. I was different. We ended the night with Communion and worship. Late into the night, I could hear the sounds of the city. As we got on the bus, heading for home, my despair turned to worship. I realized a day would come when there would be no more suffering, no more pain. For now, we had to live in the hope of the kingdom of God and the return of our coming King.

In this book, we have been very careful not to give you a prescription for spiritual formation. We believe that each of the elements in this book is essential, but how God uses them will differ according to His design for each person. When I began participating with TACT six years ago, the image I held in my mind regarding spiritual formation was the individual who had withdrawn from the world and spent his or her time practicing spiritual disciplines in isolation. Jesus modeled the importance of finding a solitary place to pray to His Father (see Mark 1:35), so there is a time and place for disciplines of solitude and prayer. Similarly, there is a time to engage the world in mission. Far too often, many of us shrink back from mission as a critical part of our spiritual formation, but it is precisely in those moments that God reshapes our hearts, minds, and inner beings. As we experience God at work in people's lives and become conduits for His love and power, the gospel of Jesus penetrates our hearts and the places where we are not aligned with Him. As the good news of the gospel flows into the world, it also flows through us, and we are changed from the inside out.

FOR REFLECTION AND DISCUSSION

1. Think about the passions of the ministry contexts you are involved in. Would you say they are oriented toward the freedom from sin that is discussed in the Bakke quote at the beginning of this chapter or toward freedom from the bondages of this world? Would a change toward the full freedom of the gospel be embraced in those ministry contexts? Why or why not?

2. We are formed *in* mission, not merely *for* mission. Given that reality, do you believe that people would engage in mission and integrate it into their lives more if they understood the importance of the "in" rather than merely the "for" linking formation and mission?

3. The embrace of the other, of your neighbor who is not like you, is among the hardest things to do for many people. What do we gain in our formation from this embrace? What do you gain from excluding those who are different from your life?

4. If the fullness of God's kingdom will not necessarily come any faster from my involvement in mission, then what are the

motivations? How would you encourage others to allow mission to break in to their already crowded lives?

5. America is becoming a more diverse country ethnically, economically, and in many other ways as well. How ready are your ministry contexts for these changes?

FOR FURTHER READING

Bakke, Ray with Jim Hart. *The Urban Christian: Effective Ministry in Today's Urban World*. Downers Grove, IL: InterVarsity, 1987.

Bosch, David. *Transforming Mission: Paradigm Shifts in Theology*. Maryknoll, NY: Orbis, 1991.

Henry, Carl F. H. *The Uneasy Conscience of Modern Fundamentalism*. Grand Rapids, MI: Eerdmans, 2005.

Newbigin, Lesslie. *The Open Secret: An Introduction to the Theology of Mission*. Grand Rapids, MI: Eerdmans, 1995.

Paul, Greg. *God in the Alley: Being and Seeing Jesus in a Broken World*. Colorado Springs, CO: Shaw Books, 2004.

Part 2

THEOLOGICAL ELEMENTS OF SPIRITUAL FORMATION

Chapter Eight

THE TRINITY AS FOUNDATION FOR SPIRITUAL FORMATION

Bruce Demarest

ELEMENT 8: The theology of spiritual transformation emerges from the Trinitarian nature of God — relational, loving, gracious, mutually submissive, and unified in will.

Description: This is the cornerstone statement. Everything that follows regarding spiritual formation flows from who God is. The God who is revealed in Scripture and who lived among us in Jesus Christ exists as a loving community of grace in three persons. From eternity past to eternity future, Father, Son, and Holy Spirit relate to each other with grace, love, mutual submission, and unity of heart and by honoring their roles practicing functional submission — the Holy Spirit to the Son and the Father, and the Son to the Father. Marvelously, this triune God has invited us, in relationship with Himself, to participate in this culture of grace.

WHAT'S AT STAKE HERE?

Theology has often been viewed as something that only people in universities do—and in the German language. It is not unusual in seminary classes for students of systematic theology to complain, "When am I ever going to use this?" And to be fair, often when the great doctrines of the church are discussed, it is done in dry, obscure ways and with the sense that no one really cares to know about these things. For many people, the doctrine of the Trinity is chief among such doctrines—obscure, poorly understood, and not entirely necessary. How unfortunate this is, because biblical truth is the foundation on which our faith and transformation rest. Rejecting the truth of the Trinity of God cuts the heart out of the Christian faith.

One seminarian, Christopher Morton, grounded the importance of the Trinity in our lives by sharing the following story:

> Having been raised in a family in which God was to be feared but never known, the idea of "three persons in one God" seemed absurd to me. After I met Jesus at age twenty, this perspective did not change, and honestly I did not think about it. But more than four years later, when a person whose life and love for God I deeply respected challenged me, I finally realized that something about how I understood God was out of whack. This person had noticed that I only talked about and prayed to Jesus. Now talking and praying to Jesus is not a bad thing, of course, but he asked me about what I thought about God the Father and God the Holy Spirit. My blank face told it all. I was four years into my new life in Christ and had never thought about why the Father of Jesus Christ and the Spirit that He promised to send mattered. It was at that point that so many of the difficulties in my faith that had driven that dear man crazy became understandable. My mentor challenged me to walk with God to see if there might be something even bigger about Him than I had thus far imagined and experienced.[1]

ARE WE REALLY TRINITARIANS?

Living models of spiritually transformed and missional people and com-munities are uncommon commodities in our self-serving, pleasure-seek-ing world. God in His surprising providence privileged me to experience such an apostolic model some twenty years ago. Encouraged by a Jesuit spiritual director, I spent extended seasons in the Pecos Benedictine Abbey, a renewal community outside Santa Fe, New Mexico. In 1995, with forty other Christians (Evangelical, Lutheran, Anglican, and Roman Catholic), I enrolled in the abbey's six-week residential School for Spiritual Direction.

In totally orthodox fashion, the men and women of the Pecos com-munity lifted up the life of the triune God. Living together, worshipping together, learning together, and ministering together, we participants encountered the awesome majesty of the Father, the grace of Jesus Christ, and the dynamism and joy of the Holy Spirit. Through the daily rhythm of prayer, study, and work, the Holy Spirit gradually purged our fleshly selves, healed old wounds, deepened love for Christ, and glori-fied the Father. During this graced season I personally sensed that I was being transported by the Spirit back into the life of the early church with its passion for Christ and power for living. I matured spiritually and emotionally more in those six weeks than in several decades of previous evangelical life.

The grace of this fresh experience of God helped me discover, to a far greater degree, the triune God. Engaging Father, Son, and Holy Spirit in the unity of the Trinity helped me know experientially the completeness of God — the love of the Father, the beauty of the Son, and the power of the Spirit — that had been deficient in my previous Christian experience. I witnessed the Holy Spirit thrusting radically transformed disciples of Jesus into new ministries of establishing retreat houses, offering spiritual direction, and caring for the poorest of the poor at home and abroad. I brought the triune-God–centered treasures of spiritual formation that I had received to my spheres of influence: my local church community and the seminary where I have taught for thirty years.

Many Christians are theoretical Trinitarians but practical Unitarians. In our busy lives we don't think much about the Trinity, and often we don't experience the transforming life of the three-in-one God. It may be that in our churches we have never heard a sermon on the Trinity and its relevance for our lives. In practice, Christ the Son may be no more than a man to emulate and the Spirit no more than the junior assistant in the Godhead. An outcome of this pragmatic approach is that the Trinity has little relevance for our daily lives. Saints who consider themselves faithfully orthodox may not be that different from liberal Christians in devaluing the three divine persons in the Trinity. The questions must be asked: Do we really believe in the Trinity we confess in the creeds? Does the Trinity play a vital role in our spiritual lives? Do we actually live in the reality—the grace, love, and power—of the Trinity? But first we need to explore what Christians mean by the Trinity of God.

GOD AS UNITY AND DIVERSITY

The triune God is both the beginning and the end of all reality. The dynamic communion of the three divine persons—Father, Son, and Holy Spirit—constitutes the very heart of Christian faith and life. The triune God, moreover, grounds the sum and substance of the church's beliefs, life, and mission in the world. Admittedly, the word *Trinity* is not found in Scripture, but neither are terms such as *session, ordination, mission board*. If not explicitly stated in the Bible, the reality of the Trinity is taught in a number of texts such as Matthew 28:19; John 14:26; Titus 3:4-6; and 1 John 4:13-15. The God of the Bible is not a solitary monad but a complex unity of three divine persons—"person" being understood as a center of conscious life and activity. God has made known His threefold reality via the names Father, Son, and Holy Spirit—names that signify dynamic relationships within the Godhead. The one true God, then, is a community of three divine persons subsisting in one infinite spirit being. As an early church father stated, "The Trinity itself is a sweet society." In terms of their work we may say that the Father is God for us, the Son is God with us, a Spirit is God in us. Deuteronomy 6:4—"Hear, O Israel: The LORD our God, the LORD is one"—highlights God's unity, albeit a unity that is complex, even as a family or a nation is both one and many.

The Christian doctrine of the Trinity sheds light on the perennial problem of unity and diversity—how the many can be reconciled with oneness or coherence in the universe. Scientists once thought that the smallest particles were protons, neutrons, and electrons. Recent research in particle physics has shown that subatomic particles known as quarks form one of the two basic constituents of matter. Quarks, however, do not exist alone but only as three pairs of two. The smallest things scientists have discovered exist only in relationship—as three interacting pairs of two.

Christian thinkers have proposed illustrations from our world of experience for the purpose of describing the Trinity. Since God is infinite, all illustrations of the Trinity are less than perfect. However, here are a few illustrations that help us better understand the Trinity's dynamic relationship. In *On the Trinity*, a great classic of the church, Augustine, in reading that "God is love" (1 John 4:16), judged that love requires a lover, a beloved, and the spirit of love that flows between them. Love in reality exists only when these three unite. He then concluded that God the Father is Lover, God the Son is the Beloved, and the Holy Spirit is the personal Love that connects them. Thus we can say that the Trinity is love revealed, demonstrating the self-forgetting, self-giving compassion often missing in the world today. Another illustration of the Trinity focuses on speech and communication: Christ is the spoken Word of the Father, but speech is made possible only by breath (the Holy Spirit). Yet another model describes Father, Son, and Spirit as "Giver, Given, and Gift/ing."[2] The Trinity might be visually represented as a triangle, where the triangle itself represents God and the three angles represent the three divine persons of the Godhead. The Christian doctrine of the Trinity, while not at all contrary to sound reason, nevertheless exceeds the limits of human reason and in this respect represents a revealed mystery.

Rocky Mountain aspen groves are noted for their quaking leaves and gloriously golden autumn colors. But a grove of aspen trees actually proves to be a single living organism. The grove of trees shares a common root system that nourishes and supports each of the seemingly individual trees in a symbiotic relationship. The *Guinness Book of Records* states that an aspen grove in a Rocky Mountain meadow represents the largest single living organism on the planet. How fitting, then, that the church father Tertullian (170–220) figuratively depicted the Trinity as a tree, with the Father as a deep root, the Son as the shoot that breaks forth into the world, and the Spirit as the beauty and fragrance thereof.[3]

The Trinity is unique among the world's creeds and religions. The biblical doctrine of the Trinity, as confessed in the church's creeds, has been opposed by cults such as Mormonism, Jehovah's Witnesses, and Christian Science. It has been the object of attack by religions such as Hinduism, Buddhism, Judaism, and Islam. And the Trinity has been misinterpreted by many within professing Christendom, particularly in the liberal theological tradition.

THE RELATIONAL LIFE OF THE TRINITY

It is not enough to gain understanding of the Trinity as a single entity with distinct parts. The three-in-one God is a *relational* God—from eternity past to eternity future, a dynamic community of three loving persons. Ancient Christian writers described the personal relations within the Trinity by the Greek word *perichorēsis*, literally meaning "dance around." The term affirms the three persons of the Trinity indwell each other such that the supernatural life of each flows among the others. A leading Eastern theologian, John of Damascus (655–749), spoke of the dynamic give-and-take of the three divine persons within the Trinity. He acknowledged the flow of person, idea, virtue, and life among Father, Son, and Spirit — each giving to and receiving from the others. This "spilling over" or "pouring back and forth" of life from one divine person to another in the Trinity is reflected in the fourth gospel's teaching that each person is "in" the other two persons. Concerning His Father, Jesus uttered the words, "Just as you are in me and I am in you" (John 17:21; cf. verse 23). The Lord added, "The Father is in me, and I in the Father" (John 10:38; cf. 14:10-11). Statements such as these amplify John's earlier teaching that "the Word was with God" (John 1:1) and that "the unique One, who is himself God, is near to the Father's heart" (John 1:18, NLT). Far from being independent, self-sufficient entities, Father, Son, and Spirit receive their personhood in and through the other two.

In talks to groups, Eugene Peterson often describes *perichorēsis* as the exchanging of partners on a dance floor: One moment we find ourselves dancing with the Father, another with the Son, and when we look again it's the Spirit who is twirling us around. In one of his writings Peterson highlighted "a giant dance, with the persons of the Father, Son, and Spirit exchanging freely with one another, with no beginning, no ending, and no stopping — a giant dance of beauty, freedom, and love."[4] The flow of love between the three divine persons of the Trinity can be further illustrated by the giving and receiving of life spiritually, emotionally, and physically between a husband and wife (although the marriage partners are two not three). In the bond of marriage, husband and wife are "one flesh," although they are two distinct and unique persons (Ephesians 5:31). Couples in marriage ceremonies often merge two candles into one larger candle, symbolizing the two becoming one flesh. As within the Trinity, relations between marriage partners are characterized by self-giving, unconditional loving, mutual affirmation, promoting the welfare of the other, and sheer delight at being together. As happily married couples can testify, this rich union often is experientially felt. The partners function as living icons of Jesus to one another.

Within the unity of the Godhead, each of the three divine persons brings a unique identity to the relationship. Jesus knew Himself to be a worthy person distinct from the Father and the Spirit. Jesus not only said, "I and the Father are one" (John 10:30), but with not the slightest hint of inferiority He also said, "The Father is greater than I" (John 14:28). (This particular saying of Jesus points to functional roles within the economy of the Trinity.) Moreover, each divine person possesses intimate knowledge of the other two divine persons. Jesus said, "No one knows the Son except the Father, and no one knows the Father except the Son" (Matthew 11:27). The compound verb "to know" (*epiginōskō*) denotes a knowledge that is intimate and complete.

The life of the Trinity, moreover, is characterized by mutual submission and complete sharing. The Son said to the Father, "All I have is yours, and all you have is mine" (John 17:10). On another occasion Jesus said to His disciples, "The Spirit will take from what is mine and make it known to you" (John 16:15). On at least one occasion the Son even issued a command to His Father (see Luke 23:34). Here we see the three persons honoring their primary roles in the economy of the Godhead via relations of loving submission. Moreover, a profound others-centeredness characterizes intra-Trinitarian relations, such that each divine person perfectly promotes the significance of the other persons. Within the social life of the Trinity, one finds no jealousy, no complaining, and no cross-purposes. The Father glorifies the Son (see John 17:1,5), and the Son glorifies the Father. As Jesus said to His Father, "I have brought you glory on earth by completing the work you gave me to do" (John 17:4). The Spirit, furthermore, brings glory to the Son (see John 16:14).

Perfect trust exists between the Father and the Son in the outworking of redemption. Jesus said, "The Father loves the Son and has placed everything in his hands" (John 3:35). Later the Son prayed to the Father, "For you granted him authority over all people that he might give eternal life to all those you have given him" (John 17:2; cf. verse 3). Intra-Trinitarian relations, finally, are characterized by unconditional love, the essence of which is mutual submission and furthering the good of the other. The Gospels teach that the Father loves the Son (see Matthew 3:17; John 5:20; 17:24) and the Son loves the Father. Feel Jesus' overflowing heart of love for His Father expressed by these words of longing: "I am coming to you now" (John 17:13).

Furthermore, open and honest communication prevails eternally between the three persons of the Trinity. The ease with which Jesus dialogued with the Father is seen in His frequent seasons of communion with Abba in remote places, as well as His extended prayer upon leaving the Upper Room as recorded in John 17. In addition, the Son of God demonstrated humility by living in dependence upon His Father with gratitude to the Spirit. By saying, "Everything you have given me comes from you" (John 17:7), the Son freely acknowledged the sufficiency of the Father's gifts. Philosopher Gabriel Marcel (1889–1973) fittingly identified the elements of Trinitarian community as availability, mutuality, and self-giving.

IMITATING THE TRINITARIAN COMMUNITY

We have examined the nature of the Trinity and its intrapersonal relations. Many at an intellectual level believe the doctrine of the Trinity but are uncertain how this great truth relates to us. It does so in two principal ways: by emulating or imitating the Trinity and by being caught up into the dynamic relational life of the Trinity.

The harmonious relations among the three persons of the Trinity offer a powerful model for imitation that advances the process of our spiritual formation. The Son embodies and reveals to us in human terms the perfections and works of God the Father. Each of the three persons of the Trinity exercises a primary function in the relation between people and the Godhead: the Father (Creator) originates the plan of salvation; the Son (Redeemer) provides the remedy for the blight of human sin; and the Spirit (Sanctifier) applies this salvation, growing new spiritual life. Yet because God is united and not divided, each of the three persons works harmoniously to accomplish the saving works of the Godhead. Jesus intentionally imitated His heavenly Father's actions: "I tell you the truth, the Son can do nothing by himself; he can do only what he sees his Father doing, because whatever the Father does the Son also does" (John 5:19). Jesus then instructed His followers to "learn from me" (Matthew 11:29) and to "follow me" (John 21:22). The apostle Paul was passionate about copying Christ. "Be imitators of me, just as I also am of Christ" (1 Corinthians 11:1, NASB). Paul's word for *imitator* literally means one who "mimics." Peter likewise commanded saints to imitate or "follow" the life of Christ (1 Peter 2:21). To follow Christ is to mimic in all respects the pattern of His speech, relationships, and actions.

Christian authorities throughout history have stressed the importance of imitating the incarnate Christ in order to be transformed spiritually and to glorify God. The early bishop and theologian Clement of Alexandria (150–215) wrote, "One truly follows the Savior by arranging everything to be like him,"[5] Thomas à Kempis (1380–1471) devoted an entire book, which has become a classic of Christian spirituality, to this theme. He urged, "Imitate Christ in life and behavior. . . . Conform one hundred percent to his life."[6] The French spiritual writer François Fénelon (1651–1715) similarly wrote, "We must imitate Jesus. This is to live as he lived, to think as he thought, to conform to his image, which is the seal of our sanctification."[7]

As apprentices of Jesus, we must intentionally and prayerfully model the others-centeredness, intimacy, trust, honest communication, and unconditional love that He exhibited in relationship with the Father and the Holy Spirit as a member of the social Trinity. To experience transformation into wholeness and holiness, we are called to cultivate, nurture, and sustain the quality of relationships experienced between the Father, the Son, and the Spirit. We do this by imitating Jesus' life on earth, which flowed from His life in the Trinity. Jesus cared greatly for people who cared little for Him or His kingdom cause. For example, Jesus dealt patiently and compassionately with the Samaritan woman who resisted His efforts to lead her to the truth (see John 4:4-30). He patiently nurtured His disciples, who were spiritually dull, strong willed, self-confident to the point of arrogance, and at times contentious with one another and with Him. He demonstrated extraordinary humility and love by washing His disciples' feet (see John 13:3-14). He dealt lovingly and nonjudgmentally with the woman caught in adultery, while dealing firmly with the scribes and Pharisees who used her as a pawn to trap Him (see John 8:1-11). He showed compassion to the rich young ruler in his misguided search for purpose and satisfaction in life (see Mark 10:17-22).

Jesus, moreover, ministered saving grace to a despised pocket-padding but spiritually hungry tax collector (see Luke 19:1-10). He ministered comfort and reassurance to His confused and distraught disciples in the Upper Room (see John 14–16) and brought encouragement and hope to two dejected disciples on the road to Emmaus (see Luke 24:13-35). The Lord tenderly restored Simon Peter to wholeness following the fisherman's cowardly denial of Himself (see John 21:15-23). Jesus earnestly prayed for His weak and frail followers on their perilous journeys (see John 17:6-26; Luke 22:32). Thus we find that imitating Jesus will involve a life that affirms, encourages, blesses, and releases the good in others.

Finally, since God is love (see 1 John 4:8,16) and love thus is the greatest virtue, God's people imitate the love of the Trinitarian community. Scripture testifies that the Father (see John 14:23; 1 John 3:1), the Son (see Romans 8:35; Ephesians 3:18), and the Spirit (see Romans 15:30) exude unconditional, unsurpassing love. Since Jesus is God revealed in human flesh, we imitate the Savior in His loving relations. Jesus loved the lowly, the unlovely, the outcasts, and the marginalized in society. As we love others in the way Jesus loved, God dwells in us and we are transformed. In the words of Augustine, "People are renewed by love. As sinful desire ages them, so love rejuvenates them." He continued, "Love . . . is the sign of our renewal as we know from the Lord's own words: 'I give you a new commandment—love one another.'"[8] To His followers today Jesus says: "Journey with Me; align your life with My life; imitate My speech and actions." As we imitate the pattern of Jesus' life, we become like Him, which is what godly transformation is all about.

Imitating the love of the Trinitarian community is not just a theological ideal but has everyday implications. Christopher Morton shared another story of his journey into the Trinitarian life:

> My wife and I were hurt at an emotional level. We had started a class for young married couples, many of whom were new to the faith, but our friends drove us from the group. As a result it was easy to complain. Members of the class had not loved us and, indeed, had failed us. For many years that experience created a deep scar on our hearts and kept us from opening ourselves to new community. But as we read about the importance of the Trinity and understood the deep love that binds the Father, the Son, and the Spirit to each other—what Peter calls "sincere love" (1 Peter 1:22)—we came to the realization that we had inculcated in that group a type of manipulative love. We had fostered a love that sought our personal interests instead of the best interests of the others. It was in that realization that finally we were able to let go of the pain, reconnect with those from that earlier community, seek their forgiveness, and begin to love them in a brand-new way.[9]

Our mandate to model the triune God recalls the story of a budding young painter who desired to create artwork as elegant as that of her teacher, a famous master of form and color. The student painted several scenes but never attained her teacher's level of excellence. Then she got the bright idea that if she used her teacher's brushes, she could paint great art. But her paintings failed to measure up to the instructor's works. Observing the young woman's struggles, her teacher said to her, "It's not my paintbrushes you need; it's my spirit."

CAUGHT UP INTO THE TRINITARIAN LIFE

In addition to imitating the persons of the Trinity, disciples are swept into the community life of the three-in-one God. Those who trust Christ and follow Him become members of God's family and participate in that family life. Saturn, the second largest planet in our solar system, is circled by seven main rings. Imagine that as Saturn traveled through space long ago, its gravitational field gathered together zillions of particles as small as grains of sand and as large as automobiles, which we observe as rings. Scientists speculate that in time these swirling bands of ice-coated particles will collapse into the planet and be joined with Saturn. Analogous to Saturn's rings, followers of Jesus by grace are swept into the Trinity, willingly joined to its transforming life.

By virtue of Christ's death and resurrection, followers of Jesus are joined to the triune God in an intimate union of life and love. The Father, Son, and Spirit live in Christians, and Christians live in the same Father, Son, and Spirit (see 1 John 4:13,15). Expressed in other terms, followers of Jesus are personally, experientially, and collectively swept into the relational life of the triune God. Although retaining our unique identities, we participate in the dynamic communal life of the Trinity, wherein we find our completeness, fulfillment, and delight. So the apostle John wrote, "As we live in God, our love grows more perfect" (1 John 4:17, NLT). Writing to the Ephesians, Paul asserted that through faith saints are seated in heavenly places in the *koinonia* of the Trinity (see Ephesians 2:6-7). Spiritual transformation, then, involves gracious participation in the divine drama that is the inner life of the Trinitarian community.

The Reformation church expressed this reality as the doctrine of union with Christ, which affirms that at the new birth the repentant person is united with Christ (see John 15:5; 1 Corinthians 15:22; 2 Corinthians 5:17) and Christ with him (see John 15:5; Galatians 2:20; Ephesians 3:17). This union of life is expressed by the frequently used New Testament phrase "in Christ" (242 times in the writings of Paul and John alone)—a phrase that becomes virtually a synonym for the Christian. In the same vein, 1 Corinthians 6:17 states, "But he who unites himself with the Lord is one with him in spirit." By virtue of this union we become, as it were, Christ's brothers and sisters (see Hebrews 2:11-12). Paul added that the church, the body, is filled with the "fullness of [Christ] who fills everything in every way" (Ephesians 1:23). Second Peter 1:4 teaches the profound truth that through Christ's redemptive work those who trust Christ "participate in the divine nature [*theia physis*]," meaning that they are incorporated into the very life of the Father, the Son, and the Spirit, which, as noted above, is a powerful force for spiritual transformation. The above Scriptures teach that followers of Jesus, through the Spirit (see Romans 8:9; Galatians 4:6), participate in the transforming dance of life and love that is the triune God.

The Eastern church represented the union between the Trinity and God's people as a "divinization"—the Greek word *theōsis* literally meaning "in-godded." The provocative term *divinization* certainly does not mean that the new Christian becomes God—literally a fourth member of the Trinity! Rather, what Athanasius of Alexandria and other Eastern theologians meant by *divinization* is that by grace disciples share in the community life of the Godhead through the energy of the Spirit—or alternatively, become a "new creation" in Christ (2 Corinthians 5:17). Robert Webber explained, "In Eastern thought, the goal of the Christian life is to so commune with God that he or she is made more and more in the image of Christlikeness, fulfilling God's purposes for humanity in God's creation."[10] From the perspective of the Eastern church, divinization is the work of God's grace by which we are drawn into the very midst of the triune life and are washed over by God's love such that we share in that joy as new creations and His beloved children (see Galatians 4:4-7). In one of his beloved hymns Charles Wesley put it this way:

He deigns in flesh to appear,
Widest extremes to join;
To bring our vileness near,
And make us all divine:
And we the life of God shall know,
For God is manifest below.[11]

TRINITARIAN TRANSFORMATION

It should be clear that spiritual transformation, like creation of the cosmos, is the gracious work of the triune God applied to our lives wherever God has placed us. Previously I noted that each of the three persons of the Godhead performs a *primary* work. (Given the unity of the Godhead, the other two divine persons participate in a secondary way in each of the primary works.) These works play distinct roles in our transformation into the image of His beloved Son (see Romans 8:29; Ephesians 4:13) through the lifelong process of Spirit transformation, or what theologians call "sanctification." Thus the Father creates all things; the Son sustains all things and redeems the lost; and the Spirit applies the benefits of salvation to those who trust Christ. As Charles Spurgeon noted,

> God the Father is the fountain of grace, God the Son is the channel of grace, and God the Holy Spirit is the cup from which we drink of the flowing stream. . . . The Father gives the great gospel feast, the Son is the feast, and the Spirit not only brings the invitations, he also gathers the guests around the table.[12]

The following details explain the roles each person of the Trinity plays in the lifelong process of spiritual transformation.

The first person of the Trinity, who bears the name Father, is the fountain of all grace (see 2 Thessalonians 2:16). He forgives our sin (see Matthew 6:14; 1 John 2:1), lavishes love on us (see 1 John 3:1), and provides for our spiritual, emotional, and physical needs (see Matthew 6:26,32). In the process of transformation the Father paradoxically is likened to a mother (see Isaiah 49:15; 66:13), who embraces, comforts, and nurtures her beloved child. The Father, furthermore, is revealed as our shepherd (see Psalm 23:1; Isaiah 40:11), who tenderly bears up, protects, and provides for His sheep. He is the "spring of living water" (Jeremiah 2:13; 17:13), the source of our spiritual sustenance and refreshment. He is our rock (see Deuteronomy 32:18; 2 Samuel 22:2-3), our source of stability, strength, and safety. The Father, moreover, is our strength (see Psalm 46:1; Habakkuk 3:19), supplying enabling power for the journey. When we are threatened, He is our refuge (see Deuteronomy 33:27; 2 Samuel 22:3; Psalm 9:9) and fortress (see 2 Samuel 22:2; Psalm 46:11; 144:2)—images that signify shelter, safety, and security. The Father, moreover, is the potter (see Isaiah 64:8; Jeremiah 18:1-6), who skillfully molds His people, as clay, into vessels of honor. He is the gardener (see John 15:1), who skillfully prunes us, the branches, thereby promoting our transformation.

The second person of the Trinity, God's Son, bears the earthly name Jesus, which is the transliteration of the Greek form of the Hebrew name Joshua, meaning "Jehovah is salvation." As "Immanuel" (Isaiah 7:14; Matthew 1:23), which means "God with us," "Jesus is the central figure in the spiritual life."[13] In love He descended from heaven to redeem, transform, and lead us to our heavenly home. The Son is the "Word of life" (1 John 1:1), who imparts fullness of life to those who trust Him. He is the "bread of life" (John 6:35,48), who nourishes, satisfies, and sustains the soul with food that will never spoil. He is the "true vine" (John 15:1), the source of life, growth, and fruitfulness, provided that we remain vitally connected to Him. The Son is the "true light" (John 1:9), who scatters the darkness of sin, illumines our hearts, and brightens the path before us. Jesus is "the power of God" (1 Corinthians 1:24), whose saving work energizes our transformation.

The Son is our high priest (see Hebrews 2:17; 3:1; 6:20), who "is able to save completely those who come to God through him" (Hebrews 7:25). The Son intercedes ceaselessly for us before the Father in heaven (see John 17:9,15-19,20-26; Romans 8:34). He is our physician (see Luke 4:23) who binds up our wounds and makes us whole. He is the "good shepherd" (John 10:11,14), who knows His sheep intimately, protecting us from danger and bringing us back when we wander from the fold. He is our teacher (see Matthew 23:10), who by His instruction enables apprentices to live well in the kingdom of God. The Son sits "as a refiner and purifier" (Malachi 3:3), burning off impurities and advancing holiness. Finally, Jesus loves us to the end, as He repeatedly reminded His perplexed disciples in the Upper Room (see John 14:21,23; 15:9; 16:27; 17:23). The Son's unfailing faithfulness and love enable us to overcome life's struggles and trials. Charles Spurgeon observed, "What the sun is to the day, what the moon is to the night, what the dew is to the flower, such is Jesus Christ to us. What bread is to the hungry, clothes to the naked, the shadow of a great rock to the traveler in a weary land, such is Jesus Christ to us."[14]

The third person of the Trinity, who bears the name Spirit, is the Father and Son's bestowal of love to the world, particularly to those within the household of faith. The word *spirit* (*pneuma*) literally means "breath," implying that the Holy Spirit is the divine person who breathes new life into us. As Michael Downey put it, the Spirit is "Love's speaking and breathing, living and loving among us."[15] Jesus repeatedly promised His followers that He would come to them formatively in a new way through the Counselor (see John 14:16-19,23,26; 15:26; 16:7). The Spirit, or Counselor, makes Jesus experientially real to those who trust and follow the Master. The Spirit's anointing illumines and enlightens our minds (see 1 Corinthians 2:12), teaching us all things spiritual (see 1 John 2:27). The "Spirit of truth" (John 16:13-15) not only provides access to, and communion with, the Father (see Ephesians 2:18) but also applies the Son's transforming provision to our lives.

The Spirit is like refreshing water splashed on a thirsty people (see Isaiah 44:3-4l). The Spirit is the wind of God (see John 3:8; Acts 2:1-4), who enlivens (see John 6:63), encourages (see Acts 9:31), and empowers (see Acts 1:8). Apart from the Spirit's ministry in our hearts, we are like branches without sap, coals without fire, and ships without sails. The same Spirit bestows enabling gifts — words of wisdom and knowledge, faith, discernment of spirits, and so on (see 1 Corinthians 12:7-11) — for the building up of Christ's body (see Romans 12:6-8; 1 Corinthians 14:1-5). The Spirit kills the unclean works of the flesh — "sexual immorality, impurity and debauchery; idolatry and witchcraft; hatred . . . factions and envy; drunkenness, orgies, and the like" (Galatians 5:19-21) — and brings forth transformational virtues such as "love, joy, peace, patience, kindness, gentleness, faithfulness and self-control" (Galatians 5:22-23).

The Spirit not only imparts the desire to pray but also enables and empowers our prayers (see Ephesians 6:18; Jude 20). The same Spirit intercedes before the Father on our behalf (see Romans 8:26-27). Prayer thus is a profoundly Trinitarian reality: Disciples pray to the Father (see Matthew 6:6), through the Son (see John 16:24), in the energy of the Spirit (see Jude 20). The Spirit is the agent of sanctification (see Romans 15:16) and transformation (see 2 Corinthians 3:18) for God's pilgrim people. Well did Augustine insist, "The body of Christ can live from nothing else but the Spirit of Christ."[16]

The lifelong process of spiritual transformation, then, is the work of the triune God. The indwelling Trinity progressively recreates justified children of the Father (see Romans 8:15-16) into the likeness of the Son (see 2 Corinthians 3:18) by the power of the Spirit (see Romans 8:2-6). Although the triune God initiates transformation, apprentices of Jesus must perform their part where God providentially has placed them. Paul acknowledged the divine/human synergy with the statement, "Continue to work out your salvation with fear and trembling, for it is God who works in you to will and to act in order to fulfill his good purpose" (Philippians 2:12-13, TNIV). Formation occurs as we "keep in step with the Spirit" (Galatians 5:25, TNIV). Peter wrote that God's "divine power has given us everything we need for a godly life through our knowledge of him who called us by his own glory and goodness" (2 Peter 1:3, TNIV). But he immediately urged people to:

Make every effort to add to your faith goodness; and to goodness, knowledge; and to knowledge, self-control; and to self-control, perseverance; and to perseverance, godliness; and to godliness, mutual affection; and to mutual affection, love. For if you possess these qualities in increasing measure, they will keep you from being ineffective and unproductive in your knowledge of our Lord Jesus Christ. (2 Peter 1:5-8, TNIV)

TRANSFORMATION, COMMUNITY, AND MISSION

The reality of God as Trinity—Father, Son, and Holy Spirit—has profound implications for Christian community and mission, both of which are inextricably bound up with spiritual transformation. Here is a brief summary of what is developed more fully in other chapters in order to show that transforming community and mission are grounded in God's three-in-one nature.

Our tendency in the Western world is to view transformation as a strictly individual or solo enterprise. We recognize that God can and does form us wherever we are on our appointed path of discipleship, even in the absence of other Christ followers and when surrounded by unbelievers. God has ordained the special place of transformation into Christlikeness, however, to be the community of the church, the *ecclesia*. Just as the institutional form of the kingdom in the Old Testament was the nation Israel, so the institutional form of the kingdom between Pentecost and Christ's return to earth is the church, with Jesus as the centerpiece and face of the present form of the kingdom. Acts 2:42-47 and 4:32-35 describe the life-giving and empowering community life that existed in the church of the first century.

Note how often Paul referred to the building up of the *body* of Christ (see Ephesians 4:4,12-13,15-16; Colossians 1:18,24). In Ephesians 5:25-27 he wrote, "Christ loved the church and gave himself up for her to make her holy, cleansing her by the washing with water through the word, and to present her to himself as a radiant church, without stain or wrinkle or any other blemish, but holy and blameless." Comparing the church to a *building*, Paul added, "In him the whole building is joined together and rises to become a holy temple in the Lord. And in him you too are being built together to become a dwelling in which God lives by his Spirit" (Ephesians 2:21-22). The mutual indwelling of the Father, Son, and Spirit—and the fact that disciples are swept into the life of the Trinity—fosters two outcomes: they share in the transformational life of the Trinity and they are united interdependently with one another in formational community life. All true disciples, notwithstanding ethnic, cultural, and economic differences, are united by the Spirit to the triune God and to one another in communities of truth and grace. How radical yet rich is this community togetherness compared with the individualism, self-centeredness, and self-reliance of contemporary Western culture.

Since God created persons in His image (see Genesis 1:26-27), the loving communication of three persons within the unity of the Godhead constitutes the basis and model for the fellowship of God's people in loving community. The unity of the Godhead (one God) corresponds to the drive to be close, to belong, and to be connected to a loving community. It ties in to the desire to overcome rivalry and conquer loneliness. The diversity of the Godhead (three persons) corresponds to the need to be acknowledged as a unique individual and to have one's own space. We need gentle, fearless space in which to move to and from each other, insisted Henri Nouwen.[17] Too much union and we feel suffocated; too much space and we feel lonely.

The ways of emperor penguins teach core truths about vital Christian community. The documentary film *The March of the Penguins* traces the emperor penguins of Antarctica on their journey through ice and snow to their mating grounds some seventy miles inland. Once the females have laid their eggs, the males abandon their competitive nature and form a team to enhance the survival of the new life. The narrator of *The March of the Penguins* related,

As the fathers settle into their long wait at the breeding grounds the temperature is now eighty degrees below zero. That's without taking into account the wind, which can blow one hundred miles per hour. Though they can be aggressive during the rest of the year, at this time the males are totally docile, a united and cooperative team. They brace against the storm by merging their thousand bodies into a single mass. They will take turns, each of them getting to spend some time near the center of their huddle where it's warmer.[18]

Spiritual transformation is also fostered by participating in the church's ordinances or sacraments. Our Lord commanded the observance of two ordinances and sacraments for our growth in grace. Ordinary elements prescribed by our Lord—water, bread, wine—signify invisible realities that foster the formation of Jesus' followers. Baptism and the Lord's Supper usher those who follow Christ into the Trinitarian life. This is reflected in the fact that Jesus commanded baptism, for instance, to be administered "in the name of the Father and of the Son and of the Holy Spirit" (Matthew 28:19), where "name" signifies the *reality* (life, love, grace, truth, power) of the triune God. Water baptism, while not regenerating, denotes forgiveness of sins (see Acts 2:38), the cleansing of defilement (see Acts 22:16), and renunciation of the Devil and his ways. Mystically, baptism signifies incorporation into Christ's death and resurrection (see Romans 6:4; Colossians 2:2) and reception of the renewing Spirit (see Matthew 3:11; Acts 19:6). Because baptism in Scripture closely follows conversion, new converts partake of Christ through the Spirit and are empowered to live transformed lives in union with Him (see Romans 6:8). As Robert Webber put it, "Baptism is . . . a *call* to live deeply into the pattern of death and resurrection in every area of life."[19] In the words of Michael Downey,

> Trinitarian spirituality is . . . a baptismal spirituality. In baptism we are conformed to Christ, anointed with the Spirit, gifted by the Father to live as sons and daughters of God, brothers and sisters in Christ. Through baptism we are invited to participate in the mission of Word and Spirit.[20]

My own "Damascus road" conversion experience occurred dramatically during my sophomore year of college. Alone in my dormitory room late one evening, I felt the Holy Spirit suddenly come upon me with incredible convicting power. I retrieved the Bible my mother had placed in my suitcase and read from it until the sun rose the next morning. Sometime during the night I gave my heart to Jesus Christ. Within a few months I was baptized in my home church in the presence of the community of God's people. As I emerged from the waters of baptism, the Holy Spirit descended upon my heart and flooded my life with a graced presence so palpable and powerful it will never be forgotten. Through water baptism I was immersed in the loving and renewing communal life of the triune God and His people.

The church's second ordinance or sacrament—the Eucharist—is a joyful recollection of Christ's atoning work on our behalf (see 1 Corinthians 11:23-26). Furthermore, the Lord's Table is a precious experience of *koinonia*—a sharing or participation in the life-giving spiritual presence of the resurrected Lord in the community of the body (see 1 Corinthians 10:16-17). As we, in faith with other disciples, make our hearts right with God, the Spirit unites us with Christ under the form of bread and wine. Augustine wrote, "What is meant by eating that food and taking that drink is this: to remain in Christ and have Him remaining in us."[21] A good meal tastefully prepared delights the soul and nourishes the body. Similarly, loving recollection of, and communion with, Christ in the Eucharist constitutes spiritual food and drink that nourishes us spiritually. As the Westminster Confession of Faith puts it, God's people who come to the table in faith "spiritually receive and feed upon Christ crucified, and all benefits of his death."[22] According to Charles Spurgeon, "The moments we are nearest to heaven are those we spend at the Lord's table."[23] Baptism and the Eucharist are powerful grace gifts from the triune God that renew us spiritually.

Transformation into Christlikeness also occurs within the context of kingdom mission. Theologians distinguish between the immanent Trinity (God in Himself) and the economic Trinity (God going out to others). In terms of the latter, the Father sent His Son on the grand mission of redeeming a lost world (see John 3:17). As the Father sent His Son in the power of the Spirit, so the Son sends His friends into the world on a mission of evangelism, kingdom building, and social justice. Compelled by the expulsive power of the Father's love revealed in Jesus, disciples are impelled into the world on a mission of compassion (see 1 John 4:9-12). As Augustine observed, "This is the rule of love: the good that we desire for ourselves we desire for our neighbor also. . . . All who love God will have such a desire toward everybody."[24] In the context of the three persons of the Godhead, Jesus said, "'As the Father has sent me, I am sending you.' And with that he breathed on them and said, 'Receive the Holy Spirit'" (John 20:21-22).

In His extended prayer to the Father upon leaving the Upper Room, Jesus seamlessly brought together incorporation into the Trinitarian life, believing community, and kingdom mission.

> I pray . . . that all of them may be one, Father, just as you are in me and I am in you. May they also be in us so that the world may believe that you have sent me. I have given them the glory that you gave me, that they may be one as we are one: I in them and you in me. May they be brought to complete unity to let the world know that you sent me and have loved them even as you have loved me. (John 17:20-23)

Spiritual transformation, community, and mission are intended to form an unbroken circle. Disciples find themselves gloriously transformed as they relate together in community in the context of kingdom mission. Often we discover that a fruitful catalyst to spiritual formation is participation in short- or long-term mission ventures with other followers of Jesus. Apprentices united in community and engaged in kingdom mission discover themselves being formed by the Spirit into the likeness of the Son. On the other hand, followers of Jesus in the process of transformation find their experience of community richer and their kingdom service more fruitful. Paul wrote that only disciples vitally related to Christ—that is, being actively transformed—"bear fruit to God" (Romans 7:4). Lacking intimate connection with the triune God and with one another, professing Christians lack the power to positively affect the unbelieving world. Clearly, then, transformation, mission, and community constitute an inseparable trinity of graces.

IN SUM

The three divine persons of the Trinity exist eternally in a loving, unified, others-centered, and mutually submissive community. Through the grace of the new birth, followers of Jesus are swept into the loving relational life of the Trinity and so participate in this radically transforming culture of grace. By imitating the loving relations of the three-in-one God as demonstrated by Jesus, followers of the Lamb experience the thrill of lifelong formation. Spiritual transformation, community togetherness, and kingdom mission exist in symbiotic relation with one another. United in loving community with fellow disciples and engaged in kingdom mission, apprentices of Jesus experience the grace of spiritual formation, and vice versa. Through the radical transformation of Jesus' missional people, the church is gathered; human destiny is fulfilled; and glory is brought to the triune God.

Authentic spirituality, then, is all about living the transforming life of the triune God. Thomas Merton observed, "The man. . . who, enlightened by the Spirit of God, discovers in Himself this union with the Father in the Son and with all men in Christ, is at the same time unified in the highest possible degree within himself and perfectly united with all who are one with Christ."[25] The Trinity has provided motivation, power, and courage to apprentices of Jesus throughout the centuries. Christians have both lived and died for the one true God, who subsists as Father, Son, and Holy Spirit. The blessed reality of the Trinity was on the lips of the apostolic father Polycarp as he was being martyred (AD 156). Looking up to heaven the bishop prayed,

O Lord God Almighty, the Father of thy beloved and blessed Son Jesus Christ, by whom we have received the knowledge of Thee . . . I give Thee thanks that Thou hast counted me worthy of this day and this hour, that I should have a part in the number of Thy martyrs, in the cup of thy Christ, to the resurrection of eternal life, both of soul and body, through the incorruption [imparted] by the Holy Ghost. . . . I praise Thee for all things, I bless Thee, I glorify Thee, along with the everlasting and heavenly Jesus Christ, Thy beloved Son, with whom, to Thee, and the Holy Ghost, be glory both now and to all coming ages. Amen.[26]

For Reflection and Discussion

1. From your own experience, put into words how you perceive that the doctrine of the Trinity has been neglected or minimized in the contemporary Christian world.
2. As you ponder the nature of the Trinity, formulate other illustrations for the God who is three divine persons in one infinite spirit being.
3. After reading this chapter, journal how you prayerfully propose to imitate the relational life of the God who exists as three loving persons.
4. How have your experiences in community and in kingdom service or mission enriched your spiritual formation in Christ?

For Further Reading

Downey, Michael. *Altogether Gift: A Trinitarian Spirituality*. Maryknoll, NY: Orbis, 2000.

Fortman, Edmund J. *The Triune God: A Historical Study of the Doctrine of the Trinity*. Philadelphia: Westminster Press, 1972.

Grenz, Stanley. *Rediscovering the Triune God: The Trinity in Contemporary Theology*. Minneapolis: Augsburg Fortress, 2004.

Johnson, Darrell W. *Experiencing the Trinity*. Vancouver: Regent College Publishing, 2002.

Knight, G. A. F. *A Biblical Approach to the Doctrine of the Trinity*. Edinburgh: Oliver and Boyd, 1953.

Wainwright, Arthur W. *The Trinity in the New Testament*. London: SPCK, 1962.

Chapter Nine

THE HOLY SPIRIT AND SPIRITUAL FORMATION

Michael Glerup

ELEMENT 9: Spiritual formation takes place by the direct work of the Holy Spirit, regenerating and conforming us to the image of Jesus Christ as the Spirit indwells, fills, guides, gifts, and empowers people for life in the community of faith and in the world.

Description: The best place to start in defining and understanding biblical formation is with Scripture passages about the Holy Spirit forming and transforming believers (see Romans 8:26-29). The Holy Spirit is at work to regenerate us and to progressively conform us to the image of Jesus Christ — reflecting purity, passion, and sacrifice and empowering us to live as salt and light in the world (see Romans 8:29; Galatians 4:19; Matthew 5:13,16). The Holy Spirit indwells and fills (see Ephesians 5:18) us as believers and communities of believers in order to guide us into all truth (see Romans 8:14; John 16:13), bringing forth the fruit of the Spirit in our lives (see Galatians 5:22-23), and gifts us for ministry in the church and in the world (see 1 Corinthians 12).

The mission of the Holy Spirit is to bring Christ to us and us to Christ. The Holy Spirit is the agent of intimacy, the divine matchmaker. —R. R. Reno

THE PUPIL MADE READY: THE PIVOT OF HISTORY

On a small hill outside the city, Christ, naked before all, was nailed to a cross and died. We are told by the early apostolic witnesses how this should be interpreted: "For God so loved the world that he gave his one and only Son, that whoever believes in him shall not perish but have eternal life" (John 3:16). The crucified Christ, having the power of eternal life, died for our sins, was buried, descended, was raised, and ascended to the right hand of the Father in heavenly intercession. The new covenant was confirmed, and the apostolic witnesses were commissioned to share the good news to the ends of the earth. Remission of sin made possible a new life available now. The pupil was made ready. This set the stage for what was to immediately follow: the coming of the Spirit.

The outpouring of the spirit at Pentecost; the calling out of God's people; the forming of the body of Christ; the introduction of the new law of holy love, a new rule of life; the gospel beginning to be preached to the whole world—all this happened within weeks after the death of Jesus. This intense series of events is called the pivot of history, the launching of the new age.

Theologically, at this fundamental pivot in history, the focus shifts from the work of the Son to the work of the Spirit applying the benefits of the work of the Son in the church. In Christ, we speak chiefly of "God for us." Now we speak more purposely of "God working in us." We speak not of events addressing us, as if it were from outside our experience, but more intentionally of active inward processes and events by which persons in community are convicted, transformed, regenerated, justified, and brought into union with Christ, one by one. The Holy

Spirit acts as the agent of intimacy. No longer spiritual orphans, all those who trust in the risen Christ are incorporated into His spiritual body.

The forgiveness of God the Son, having been offered on the Cross once for all, must be ever again received, and at each stage we must be enabled to receive it. In Christ we learn what God has done on our behalf. By the Spirit, we are being enabled to reshape our doing in response to what God has done, to restructure our loves in relation to God's incomparable love, to allow God's redeeming activity to affect every aspect of our broken lives. With this pivot, our own decisions and actions become a crucial part of the salvation story, the history of the body of Christ.

God not only forgives sin through His Son but through the Spirit works to overturn the power of sin and actual daily interpersonal behavior and life in community. The gospel not only announces the death and resurrection of Christ but calls us to die to sin and live to God by the power of the Spirit. Thus, by death, we receive true life. By the Spirit, we are called consciously and unconsciously, actively and passively, to enter the sphere of God's saving work.

PENTECOST AND PAUL

An important aspect of the early church's understanding of Pentecost that regularly goes unnoticed by Protestant Christians is the connection between the Jewish feast of Shavuot and Pentecost. Shavuot, celebrated fifty days after the Passover, commemorates God's giving of the law to Moses and Israel on Mount Sinai. On the Passover, the Jewish release from captivity is remembered; fifty days later on the Shavuot, the giving of the law and the formation of the people of God are celebrated. Pentecost, celebrated fifty days after Easter, celebrates the descent of the Spirit onto the apostolic community and the formation of the church. Typically the Spirit and the law are held up as opposites, but in the memory of the early church the descent of the Spirit recollected the descent of the law.

Before discussing this connection further, let's briefly recall the events surrounding the giving of the law. Soon after the Israelites' departure from Egypt, following the lead of Moses, they entered the

Sinai wilderness and camped at the base of a mountain. Moses made repeated trips up the mountain to meet with God. It was on one of these occasions that Moses received the tablets of stone "written with the finger of God" (Exodus 31:18, NKJV). Moses descended the mountain with these stone tablets only to find the Israelites engaged in debauchery and pagan calf worship. In anger, Moses threw down the tablets, thus destroying them, and ordered the death of three thousand men in accordance with the divine prohibition against idolatry.

Soon after, following the command of the Lord, Moses cut out a second set of stones and ascended the mountain (see Exodus 34:1,4). After forty days and nights in the presence of the Lord, in which he neither ate nor drank, Moses returned from the mountain "with the two tablets . . . in his hands" (Exodus 34:29). He was unaware that his face was radiant because of his encounter with the Lord. Aaron and the Israelites were fearful to approach the radiant Moses, but he encouraged them to come near. He shared with them all that the Lord had commanded during his stay on Mount Sinai. Afterward, he covered his face, but the text states,

> Whenever he entered the LORD's presence to speak with him, he removed the veil until he came out. And when he came out and told the Israelites what he had been commanded, they saw that his face was radiant. Then Moses would put the veil back over his face until he went in to speak with the LORD. (Exodus 34:34-35)

Based on the scriptural text just quoted, why did Moses veil his face? The simple answer is to hide his face. Yes, but why? Did he hide his face because the Israelites were afraid to approach him because his face glowed? Read the passage carefully. He places the veil over his face only after speaking to the people. Why? In order to hide something. What? Moses veiled his face to hide his fading radiance. Why would Moses want to conceal the fact that the radiance of his face was fading? We'll come back to this thought in a moment.

The Law and the Prophets

What is the law to the Jewish people? It is God's gift to His people. The law is light, wisdom for the unlearned, and the means by which the Israelites will be able to demonstrate that they really are God's people. Most important, the law is God's proscribed manner for entering the blessed life. Two passages illustrate this point. The first is Leviticus 18:5: "You shall keep my statutes and my ordinances; by doing so one shall live: I am the LORD (NRSV). The ordinances given to Moses for the people of Israel are such that if followed they will lead to life. Second is Moses' farewell address:

See, I have set before you today life and prosperity, death and adversity. If you obey the commandments of the LORD your God that I am commanding you today, by loving the LORD your God, walking in his ways, and observing his commandments . . . then you shall live. . . . I call heaven and earth to witness against you today that I have set before you life and death, blessings and curses. Choose life so that you and your descendents may live, loving the LORD your God, obeying him . . . for that means life to you and length of days. (Deuteronomy 30:15-16,19-20, NRSV)

As illustrated in these passages, the law is the way provided to the Israelite people to guide them to life and prosperity. It is the means of transformation—the transformation of a small Semitic tribe formerly enslaved to the most powerful government on the face of the earth into the people of God.

Also, the prophetic tradition exemplified by Jeremiah and Ezekiel sheds light on this event. In Jeremiah the Lord declared, "I will put my law in their minds and write it on their hearts. I will be their God, and they will be my people" (Jeremiah 31:33). And soon after, through the prophet Ezekiel, the Lord proclaimed, "I will give you a new heart and put a new spirit in you; I will remove from you your heart of stone and give you a heart of flesh. And I will put my Spirit in you and move you to follow my decrees and be careful to keep my laws" (Ezekiel 36:26-27). The backstory of the Lord's declaration in Jeremiah is the unfaithfulness of the Israelites' forefathers in the Exodus. The promise of Ezekiel is announced to the house of Israel in captivity. In both instances, these promises were followed by another promise to forgive the iniquities of the people.

These passages partially formed the interpretative framework employed by the early apostolic community as they discerned the movement of God in the descent of the Spirit at Pentecost. Accordingly, it is appropriate to interpret Acts 2 in the context of Israel's reception of the law, the meaning of the law, the unfaithfulness of their ancestors, and their anticipation of the coming time in which a new covenant was to be made.

At the previous Passover, Jesus was handed over to the local authorities, beaten, condemned, crucified, and—to the astonishment of His disciples—raised from the dead. The bonds of sin were broken, and those previously held captive to sin and death were set free. Fifty days later, Jesus ascended to heaven. He returned to His people, as promised, in the outpouring of the Holy Spirit at Pentecost.

What I am suggesting is that the backstory to Pentecost is the giving of the law and its subsequent promise of life. I believe this interpretive framework provides fresh insight into the heart of God and His workings in the world. I wouldn't be surprised if you were asking, *But what does this all mean?* My suggestion is that we turn to Paul's second letter to the Corinthians for clarification.

In 2 Corinthians 3:7-8, Paul asked, "If the ministry of death, chiseled in letters on stone tablets, came in glory so that the people of Israel could not gaze at Moses' face because of the glory of his face, a glory now set aside, how much more will the ministry of the Spirit come in glory?" (NRSV). Paul employed the phrase "ministry of death" as a shorthand reference to the context of Moses' first presentation of the tablets—the immediate death of the three thousand participants in idolatry. Next, he contrasted the reception of the law with the gospel. Paul associated the reception of the law with the following imagery: chiseled on stone, fading, and condemned. In contrast, he described the ministry of the Spirit as written on human hearts, unfading, and justifying. The imagery of the former suggests that it was external, temporary, and inadequate. The latter is described as internal, everlasting, and sufficient. Paul's life experience and reading of the Scripture convinced him that the law, originally received as a means to life, did not produce the life it promised. Therefore the glory of the Spirit surpassed the glory of the law. The glory of the ministry of the Spirit, whose validity he now boldly proclaimed, was that the life promised by Moses was now available in Jesus through empowerment of the Holy Spirit.

Before we move on in our discussion, it is important that we do not deny the glory of the law and God's activity through His Spirit in the people of Israel. The Old Covenant, using Paul's term, was glorious, even though in comparison to the new work of God through Jesus Christ, its glory seemed insignificant. Think of it this way: When I am walking home at night, I am very thankful for street lights, the moon, and a good headlamp because they provide enough illumination for me to find my way home. But during the day, in the bright Colorado sun, they become unnecessary. In the same way the law as a means to life no longer provides the illumination it once did.

The prophet Jeremiah anticipated this new arrangement: "No longer will a man teach his neighbor, or a man his brother, saying, 'Know the LORD,' because they will all know me, from the least of them to the greatest" (31:34). This knowledge of the Lord is now made manifest in the life, death, and ministry of Jesus. In His final conversation with His disciples before His death, Jesus boldly made the claim that He is the way, the truth, and the life and that anyone who knows Him knows His Father in heaven (see John 14:6-7). Concluding this conversation, Jesus encouraged His disciples not to worry about His impending departure because He would ask the Father to send an Advocate, who would be with them and bear witness to the Son. The Spirit of truth would continue the ministry of Jesus, communicating knowledge of God to His followers. This knowledge, now available through the Spirit, is internal and available to all, from the least to the greatest, who continue in the way of the life of Jesus.

Paul's confidence in the surpassing ministry of the Spirit derived not only from his experience of the risen Christ on the road to Damascus but his reading of the Torah—the means to life. For any close reading of Exodus 34, the veiling of Moses is problematic. As we recall from the earlier discussion, it was customary for Moses to remove the veil whenever he went before the Lord. After speaking to the Lord, he would communicate to the Israelites everything the Lord had commanded him. Afterward, he would veil his face until he returned to the presence of the Lord. Question: Why did Moses veil himself after he had spoken to the people? More to the point: Why did Moses hide his face? Paul's answer: He veiled his face to cover the fact that the glory of his face was fading (see 2 Corinthians 3:13). Moses' veil concealed the fact that his face was not permanently transfigured. Moses' veiling led the Israelites—and their future generations—to erroneously conclude that the law given by Moses was eternally valid. But as Paul made clear in verse 15, Moses' veil hid the end of that which was fading—the law. The law received by Moses came to an abrupt end in the incarnation—birth, life, death, and resurrection—of Christ, the fulfillment (*telos*) of the law. Paul most likely employed the term "end" (2 Corinthians 3:13, NASB) to express the double fact that the law was fulfilled in Christ—it had come to its goal—and that the law ceased to operate as a governing authority for the people of God.

Paul, illumined by the glory of the risen Christ, read the veiling of Moses symbolically, similar to his reading of the Sarah and Hagar story. In the person of Moses, it is acknowledged that the law was not being completely open about its temporal nature—that is, its glory was fading and would eventually be overshadowed at the coming of the Messiah. Consequently, Moses' veiling may be properly understood only in the context of the surpassing glory of the risen Christ. Subsequently, the scriptural text remains veiled until, as Paul taught, one turns to Christ, for only in Christ is the veil removed. Jesus articulated this same principle when He suggested to the Jewish scriptural interpreters, "You diligently study the Scriptures because you think that by them you possess eternal life. These are the Scriptures that testify about me, yet you refuse to come to me to have life" (John 5:39-40). The life promised by Moses is available only in Christ through the life-giving Spirit.

THE SPIRIT OF FREEDOM

In his discussion of the veiling of Moses, Paul said that the veil covers Moses (a reference to the Torah) and the hearts of those who hear the Scriptures read without Christ. Many commentators disregard Paul's shift of the veil from the face of Moses to the hearts of the hearers, which is understandable for it is very difficult to make historical or grammatical sense of this transfer. I suggest that Paul was offering a brief comment in reference to the heart of stone mentioned in Ezekiel 36:26. In 2 Corinthians 3:3, Paul claimed that his Corinthian readers were his recommendation letter, written not on tablets of stone but on human hearts by the Spirit of the living God. For Paul, the people of God who received the Spirit through the apostolic testimony were recipients of the promise made in Ezekiel. Their hearts, formerly hardened by rebellion, were softened and made new by the life-giving Spirit. They had become living letters of recommendation and, as a result, had become Christ's message to the world.

Paul continued, "Now the Lord is Spirit, and where the Spirit of the Lord is, there is freedom" (2 Corinthians 3:17). According to Paul, the risen Lord is present and available in the community as the Spirit—for *the Lord is Spirit*. The truth, power, and life demonstrated in the life and ministry of Jesus are now available in the Spirit. Yet the Spirit remains distinct, for the Spirit is the *Spirit of the Lord*.

Now what did Paul mean when he said, "Where the Spirit of the Lord is, there is freedom"? First, Paul's reference to "freedom" recalls the Exodus story—the Israelites' journey out of Egyptian captivity. As a result, we may conclude that Paul viewed the events of his day—the Incarnation and the descent of the Holy Spirit—as the new Exodus. Analogous to the Israelites' journey out of slavery under the Pharaonic regime, the people of God now make the journey out of slavery and captivity to sin, the consequence of Adam's rebellion. Guided and empowered by the Holy Spirit, the people of God are no longer defined by Adam's transgression; they now are defined by Christ. No longer in bondage to the skewed stories of their families of origin conforming to social influences, they are *set free* to pursue the life originally promised and available through the Spirit. Paul employed the term *parrhesia*, typically translated as "confidence" or "boldness" (see 2 Corinthians 3:12), to summarize an important facet of human freedom. In this sense, *freedom* means "frankness with God" or "a trusting intimacy." As a result, where the Spirit of the Lord is, there is confidence to approach God in prayer and with a life characterized by a trusting intimacy.

The Spirit does not set us free to pursue a life of license or autonomous self-indulgence; the Spirit sets us free by internalizing the law in our hearts or, to use Paul's language, by writing the law upon our hearts. And what is this law? It is the twofold law of love: love God and love your neighbor. Unlike the law given through Moses, this is an empowered law, empowered by the love of God that is poured out into our hearts by the Spirit (see Romans 5:5). It is this love that provides the energy to fulfill the law (see Ezekiel 36:26). Thomas Aquinas wrote,

> It is here that the Holy Spirit works, inwardly perfecting our spirit by communicating to it a new dynamism [energy], and this functions so well that man refrains from evil through love, as though divine law were ordering him to do this. He is therefore free not because he is not subject to divine law, but because this inner dynamism leads him to do what divine law prescribes.[1]

The new law is simply the Holy Spirit, who provides not only the content but also the energy to accomplish what is required.

So, through the Spirit we are set free to pursue the life promised. But what does this life look like? It is defined by the image we behold: *the Lord's glory*. The image is the image of the risen Christ, who gave Himself up for us. As we gaze on this image, we are conformed to it by the Spirit. Here we gain a glimpse into the work of the Spirit. The Spirit guides us to the truth of Christ through the illumination of the Scriptures and then empowers us to be transformed into the image of Christ.

Two parts of this process — (1) "we all . . . beholding as in a mirror the glory of the Lord" (2 Corinthians 3:18, NKJV) and (2) "from glory to glory" (2 Corinthians 3:18, NKJV) — describe the process of transformation that comes from the Lord, who is Spirit. We'll proceed by first discussing the latter phrase, which describes the transformation process as a movement from glory to glory. Early interpreters described this as a movement from a glory according to our person to a glory according to the Spirit. At the deepest core of a human being is the gift of God that has been renewed by the Spirit of Christ. It is a gift that is not truly "of" us but "in" us. It is the part of our humanity that enables us to respond to God's initiative in Christ. It is the locus of our desires, imagination, and attention and makes possible our contemplation of God. This deepest part of our being is a gift from God, but it remains "ours." The work of the Spirit is the purifying and reshaping of our desires (see Galatians 5:22-23) and imagination such that our internal make-up and external action are progressively conformed to the image of Christ. The movement is from the glory of our personhood to the glory of a personhood progressively shaped by the Holy Spirit.

Early Christian teachers, developing ancient concepts, suggested that Scripture functioned as a mirror to the human soul. It is in the mirror of Scripture that we behold the face of God. Augustine taught, "In this life, treat the Scripture of God as the face of God."[2] In the mirror of Scripture, our hearts are revealed. The word becomes active through the power of the Spirit allowing the purifying work of God to penetrate the depths of our soul. Our hearts are not only revealed through the gentle guidance of the Spirit in the mirror of Scripture, but we also learn how to live as God intended. By extended study of the Scriptures and continued conforming to the life of Christ, we receive through Scripture's narrative of transformation a model to understand our experience and walk with God.

THE HOLY SPIRIT IS HERE TO STAY

At Pentecost, the great prophetic tradition—the promise of God's universal presence through His Spirit—was fulfilled. The community of God was indwelt with the Spirit as living temples of God. No longer a "transient visitor," the Spirit resides among His people until the end of time. The Holy Spirit poured out at Pentecost is the promised Spirit. Peter's speech specifically linked the sending of the Spirit with the exalted Jesus at the right hand of God, affirming that Jesus fulfilled His promise. The Spirit is the promised Advocate who is to be with the people of God forever. He is the Spirit of truth who indwelled the disciples and will "teach you all things and will remind you of everything I have said to you" (John 14:26).

The Spirit entered into history in a powerful way at Pentecost and inaugurated a new age—the age of the Spirit. There can be no doubt something was different. Everyone agrees that there was a difference in the way the Spirit was present after Pentecost. The question is how it should be interpreted.[3] An example of this difference may be observed in the contrasting responses of the priest Zechariah (see 2 Chronicles 24:17-22) and Stephen (see Acts 7:55-60) to their persecutors. Both were Spirit led; both were stoned to death because they spoke truthfully; and both cried out to the Lord before they died. Zechariah said as he died, "May the LORD see and avenge!" (2 Chronicles 24:22, NASB). Stephen, before he fell asleep, cried out, "Lord, do not hold this sin against them!" (Acts 7:60, NASB). Both acted righteously in accordance to the revelation they had received, but Stephen had received the Holy Spirit, who is the gift of God, who is love, and was made capable of imaging in his death the care and love of God for His creation.

Before the Incarnation, the ministry of the Spirit was anticipatory. After the Incarnation, the Spirit was present in Jesus. And only after the Ascension does the indwelling of the life-giving Spirit become a historical event. As Peter stated to the eyewitnesses of Pentecost, "God has raised this Jesus to life, and we are all witnesses of the fact. Exalted to the right hand of God, he has received from the Father the promised Holy Spirit and has poured out what you now see and hear" (Acts 2:32-33). The ministry of the Spirit takes distinctive form. The Spirit accurately remembers the work of the Son, advocating and completing His mission on earth and forming actual living communities of grace and trust.

At Pentecost, the Spirit-empowered preaching of Peter "cut to the heart" of his hearers (Acts 2:37). In anguish they asked, "'Brothers, what shall we do?' Peter replied, 'Repent and be baptized, every one of you, in the name of Jesus Christ for the forgiveness of your sins. And you will receive the gift of the Holy Spirit'" (Acts 2:37-38). Peter's admonition suggests two responses — repent and be baptized — and two promises — the remission of sins and the reception of the Holy Spirit. In the historical event of Pentecost we can discern the sequence of the ministry of the Holy Spirit in personal transformation. In fact, the remainder of Acts and the letters of Paul illustrate the work of the Spirit in transformation: conviction, repentance, regeneration, indwelling, baptizing, sealing, and filling.

THE TRANSFORMATIVE WORK OF THE SPIRIT

Conviction and Repentance

The Holy Spirit acts interiorly to convict (see John 16:8), awakening the desire for repentance. The conviction the Spirit works within us is deeper than that of mere regret. The Spirit offers us an awareness of the selfish ambition and dissatisfaction that characterize our lives. It is here we experience the duality of judgment and grace. We become attentive to our impending judgment, but before we are devastated by despair, grace preemptively offers the possibility of forgiveness. Our excuses and rationalizations for our actions are silenced, and we respond in the only manner appropriate — gratitude. Conviction and repentance are not only the work of the Spirit in conversion but in the continuing process of sanctification or the Spirit's work of conforming us to the image of Christ.

Julian of Norwich

At thirty years old, Julian of Norwich became sick to the point of death. Convinced of her imminent death, her local priest performed last rites. After a few days she was again visited by her priest; amazingly the pain suddenly left her and a series of wonderful "Revelations" or "Showings" began. The following is a reflection on what she learned concerning God's outlook toward His creation:

> I had been taught that we must see our sin and turn from it, and *then* God's anger is turned away, then we are forgiven and experience His mercy. . . .
>
> But in the Lord's revelation of His love to me, I had not detected *any* holding back of love. It seemed impossible that God, who is love, could withhold any part of love for us until *after* we turn to Him. I saw only love.
>
> So I sought Him in contemplation. And now I shall describe as best I can how God's mercy operates, if God will give me the grace to do so.
>
> In this life, we are so unstable—even the best Christian among us. We say we love God one minute, and truly do love Him. And in the next minute we fall into sin—one minute speaking well of people, then slandering them behind their backs, or freely overlooking the sins of those we favor and refusing to forgive those we do not think "worthy" of forgiveness. We fall into these sins because we are blind to ourselves, ignorant of the great evil we are doing. We are weak and foolish in our self-centeredness. Add to that all the sickness and sad events of life that overpower our good intentions.[4]

Julian reasoned that humans fall back into these negative patterns of relating because we suffer from spiritual blindness—that is, we do not continually see God as God is. If we perceived the compassion and generosity of God, how could we hold grudges or treat others with contempt? Yet we do, and before long we no longer perceive the mercy of

God and are overwhelmed by our sin. We mistakenly believe that our sin is deeper and truer than the redeeming love of God. She continued,

> That is why our good Lord, the Holy Spirit who is endless life, dwells within our soul. He protects us as we stumble around, blindly forgetful of the love of God. He produces in us a longing for peace, a longing for freedom from restlessness. By His working within us, which we call grace, He brings us to rest. He works in us, and He does so to reveal our own dissatisfaction to us. Once we see we are dissatisfied we are then willing to turn and become obedient under the hand of God.[5]

The indwelling Holy Spirit protects and convicts. The Spirit protects by reminding us of the love of God, which characterizes the internal dynamics of the Trinity. The Spirit can be trusted because the Spirit knows the mind of God. The Spirit convicts not in the sense of heaping on loads of guilt and shame but in revealing to us our own dissatisfaction with a life lived displaced from God. Then again, not out of guilt but out of appreciation, we return to God, desiring to take His light yoke upon us. God is not lurking in the distance waiting for us to recognize our sin and turn from it but is always present in the Holy Spirit, drawing us back to Him and generously producing in us the desire to obey.

TACT Reflection on Julian

In the process of compiling this book, each group of authors would present parts of their chapter for feedback and critique. Sometimes the feedback was positive, and at other times it was critical. When this selection from Julian was presented, to my surprise, it invoked a negative reaction in a number of participants. Though there was some variation in reaction, their critique may be simply summarized: Julian's vision is too permissive. Julian is presenting a picture of Christianity that elevates God's accepting love at the expense of the justice of God.

I took seriously their assessment because in most instances their analysis was true and protected me from my own ignorance. But on further reflection I remembered a quote at the end of the movie *Babette's Feast*[6]: "Mercy and truth have met together; righteousness and bliss shall kiss" (Psalm 85:10). Reading the verse in its literary context indicates mercy and truth meet when God's glory (*kabod*) dwells in the land. Likewise, when the glory of the Spirit dwells in our hearts, mercy and truth shall meet—that is, God's accepting love and justice will come together. Mercy motivates faithful obedience.

It seems that much of contemporary discipleship or formation usurps the convicting work of the Spirit, which leads to repentance. The internal motivating force of the mercy of God—the indwelling Spirit—is replaced with human forms of manipulation—anger, guilt, and shame. Why? Because we are miserable wretches? No. As Julian suggested, in this life we are unstable—one minute loving God and the next forgetting that love. Our self-centeredness mingled with the wounds and disappointments of life veils the love of God available to us, individually and corporately, through the indwelling Spirit.[7]

Faith, Generation, and Indwelling

Augustine, the bishop of Hippo in North Africa, may very well be the most influential thinker in Western history. Though he is primarily known for his theological reflection on issues concerning predestination and original sin, his work also had a significant influence on Western theological understanding of the Trinity and the nature of the Holy Spirit.

Two texts were particularly instructive to Augustine's theological reflection on the nature of the Holy Spirit: Romans 5:5, "God's love has been poured into our hearts through the Holy Spirit that has been given to us" (NRSV), and 1 John 4:13, "We abide in him . . . because he has given us of his Spirit" (NRSV). Based on these passages, Augustine suggested that the unique work of the Holy Spirit is to makes us abide in God and Him in us. In addition, the means of our abiding in God through the Holy Spirit is love. It follows that the distinctive characteristic of the Spirit is *love* and that the Holy Spirit is the gift of God, who is love. Robert Louis Wilken said, "What is given enters into the life of the believer and becomes his or her own and turns the believer toward the Giver. *Gift* and *love*, as used in the Scriptures, are relational terms and have built into them reciprocity and mutuality."[8]

The gift of Holy Spirit forms the *bond* or *communion* between God and the believer. Yet, as Augustine argued, the Spirit also is the *bond* between the Father and the Son. The bond of love between the Father (Lover) and the Son (Beloved) is the Holy Spirit. Consequently, the sending of the Holy Spirit not only forms the bond of fellowship between God and humanity, it also reveals to us the love that unites the Son and Father eternally. The Holy Spirit, then, is the gift of God, who is love. And because the Holy Spirit is poured into our hearts (indwelling), we experience fellowship with God, whose nature and internal relations are love. Not only does the Holy Spirit enable us to put our trust in the risen Christ, He generates new life in us and indwells us with the loving presence of the Father and the Son. If this isn't enough, not only do we receive the benefits of new life, we actually experience God's internal nature — self-giving love.

Sealing and Assurance

Though it wasn't until the summer of 2007 that I visited the mainland of China, I have been always curious about the experience of Christians in China. Before my trip to Southeast Asia, I grabbed a paperback book, which I thought would be a relaxing read on the twelve-hour flight from Los Angeles to Hong Kong. Though unfamiliar with the story, I thought the book had an interesting title: *The Heavenly Man: The Remarkable True Story of Chinese Christian Brother Yun.* I attempted to finish the book in one reading, but I was emotionally spent after a few hours. I was overwhelmed with the difficulties that Chinese Christians face on a daily basis. Though the authenticity of some of the trials and miracles described in the book have been called into question, it doesn't necessarily undermine the value of its spiritual insights.

I am a strong advocate for Christians to enter into empathic relationships with Christians living in different cultural situations, not only historically but also geographically. The wisdom gained from these encounters helps us to remove the veil of our cultural blind spots. As I experienced other Christian cultures through my studies, I began to recognize that knowledge of God (truth) acquired through learning that was not practiced was not true knowledge of God. Yet my experience of American Christianity suggested that practice was optional and not necessary, especially if it involved emotional pain or sacrifice. I think that is why I appreciated Brother Yun's response to Western visitors' and missionaries' query: "What seminary had he attended?" He replied that he had years of training in the Holy Spirit Personal Devotional Bible School—that is, prison. He continued,

> Sometimes our Western friends don't understand what we mean because they then ask, "What materials do you use in this Bible school?" We reply, "Our only materials are the foot chains that bind us, and the leather whips that bruise us." In this prison seminary we have learned many valuable lessons about the Lord that we could never have learned from a book. We've come to know God in a deeper way. We know his goodness and his loving faithfulness to us.[9]

In the midst of difficult personal circumstances, the Holy Spirit taught imprisoned Chinese Christians the goodness and faithfulness of God. They understood that Christians who are in prison for the sake of the Lord are not the ones who are suffering. Yun wrote,

> The people who really suffer are those who never experience God's presence. . . . The way to have God's presence is by walking through hardship and suffering—the way of the cross. . . . The first time I went to prison I struggled, wondering why God had allowed it. Slowly I began to understand he had a deeper purpose for me than just working for him. He wanted to know me, and I to know him, deeply and intimately.[10]

The Spirit wants to teach us a personal knowledge of God — deep and intimate. I love what Brother Yun said: "We know his goodness and his loving faithfulness to us."[11] I think this short sentence holds one of the keys to a deeper life. The path to this knowledge is by entering the way of the Cross in companionship with God. It is here that we learn that those who really suffer are those who do not experience God's presence. It is here in these difficult and dark experiences that we are assured of God's active presence of comfort and love — in the person and power of the Holy Spirit. It is here that we know we are sealed for the day of redemption.

The metaphor of sealing is helpful to understanding the work of the Holy Spirit in spiritual formation. Levitical priests inspected lambs presented for sacrificial offerings for defects. Animals that were found to be without blemish were marked with a temple seal that indicated they were acceptable as a sacrificial offering. John applied this symbolism to Jesus, the Lamb of God, as the one on whom "the Father has placed his seal of approval" (John 6:27). Paul extended this metaphor to those who are included in Christ. He wrote, "Having believed, you were marked in him with a seal, the promised Holy Spirit, who is a deposit guaranteeing our inheritance until the redemption of those who are God's possession" (Ephesians 1:13-14). Those sealed with the Holy Spirit may be assured that they will receive the promised gift of eternal life — that is, knowledge of God. In the obscure prisons of rural China, Christians were provided with a deep knowledge of God — the Holy Spirit. In this knowledge, they knew their hopes for continued life with God were secure.

Filling and Sanctification

Bernard of Clairvaux, the third son of a knight, was born in 1090. His brothers were trained as soldiers, but from youth Bernard was destined for more scholarly pursuits. At twenty-two, he entered the monastery of Citeaux. The order of monks was committed to arranging their lives according to the simple rhythms of work, study, worship, and prayer.

Similar to our situation today, spiritual leaders in Bernard's day offered a weak gospel that pacified rather than provided spiritual benefit. Instead of instructing in the means and ways of God, they offered words of assurance that lulled their members into a spiritual slumber. You might say they taught that you could be a Christian without becoming a disciple. Against this practice Bernard argued,

> We must beware of this misstep so that we do not fall asleep in our faith. I warn you—do not become one of those who has a head full of "the right" Christian doctrines while failing to go on by working truth into everyday practice. For as the apostle James warned, faith that does not show itself in good deeds is not true Christian faith at all. For when we truly believe something, we give our whole self to it—not only our minds—and gradually all of our actions are changed.[12]

The first sign that our faith is true, living, and active is when we ask that the light of the Holy Spirit shine into the dark corners of our soul. When we love someone, as we claim to love God, we want to please that one and not offend. Therefore, we ask the Spirit to show us how our many spiritual hungers—for power, security, and comfort—drive us to sin. We ask God to show us how to feed these needs by filling us in new ways every day with Himself. In this way, we drive out the hungers that cause us to use other people wrongly and to fill our lives with worldly pursuits and treasures that can never satisfy, because some set out on the path of Christ but remain captive to the empty cravings of the soul.

As the hidden motives of our hearts are exposed and changed, we will no longer speak with the tongue of our first parents; we will stop using excuses, blame, and self-pity to cover our shame. Lying to cover our sin is what it amounts to when we refuse to own up to the truth about ourselves.

CLOSING PRACTICAL SUGGESTIONS

The apostolic memory of Pentecost has a number of corollaries to the Spirit's work in Mosaic ministry described in Numbers 11. Let me explain. Moses, overwhelmed with the burden of ministry, complained to the Lord, asking for relief. The Lord answered, saying He would "take some of the spirit that is on you [Moses] and put it on them [the elders]" (Numbers 11:17, NRSV). So Moses gathered the elders as commanded, and the Lord came down in a cloud and took some of the spirit that was on Moses and put it on the elders. "And when the spirit rested upon them, they prophesied. But they did not do so again" (Numbers 11:25, NRSV).

Two of the elders refused to gather at the tent as they were instructed, but they also prophesied. Moses' assistant, Joshua son of Nun, seeking to protect Moses' authority, demanded that Moses stop them. But Moses' responded, "Are you jealous for my sake? Would that all the LORD's people were prophets, and that the LORD would put his spirit on them!" (Numbers 11:29, NRSV).

Moses, the greatest of prophets, looked forward to the day when *all* the Lord's people would be prophets and the Lord's Spirit would be upon them. In Moses' day the Spirit was shared with the elders to demonstrate God's power and to confirm their leadership of God's community.

What I have been suggesting through this chapter is that *just as* Paul employed a form of Jewish exegetical argumentation (*qal vahomer*—that is, an argument from the lesser to the greater) in 2 Corinthians 3 to defend his ministry, the author of Acts is arguing through historical events the superiority of the new covenant in Jesus Christ to the Mosaic covenant. Two areas of superiority are clearly shown. First, the apostles acted with great *boldness* and spoke with confidence, unlike Moses, who veiled his face before the Israelites. When faced with the task of confronting Pharaoh, Moses asked the Lord to send someone else because he lacked eloquence and was "slow of speech and tongue" (Exodus 4:10). Peter and the other disciples did not shrink from the task assigned to them. They acted confidently because they knew Jesus was the Holy One of God and spoke the words of eternal life (see John 6:68-69). They were confident because God had raised Jesus from the grave (to which they were eyewitnesses) and had poured out the promised Holy Spirit (which was witnessed by those present on the day of Pentecost).

Second, the first law was written on stone; the second law was written on the hearts of the people by the Spirit of God. When the first law came, there was condemnation. The second came inwardly in order that the people of God might be justified. Jesus contrasted the internal difference of the law associated with the kingdom of heaven with the law given through Moses. He said, "You have heard that it was said to those of ancient times, 'You shall not murder' . . . but I say to you that if you are angry with a brother or sister, you will be liable to judgment" (Matthew 5:21-22, NRSV). Likewise Paul argued that the commandments received at Sinai could be summed up: "'Love your neighbor as yourself.' Love does no wrong to a neighbor; therefore, love is the fulfilling of the law" (Romans 13:9-10, NRSV). This fulfilling of the law of love is accomplished by God's love, which has been poured into our hearts through the Holy Spirit (see Romans 5:5).

The gifts of confidence and the interiorized love of God empowered the community of disciples for mission and to share a common life characterized by love of God (worship) and love of neighbor (glad and generous hearts). A missional transformation community then is first and foremost a community shaped and empowered by the Holy Spirit.

I would like to finish this chapter by suggesting three practices, guided and empowered by the Spirit, which will enable each person and his or her respective communities to become missional.

The first is daily obedience in community. Jesus' statement, "If you love me, you will keep my commandments" (John 14:15, NRSV), is united with the coming of the promised Comforter, the Spirit of truth. Obedience leads to understanding; likewise, understanding leads to obedience. Initially our obedience might be motivated by fear of punishment or the gain of some benefit, but in the end it will be motivated by our love for Christ. Obedience and understanding are acquired in community.

A second practice is meditation on passages of Scripture in relation to the movement of God in history. A surprisingly fruitful practice that I learned from early Christian writers is to mediate on Scripture in light of the Pauline mystery. Let me explain. Peter in his Pentecost address spoke of the "definite plan" of God (Acts 2:23, NRSV). Later, Paul stated his vocation as to make fully known "the mystery that has been hidden throughout the ages," which is "Christ in you, the hope of glory" (Colossians 1:26,27, NRSV). The "definite plan" of Peter and the "hidden mystery" of Paul are one and same movement of God through history. I would summarize the Pauline mystery this way: Humanity was created to be intimately related to God, but they rebelled. In the fullness of time and in accordance with His eternal purpose, God demonstrated His love for us in that Christ died for the ungodly. Therefore we now are justified by faith; we have peace with God through our Lord Jesus and our lives are hidden in Christ. This divine love, the love with which He loved us in Christ, has now been poured forth into our hearts through the Holy Spirit, which has been given to us. This Spirit, the spirit of adoption, has been poured out in order that we might become children and heirs according to the hope of eternal life. Intimately related to God through His Spirit, we become capable of this same love and thereby are the image God to His creation.

Third is a practice that characterized the very earliest Christian community: the prayer of dearly loved children to the Father of Jesus through the Spirit. Paul taught that when we call out "Abba! Father!" to the Lord in prayer, "it is that very Spirit [spirit of adoption] bearing witness with our spirit that we are children of God" (Romans 8:16, NRSV). Because we are children of God, the Spirit helps us in our weakness and "intercedes with sighs too deep for words" (Romans 8:26, NRSV). The Spirit, so intimately related to our spirit, prays on our behalf. Many times in life we will face difficult circumstances in which we do not know how to pray, but we can be confident that the Spirit will pray for us according to the will of God.

In summary, the three steps are obedience in community, scriptural meditation in light of the Pauline mystery, and prayer that relies on the Spirit. I urge you to practice these in a spirit of reverence, gratitude, and joy.

For Reflection and Discussion

1. Reflecting honestly, how much does your ministry context require the work of the Holy Spirit and how much of it runs on the natural work of people and their giftings?
2. How do you connect the written law with the law written on the hearts of God's people through the Spirit? In what ways do these connections influence both the "how" of spiritual formation and the "what does it look like" that the community has set its intention on?
3. Can a formational community be directed toward formation and holiness yet leave room for the unique work of the Holy Spirit in each person's life? What might this look like?
4. How does a community committed to being formed spiritually experience the presence of God within them in the Holy Spirit? What kind of things can you imagine being done to provide openings for the work of the Spirit? What kind of things crowd out the work of the Spirit?

For Further Reading

Elowsky, Joel C., ed. *We Believe in the Holy Spirit*. Ancient Christian Doctrine, vol. 4. Downers Grove, IL: InterVarsity, 2009.

Furguson, Sinclair B. *The Holy Spirit: Contours of Christian Theology*. Downers Grove, IL: InterVarsity, 1997.

Smith, Gordon. *The Voice of Jesus: Discernment, Prayer and the Witness of the Spirit*. Downers Grove, IL: InterVarsity, 2003.

Chapter 10

THE BIBLE IN SPIRITUAL FORMATION

Richard E. Averbeck

ELEMENT 10: Spiritual formation is based upon the Bible as God's reliable and authoritative revelation. The Bible, our primary source of truth, guides and informs the use of spiritual disciplines and models of spirituality as they have emerged worldwide and throughout time.

Description: The Bible is God's special revelation, so we need to rely on it and align with it as we study, practice, and teach spiritual formation (see Ezra 7:10; 2 Timothy 3:15-17). The Scriptures are living and active in penetrating, exposing, and transforming our hearts and lives as the Holy Spirit brings to bear upon us individually and together (see Hebrews 4:12-13). The Bible calls us to, and illustrates the use of, spiritual disciplines as invitations to grace and ways and means of living well in the kingdom and in the world (see Joshua 1:8; Matthew 11:28-30). The historical and contemporary models of spirituality from various traditions and ethnic contexts can be valuable sources for stimulating thought and progress in spiritual formation as they correspond to the teachings of Scripture.

❧ ❧ ❧

We do not worship the Bible. We worship the God who has revealed Himself to us through the Bible. And that is why we take the Bible so seriously. It is the revealed word of the God we worship. I came to know the Lord during my first semester in college in the fall of 1969. Those were the days of the hippie and the Jesus movements, and both were related for me. Though I was not a hippie, I held in common with them the same feelings of despair and the meaninglessness of life. When I first heard about knowing and trusting Jesus personally, it was immediately clear to me that this was what I had been looking for. For me, coming to the Lord had little to do with escaping hell but everything to do with having something and someone to live for.

If you love someone, you take what he or she says seriously. Having grown up on a dairy farm in Wisconsin, I was studying agronomy, the science of agriculture. It was not long, however, before I lost all interest in everything except knowing and serving Jesus. For me, this centered on Bible study, prayer, fellowship with other believers, and evangelistic witnessing. Along the way, I found out that the Old Testament was written in Hebrew and the New Testament in Greek, so it seemed natural to me that I should learn Greek and Hebrew. Not long after that, I transferred to a Bible college to study the languages. I met my wife, Melinda, there. One thing led to another, and we ended up going on to seminary and then PhD work in Old Testament and ancient Near Eastern studies.

The great *shema* of Deuteronomy 6 begins with the proclamation, "Hear [Hebrew *shema*], O Israel: The LORD our God, the LORD is one" (verse 4). What has come to be known as Jesus' first great commandment (see Matthew 22:37-38) follows immediately: "Love the LORD your God with all your heart and with all your soul and with all your strength" (verse 5).[1] The implication is that there is no room for divided loyalties. We owe no devotion to any other god. That, in turn, brings us to the next verse and the main subject of this chapter: "These commandments that I give you today are to be *upon your hearts*" (verse 6, emphasis added). If we truly love God, His Word will be upon our hearts. It is what we become preoccupied with. And, therefore, the Word of God becomes what we will most naturally talk about to our children (see verse 7). It will become a guide for life in the world (see verses 8-9). In another place, Jesus said it this way: "Whoever has my commands and obeys them, he is the one who loves me. He who loves me will be loved by my Father, and I too will love him and show myself to him" (John 14:21).

The second great commandment is "Love your neighbor as yourself" (Matthew 22:39; from Leviticus 19:18; cf. 19:34 and especially Matthew 7:12, the so-called Golden Rule). Yes, the Bible is about God's love for us and our loving Him back. But it is also about our loving other people the way we would want them to love us. As Jesus put it, "All the Law and the Prophets hang on these two commandments" (Matthew 22:40). Ultimately, the Bible is a relational book about *both* God and us. It exists because God wants good relationships with us and among us.

Our discussion in this chapter will fall into two main parts. First, we will consider *spiritual formation in the Bible.* Here our concern is a clear understanding of what spiritual formation is, or should be, and how it should work specifically, according to the Bible. There are two main points here. First, as the element or key concept and its explanation cited above declare, the Bible contains reliable divine revelation about spiritual formation. We can know the truth about spiritual formation from the Bible. In fact, this is what the Bible is all about in the first place. Second, the goal of spiritual formation as revealed in the Word of God is the (trans)formation of our hearts and lives into the very image of Jesus Christ Himself, which is the will of God the Father. The Bible as a whole, and everything in it, is designed to contribute in some way to our individual and communal spiritual formation, including what it says about the so-called spiritual disciplines.

The second major section of this chapter will treat *the Bible in spiritual formation.* The focus there is on the ways and means of using the Bible in the actual practice of doing spiritual formation. There are three main points here. First, the same Holy Spirit who originally guided the writing of Scripture as revelation also indwells us individually and corporately in order to bring His written revelation to bear upon us. This is called illumination. Second, there is a kind of reading of the Bible that is called spiritual reading. Properly understood and practiced, this kind of Bible reading does not bypass basic study and interpretation but goes on to serious meditation on implications for how a person or group should bring a particular word or passage to bear in his or her personal life or community of faith. Third, the Bible is also the primary authority for discernment in spiritual formation and, therefore, the evaluation of various historical and contemporary theories and practices of spiritual formation, along with the theology that informs them.

SPIRITUAL FORMATION IN THE BIBLE

One of the things I have appreciated most about working with the TACT team over these past several years has been the ongoing determination to understand what spiritual formation is from a specifically biblical point of view. From the start, we called our key elements "*biblical* descriptors of spiritual formation." We have been committed to and relied on the fact that the Holy Spirit inspired the writing of the Bible as God's reliable and authoritative revelation of truth about Himself, us, the world, and, for our purposes, spiritual formation in particular.

We all realize that God has also revealed Himself in other ways — for example, through nature and the human conscience. The Bible extols these forms of revelation in such places as Psalm 19:1-6 and Romans 1:18-23; 2:14-16. Appreciation and enjoyment of the beauty of God's creation as well as human creativity (see Psalm 8) are often powerful forces the Holy Spirit uses for transforming our hearts and lives. Who among us has not been overwhelmed at times by the wonder, beauty, and vastness of God's creation? A whole chapter in this book could be given to this side of the way God can reach us and transform us.

But in its most defined form, God's revelation has come through the inspired writings of Moses and all the other prophets in the Old Testament and, most importantly, through God's own divine Son, Jesus Christ, the ultimate prophet, priest, and king, as revealed in the New

Testament (see Hebrews 1:1-3). Psalm 19, for example, combines the glory of God's self-revelation in the wonders and beauty of nature (verses 1-6) with the radiance and sweetness of the law of the Lord (verses 7-11). Psalm 119, the longest chapter in the Bible, is devoted entirely to the praise of the divinely inspired written Word for all its benefits to us.

The Bible as Divine Revelation for Spiritual Formation
There are two key New Testament passages on the inspiration of the Bible that require special treatment here. One of them is 2 Timothy 3:16-17: "All scripture is inspired by God [Greek *theopneustos*, literally 'God-breathed'; note *pneus* and recall *pneuma*] and is useful for teaching, for reproof, for correction, and for training in righteousness, so that everyone who belongs to God may be proficient, equipped for every good work" (NRSV). Thus, Timothy could rely on Scripture both to say what is true and to use as his divine authority in teaching, exhorting, and training people to live godly lives in Christ Jesus. Interestingly, he had known these writings "from childhood" (verse 15, NRSV), which means that this passage is talking (at least primarily and most directly) about the Old Testament Scriptures, since the New Testament had not even been written yet when Timothy was a child. Moreover, Paul, who along with others had already written much of the New Testament by the time he penned this particular passage and was near the end of his ministry (this is probably the last New Testament letter he wrote), still viewed the whole Old Testament as not only inspired but useful for instructing and guiding Christians. These were still the inspired Scriptures as far as he was concerned.

We need to take note here that Paul never came to the point of leaving the Old Testament behind in favor of the New. Neither should we. We need the whole Bible for our spiritual formation, including the Old Testament. It is true that a large part of the problem we have in the church today arises from a reduced gospel that is not really the "good news" because discipleship is left out.[2] But one of the reasons this problem has arisen in the first place is that, practically speaking, we suffer from a reduced canon—reduced to the New Testament, perhaps with the addition of certain portions of the Old Testament. Neither Jesus nor the apostles would have ever conceived of, or put up with, such a thing.

There are at least two reasons for emphasizing here the importance of a whole-Bible approach to spiritual formation. First, the New Testament was never intended to be read without the Old Testament, on which it relies so heavily. All the writers of the New Testament assumed that their readers would have been saturated with the Old Testament and devoted to it as the Scriptures of the church. Recall that the Bible of the earliest church was, in fact, the Old Testament, whether in Hebrew or translated into Greek. Ignoring the Old Testament leaves us with serious potential for misunderstanding the New Testament, or not understanding it all. Second, a serious study of what the Bible actually teaches about Christian spiritual formation shows that it has its roots sunk deep in the soil of the Old Testament.[3]

Another key New Testament passage about the divine inspiration of the Bible is 2 Peter 1:21: "Prophecy never had its origin in the will of man, but men spoke from God as they were carried along by the Holy Spirit." This tells us that the inspiration of the Old Testament prophets as writers of Scripture came through the Holy Spirit carrying them along, like the wind in the sails of a boat. Since the words for "spirit" in the Old Testament and New Testament can and do often mean "breathe" or "wind" as well, this metaphor helps us to understand the nature of inspiration. Consider the English word *aspirate*, and compare Ezekiel 37:5-6,9-10,14 and John 3:8. In these verses the words rendered "wind," "breathe," or "spirit" are all the same word. The Old Testament prophetic word was created by, and lives and breathes, the life of the divine Holy Spirit.

In its context, unlike 2 Timothy 3:16, this passage does not restrict itself primarily to the Old Testament. Peter's main point is that the apostolic eyewitness of the transfiguration (see 2 Peter 1:16-18; cf. Matthew 17:1-13 and parallels) results in "the word of the [Old Testament] prophets made more certain" (2 Peter 1:19), to which the readers need to pay close attention until it actually comes to pass (see end of verse 19). Jesus is yet to come in all His glory and power. We need to be ready for that coming, knowing first of all "that no prophecy of scripture is a matter of one's own interpretation" (verse 20, NRSV).[4] The point here is that the apostolic witness needs to be followed in the interpretation rather than anyone's own opinion. No one has the right to read the prophetic Scriptures just any old way, according to his or her own will. This is because they were not written just any old way. In fact, "Prophecy never had its origin in the will of man, but men spoke from God as they were carried along by the Holy Spirit" (verse 21). The apostolic eyewitness report recorded for us in the New Testament is the inspired guide to the interpretation of the inspired Old Testament prophetic word. The New Testament apostles and the Old Testament prophets are bound together in 2 Peter 1:16-21.

Second Peter 2:1 brings the main point into full focus: "But there were also false prophets among the people, just as there will be false teachers among you." The remainder of the book, by and large, addresses the problem of these false teachers and the effects of their teachings. The prophets and apostles are also paired together in 2 Peter 3:2: "I want you to recall the words spoken in the past by the holy [Old Testament] prophets and the command given by our Lord and Savior through your [New Testament] apostles." Peter even brought the apostolic authority of Paul's writings into the discussion. Near the end of the letter, he wrote, "Bear in mind that our Lord's patience means salvation, just as our dear brother Paul also wrote you with the wisdom that God gave him" (3:15). He pointed out that some of what Paul wrote contained "some things that are hard to understand" (verse 16) and alerted them to the fact that some "ignorant and unstable people distort" Paul's writings too, "as they do the other [Old Testament] Scriptures, to their own destruction" (verse 16). The salient point here is that since the Old Testament writings are referred to as the "other" Scriptures, therefore, the writings of Paul (and, by implication, the other apostles) are considered to be inspired Scripture as well.

A Biblical Understanding of Spiritual (Trans)Formation

The Bible, Old Testament and New Testament together, should be the primary guide for how we define and understand spiritual formation.

From a biblical point of view, the best way to define Christian spiritual formation is from passages that refer to the Holy Spirit in the context of "(trans- or con-)forming" one's life toward Christlikeness (see Galatians 4:19).[5] Understood in this way, spiritual formation is first of all, above all, and throughout the shaping (i.e., forming) work of the divine Holy Spirit, carried out according to the will of God the Father for the purpose of conforming us to the image of Jesus Christ, His Son: "The *Spirit* intercedes for the saints in accordance with God's will. . . . For those *God* foreknew he also predestined to be conformed to the likeness of his *Son*" (Romans 8:27,29, emphasis added). Biblically speaking, therefore, spiritual formation consists of the Trinitarian work of God in the lives of genuine believers in Christ through the presence and power of the Holy Spirit. Our part in this is to devote ourselves to seeking, inviting, stimulating, cooperating with, and participating in this work of the Holy Spirit.

It is important to understand the relationship between the work of the Holy Spirit and our own effort in spiritual formation. We do not earn our salvation (I will say more about this later), but we do indeed put effort into working the effects of it into our hearts and lives. Our transformation is an imperative addressed to us: "Do not conform any longer to the pattern of this world, but be *transformed* by the renewing of your mind" (Romans 12:2, emphasis added). The Bible also talks about the ways and means of it. But we need to understand that the real empowerment is provided by the Holy Spirit, not our own will or effort. As 2 Corinthians 3:18 puts it, for example, we "are being transformed into his likeness with ever-increasing glory, which comes from the Lord, who is *the Spirit*" (emphasis added). This is something that is worked in us by the Lord Himself, the Holy Spirit.

An illustration used in the Bible helps us here. As the divine "wind" or "breath" of God ("spirit" can also mean "wind" or "breath" in Old Testament Hebrew, the word *ruakh*, and in New Testament Greek, *pneuma* — see, for example, our word "*pneum*onia"), the Holy Spirit can be compared to the wind — wind that, as said earlier, catches the sails of a boat to drive it along. In fact, this is the image used for the composition of Scripture in 2 Peter 1:21, where we read, "Men spoke from God as they were carried along by the Holy Spirit." The same Greek word for "carried along" appears in Acts 27:15,17 for the wind by which Paul's ship was "driven along." The Hebrew word, for example, is used in Psalm 1:4, where the wicked are likened to chaff that "the wind [*ruakh*] drives away" (NRSV). Jesus used this image in a play on words with Nicodemus in John 3:8: "The wind [*pneuma*] blows wherever it pleases. You hear its sound, but you cannot tell where it comes from or where it is going. So it is with everyone born of the Spirit [*pneuma*]."

The main point of the illustration is that we do not supply the power for our transformation. The Holy Spirit (the wind of God) does that. But we can put up the sails to catch the enablement provided by the Spirit of God. The Bible tells a great deal about how to put up the sails, so to speak (see the remarks on the spiritual disciplines below). But we need to avoid any illusion that the real power or enablement somehow comes from us. We are as dependent on the Holy Spirit for progress in our spiritual formation, both individually and corporately, as a sailboat is on the wind for making progress through the water. We can raise the sails and are in fact commanded to do so, but we cannot make the wind blow. We are dependent on the Holy Spirit all along the way, from beginning to end. The Bible tells us so.

In light of all this, we need to concern ourselves here with a whole-Bible approach to spiritual formation that treats the Bible as a script for our lives as we are guided and empowered by the Holy Spirit.[6] There is an old saying that "history" is really "His-story"—that is, God's story from creation to consummation. Everything that exists and occurs is part God's larger story. This means, among other things, that there really is no story that does not belong within the confines of this one, so the story of humankind collectively as well as each and every one of us individually is part of "His-story." This is a good starting place for understanding what the Bible is, what it is about, and how God intends it to function in our lives.

First of all, the Bible is an authoritative canon that tells a story, but not just any old story. It is a true story, and, most important, it is a story that we are all part of whether or not we know it, and whether or not we like it. We have joined the story in progress—along the way, so to speak. And it is the script of our lives, both in terms of what we face in life and how we would best face it. It is true, of course, that the Bible is a very ancient composition, from a remote time and culture. We need to pay serious attention to that fact. Nevertheless, the Bible tells the story in a way that focuses its primary attention on the main issues in the lives of all people of all times, ancient and modern. In that way it connects directly to each of our personal stories.

Ultimately, God's story is the only real story in town because, at the end of the day, all other stories are part of it. This is what God's providence is all about. No one and nothing stands outside of this script because it is the script that God has written, and He is also the one and only director of the action. It is all under the hand of His creative, providential, omniscient, omnipotent, and directive management. As the director, He has control and is dynamically involved in seeing that all things happen according to His will so that they turn out as He intends. We are the actors—all of us, both the lost and the found.

It is a story not only about individuals but also families, communities, faith communities, and the world at large. People are so bound up within their matrix of cultures and communities that they do not read the Bible apart from that set of circumstances. As with individuals, the experiences of communities profoundly shape how they read the Bible. The Bible speaks from and to all levels and experiences of community, ancient and modern, so all communities are part of the story too, whether or not they know it, and whether or not they take it seriously. Those who take it seriously form faith communities in the midst of the culture and the complex of communities where they live and testify to the grace of God in Jesus Christ.

Second, for the individual and the community of faith, the Bible is not just *descriptive* of what happened in the past but also *prescriptive* for how we should live now. It is a script that deals with both of these. It simply tells the story about how things really are, and always have been since the foundation of the world. Our whole life, in its many seasons and dimensions, belongs to this script. Of course, on the one hand, paying attention to the ancient context of the writing and reading of the Bible is basic and essential in reading the Bible well today. After all, in the first instance, the Bible was written in ancient times to ancient readers. We should read it with vigor, rigor, and penetration, paying due attention to the fact that this is an ancient set of writings eventually collected into a book.

On the other hand, in reading the Bible well as a scriptive story, we will also pay attention to what it says about human life in general, whether ancient or modern. It will describe and explain the text as a way of making sense of life. It will meet people where they are with the text, and it will also take people where they need to go from where they are—again, with the text as our guide. As a script, Scripture both locates us descriptively and directs us prescriptively. The way we read the Bible also needs to do both. The narrative framework of the Bible consists of a story, and the story of our personal lives follows a trajectory from that one. This story, therefore, instructs us about our lives as we are living them. Stories instruct in their own peculiar way, of course. There are also other genres of literature in the Bible, and all of them have their own way of instructing us: laws command, rituals enact, poems elaborate, proverbs train, and eschatology hopes. All of these instruct and are important in God's work in our lives, but they instruct in ways that are different from narratives.[7]

As we all know, sometimes there are serious difficulties in grasping the historical meaning of the text descriptively to begin with. Exegetical difficulties and diverse interpretations abound. Sometimes we end up confused and uncertain about the overall meaning or a specific point in a verse or passage, and this can make it difficult to know how to live it out. The problems are not usually completely insurmountable, however, so we can often come up with reasonably sound conclusions regarding the basic meaning of the text and its significance in its literary and historical context. Moreover, on the main points about who we are, how we fit into God's story, and how we ought to live, the Bible is profoundly clear. The real problem is not in understanding it but in believing it, committing to it, and connecting it to our daily lives in such a way that we actually live according to it.[8] This brings us to the second main section of this chapter: how we use the Bible in spiritual formation.

THE BIBLE IN SPIRITUAL FORMATION

As is well known, one of the features of postmodern culture is its "incredulity toward meta-narrative."[9] Pluralism rules the day. Personal stories overrule everything else, so what is true for you might not be true for me. A scriptive biblical theology will penetrate deeply into the biblical story to show how it explains local stories of persons and communities so well that their incredulity toward metanarrative is overcome by the sheer force of the way the Bible explains the experience of individuals, families, and communities and provides a profoundly meaningful way forward for them in the midst of that experience. Those with ears to hear and eyes to see are called to a personal life that is continually renewed, a new community life in fellowship with God's kingdom people here and now, and a new mission in life in which we stand out as light in the midst of a world that lives in profound darkness. The light that shines forth from God's story comes into the world through us as well. After all, our lives are the continuation of the story.

Illumination in Spiritual Formation

Illumination is about how the Holy Spirit, who inspired the writing of the Bible, also brings it to bear upon us individually and together as the indwelling divine personal agent. He enlightens our lives through the Bible and thereby motivates us to live it out.[10] The term derives from such passages as Psalm 119:105, where God's word is described as "a lamp to my feet and a light for my path." Similarly, in the New Testament we have passages such as Ephesians 1:17-18, where Paul prayed that God would give the Ephesians "a spirit [or 'the Spirit'] of wisdom and revelation" and that the eyes of their hearts would be "enlightened" (Ephesians 1:17,18, NRSV; cf. 2 Corinthians 4:4).

Illumination is about God's story in God's Word as the light of our life. In the beginning God said, "'Let there be light,' and there was light" (Genesis 1:3). God just spoke the word and it was so. This divine creation word comes to its fullest expression in the incarnation of the divine Son of God:

> In the beginning was the Word, and the Word was with God, and the Word was God. . . .
> Through him all things were made; without him nothing was made that has been made. In him was life, and that life was the light of men. The light shines in the darkness, but the darkness has not understood it. (John 1:1,3-5)

John went on to draw from the Old Testament pattern of the glory cloud dwelling in the tabernacle and temple (see Exodus 40:34-38; cf. Leviticus 9:22-24; 16:1-2; 1 Kings 8:10-11): "The Word became flesh and made his dwelling [i.e., 'tabernacled'] among us. We have seen his glory, the glory of the One and Only, who came from the Father, full of grace and truth" (John 1:14). Jesus, the Word of God, "tabernacled" among us.

In His high-priestly prayer Jesus passed this glory on to us: "I have given them the glory that you gave me, that they may be one as we are one" (John 17:22). We are now the means by which His glory shines in the earth through the Holy Spirit in us and among us:

> Now the Lord is the Spirit, and where the Spirit of the Lord is, there is freedom. And we, who with unveiled faces all reflect the Lord's glory, are being transformed into his likeness with ever-increasing glory, which comes from the Lord, who is the Spirit. (2 Corinthians 3:17-18; cf. 3:7-16 and its continuation in 4:6-7,16-18; 5:5).

We actually become the glory of God shining into the world as we worship and serve our Creator and Redeemer. We are God's temple indwelt by the shining glory of God. This is true both individually (see ı Corinthians 6:19-20) and corporately (see 1 Corinthians 3:16-17; Ephesians 2:19-22; 3:14-21).

Spiritual Reading of the Bible in Spiritual Formation

The Bible serves as our main guide in the transformation of our lives, tearing out what is old and corrupt and refurbishing us with what is new, holy, and alive in Christ Jesus (see, for example, "putting off" and "putting on" in Romans 13:11-14; Ephesians 4:20-25; Colossians 3:8-11). The Scriptures speak of various individual and communal spiritual disciplines that are the main tools in this living renovation project. We are not talking here about a self-help plan but a new road to walk and a new way to do the walking. These disciplines are means of training, not behavioral but spiritual training — that is, training the human spirit under the influence of the Holy Spirit for the transformation of the whole life, inside and out. It is a whole new life that goes other places than where we have trod before, and we go there because we are walking with Jesus, who takes us there. The disciplines, rightly understood and practiced, are ways and means of walking with Jesus right in the middle of life, no matter what happens.

One helpful approach to the disciplines is to divide them into two categories, corresponding to human breathing. Recall that "spirit" also means "breath." Like human breathing for physical life, doing spiritual life with God and one another requires an ongoing pattern of breathing in and breathing out. There is a life-giving dynamic relationship between them: (1) *inhaling*: breathing in from God by reading, studying, memorizing, and meditating on Scripture; solitude and silence; fasting; and (2) *exhaling*: breathing out toward God and others through prayer and worship; fellowship, service, and mission; living the fruit of the Spirit. Like physical breathing, doing one without the other is to lose life. Numerous biblical passages could be cited for each of the disciplines mentioned here and others as well. Sometimes they are found in various combinations. For example, consider the description of life in the first-century church right after Pentecost: "They devoted themselves to the apostles' *teaching* and to the *fellowship*, to the *breaking of bread* and to *prayer*" (Acts 2:42, emphasis added).

Since this chapter is about the Bible in spiritual formation, we will focus our attention on the reflective reading of Scripture known as spiritual reading, or Christian meditation. It is slow, thoughtful praying of the Scriptures—reading the Word of God prayerfully in the presence of God, letting the content of the Scriptures inform what you are hearing from God, and speaking it back to God. Christian meditation is deliberate dwelling upon a passage, with the aim of encountering God in it. Psalm 1 indicates that the one who meditates day and night will know stability and fruitfulness in his or her life that is not dependent upon circumstances. The chief aim of Christian meditation on the Bible is not to learn more information about God but to encounter God in His Word. While Christian meditation includes discovering the meaning of a passage, it does not stay there but moves naturally to prayerful hearing or responding to the Lord based on the implications of the particular Scripture passage.

In one of its traditional historical forms, this kind of meditation has come to be known as *lectio divina* (Latin for "divine reading"), although many people have done it without knowing the terminology or sequence.[11] In any case, as Eugene Peterson put it, this is the "core curriculum" in the school of the Holy Spirit. It is a "way of reading that intends the fusion of the entire biblical story and my story." Spiritual reading, therefore, binds our personal and communal stories to the nature and content of "His-story." It is "a way of reading that becomes a way of living." Since the Bible is "spiritual writing," to read it well we need to do a kind of "spiritual reading" that corresponds to the nature of it. It is a "forbidding discipline" because it requires all of us, our whole body and mind, our whole life, daily and perpetually.[12]

Here it becomes important to deal with a particular problem I and others have run across: a forced and false dichotomy between "spiritual" reading and "informational" reading of the Bible.[13] Unfortunately, spiritual reading is sometimes placed in contrast to the disciplines of study, exegesis, hermeneutics, and theological reflection. I recall one instance in which a person who was describing the practice for group ministry remarked that in group *lectio divina*, any person's reflections on the text are to be considered as legitimate as the next person's, even if he or she is misunderstanding the text. In another case, an elder in a church called about a conflict on the board of elders. Certain people were using the words of a particular writer on the subject to argue that one should intentionally deny the "rational, cognitive, intellectual faculties" used in informational reading and turn exclusively to reading "spiritually" with the "heart and spirit."[14]

The problem is that this brings a kind of subjectivism to the reading of the Bible that often imposes the thoughts and imaginations of the readers on the text rather than discerning what God has to say to us from the text. People, of course, come at the Bible from where they stand in life, from their own cultural or educational or ethnic backgrounds, worldviews, or missional contexts. This is the nature of things, and there is nothing wrong with it. In fact, we can often learn new things from the Bible through such readings by those who stand in other places or positions. What people from other settings see is often truly there in spite of the fact that we may have not seen it there before. Our own lives and experiences have not opened our minds and hearts to some of the things that Scripture says because we are not looking at it from a place where we can see it. But notice that we are talking here about things that really are in Scripture, not meanings put there by one's own imagination or experience imposed on the text and contrary to it.

The best writers on spiritual reading emphasize the importance of serious interpretational (i.e., informational) reading of the Scripture. Richard Peace went so far as to recommend and work out a plan for group *lectio divina* where there are two sessions on each passage, the first devoted to understanding what the text really says and the second to listening meditatively to the spiritual impact of the text for life.[15] Eugene Peterson spent an entire chapter on the Bible as a text that requires exegesis (a Greek word for explaining something or someone; see John 1:18 — Jesus "has made [the Father] known"). He defined *exegesis* as a means of "submitting" to the text and God's intended meaning in it, rather than our own imaginations:

Without exegesis, spirituality gets sappy, soupy. Spirituality without exegesis becomes self-indulgent. Without disciplined exegesis spirituality develops into an idiolect in which I define all the key verbs and nouns out of my own experience. And prayer ends up limping along in sighs and stutters.[16]

Spiritual reading is not a "less than" but a "more than" approach to the reading of the Bible. Informational and spiritual reading should function together as two modes that modulate each other—moving back and forth between them, sometimes digging into what the passage means and sometimes stopping to dwell on its implications and impact on our lives. There will be times when dwelling on the implications will cause us to see something in the text that we need to study further, and vice versa. We leave neither our intellect nor our spirituality behind when we do spiritual reading. On the contrary, we bring all that we have and are to the text. Anything less is artificial reading, whether in intellectual or spiritual form.

I recall having the opportunity, with other leaders in spiritual-formation ministry, to visit and learn from Neighborhood Ministries in the inner city of Phoenix, Arizona. I and the others were shocked by the work of God happening there right in the middle of profound poverty, the chaos of lives and families blown apart by drugs and violence, and the despair of living without hope. Those serving there saw transformation happening and experienced it themselves. The weeping for others was real. In the midst of all this, the leader of the ministry sat in front of the group facilitating a meditation and interaction over Scriptures about the poor. What struck me most during this time of spiritual reading was the realization that in the midst of this ministry they felt the need for understanding the depths of God's heart just to make it from one day to the next. A superficial look at God's Word simply would not do. Real mission calls for real study and meditation of the Word of God that goes deep and stays long.

Taking God seriously in His Word must involve taking seriously what He actually means to say in His Word, not what we might see in Scripture if we read it in a way that takes God's intended meaning lightly. To take the divinely intended meaning lightly, practically speaking, amounts to denying the fact that it is revelation in the first place. Moreover, it undercuts the Holy Spirit's illumination of our lives by means of the text, since the Spirit is the one who inspired it with the intention of affecting our lives with what He means to say to us. Yes, sometimes there are legitimate differences of opinion on what a particular passage means. Some level of subjectivity is unavoidable, but we are looking for a well-informed subjectivity.

The problem goes the other way too, however. Among us there are some who react strongly to what they perceive as "mystical" practice of any kind. Spiritual reading, *lectio divina*, is sometimes associated with such mysticism. As someone has said, "mysticism" begins in "mist" and ends in "schism." I would submit, however, that when all is said and done, there is still much about God that is a mystery to us, and there is indeed something that is properly mystical about practicing His presence day by day, moment by moment.[17] I am not talking here about Eastern mystical traditions of spirituality common today in New Age forms of spirituality. The plain fact of the matter is that there is a proper Christian mysticism that pays attention to the work of the Holy Spirit in the human spirit in scriptural ways.

Paul explained it this way: "For you did not receive a spirit that makes you a slave again to fear, but you received the [literally 'a'] Spirit [or 'spirit'] of sonship. And by him we cry, '*Abba,* Father.' The Spirit himself testifies with our spirit that we are God's children" (Romans 8:15-16). The Holy Spirit does work in the human spirit of the believer that only the divine Spirit can do. It is mystical, yes, but no less real because of it. A serious problem arises when what is mystical loses its anchor in the Word of God. But the same is true when what the Holy Spirit intends to do subjectively in the human spirit through the inspired Word is ignored or treated as if it were only of secondary importance. Those who devote themselves to the cognitive understanding of the Bible sometimes so focus their attention on it that they disengage at the point where things become more subjective. But God created us not only to think cognitively of Him but also to feel, experience, practice, and act out His immediate presence in our lives.

Encountering God more fully in our experience is precisely what Christian meditation is all about. It is more than Bible study; it is encountering God Himself. He speaks by His Spirit through His Word, and when He speaks to us, we get more than information—we get transformation. When He speaks to us, our hearts are enflamed in worship; our perspectives about life are recalibrated; and we love His glory and yearn to be made more like Him. In fact, according to Psalm 1, the one who meditates "day and night" is "like a tree planted by streams of water . . . whose leaf does not wither" (verses 2-3) even in a season of draught and who does not cease to bear fruit. In other words, there is sustenance for us through meditation that promises to bring stability and reliable fruitfulness regardless of the circumstances we face. The same kind of terminology is used in Joshua 1:8. Interestingly, in the three-part Hebrew Bible, which is a different arrangement of the books than our English Bibles, Joshua 1 stands at the intersection between the Torah (Pentateuch, the first five books of the Old Testament) and the Prophets (Joshua through Malachi), and Psalm 1 stands between the Prophets and the Writings (Psalms through Chronicles). Thus, the notion of meditating on the Word of God binds the Old Testament canon together.

Spiritual reading is slow, thoughtful, a conscious interaction with the Lord along the way. *Lectio divina* arose in the monastic world of the early church and was formally clarified by a monk named Guigo the Second (in the twelfth century):

Reading, as it were, puts the solid food into our mouths, meditation chews it and breaks it down, prayer obtains the flavour of it [and swallows it] and contemplation is the very sweetness which makes us glad and refreshes us [digesting it as we go about our daily life].[18]

The descriptions of *lectio divina* sometimes vary, but it is usually broken down into steps or stages in the process, whether it is practiced in private or in a group setting.[19] The stages usually include:

1. *Lectio*—Listen to and interpret the biblical text, ten to twenty verses perhaps, reading it through several times, slowly. Take whatever time and measures are necessary to understand the passage well. Especially watch for helpful metaphors and images to dwell upon. See the spiritual reading of Matthew 11:28-30 on page 296.
2. *Meditatio*—Take the message deeply to yourself in terms of its implications for your own situation in life. This is entering the world of the text, taking the Bible to be the script for your life (see the discussion of the scriptive approach to the Bible on page 281.
3. *Oratio*—Transform the Word of God into prayer by praying its impact and implications back to God for your own life or that of the group. Note: Prayer actually permeates the process of *lectio divina* all along the way.
4. *Contemplatio*—Submit to the Word by taking what you read and meditating and praying over it for the whole day, living it plainly and humbly in your personal life and relationships.
5. *Collatio*—Share its impact on yourself with others if you are practicing it in a group setting. (This usually fits between stage 2 and 3 in a group setting.)

Sometimes it is practiced in a rather linear fashion; there really is a natural sort of progression to it. But if one is paying close attention along the way, then the meditation may bring up something that one needs to study further. Praying about it may prompt further meditation or study; contemplating it throughout the day may cause one to go back to it again in study, meditation, prayer, or discussion with others. Reading and living the Bible on all these levels is one of the main ways God has given us to live well His story by intentionally becoming part of it ourselves, right now in this day and age, under the empowering and guiding influence of the Holy Spirit.

There can be no true Christian spiritual formation without taking the Scriptures seriously and personally. Reading the Bible responsibly and responsively is indeed the core curriculum of the disciple. This is what spiritual reading is all about. Practices like this can take our personal and communal reading and study of Scripture to a new level. It uses serious, careful, and slow reading of the text as a means of enabling us to take the time to be with God in the text — to really encounter Him there. It also encourages authentic (re)consideration of our own lives as we meditate on the Bible in private or in a group setting. Thus, it enables us to be genuine people before God and one another as we are in His Word. It drives us to pray God's will into our own lives in a "pray without ceasing" sort of way (1 Thessalonians 5:17, NKJV). Moreover, it encourages a taking of the Word with us into our daily lives for transformation in our walks and talks, our relationships with God and one another. As a way of reading the Bible, this discipline brings spiritual breathing (inhaling and exhaling) together.

The Use of the Bible for Evaluation in Spiritual Formation

Finally, the Bible is our basis for evaluating the many models, approaches, and classical texts of spiritual formation that have arisen from various traditions in the history of the church. We are, of course, challenged to recognize and make use of all that is of value in these traditions or streams. We want to bring these valuable but sometimes disparate concepts, models, and practices together in one unified whole, with each element making a meaningful contribution to the whole. It is about diversity within unity or, perhaps better, a unity with diversity. But there are certain kinds of spirituality and spiritual formation that we should not even try to integrate with biblical Christian spirituality and spiritual formation. Therefore, we need to evaluate what we find in the traditions, with the Bible as our standard of evaluation.

I have heard it said that "everyone gets a spiritual formation; the question is what one they get." Certain ones are not Christian at all, much less biblical. I am thinking specifically of the kind of Western spirituality that James Herrick wrote about in his book on the "New

Spirituality,"[20] which really consists of a set of new spiritualities, some newer than others, put together in various combinations. It is in the air we breathe, at least in Western culture, and it is promoted by powerful cultural forces developed since the 1700s, including the Enlightenment, corrosive biblical criticisms, scientific advances used to promote spiritual science and scientific religion, psychoanalytical humanistic spirituality, occult spiritualities, and the influence of Eastern spiritualities (especially Buddhism and Hinduism). The kind of integration we are interested in here is one that collects what is good and beneficial from the history of specifically *Christian* spirituality and arranges it under the umbrella of a focused *biblical* spirituality.

For example, not long ago I was reading "Of the Intimate Friendship with Jesus" in *The Imitation of Christ*, a work commonly attributed to a fifteenth-century monk known as Thomas à Kempis but deriving originally from the spirituality of the founders of the Brethren of the Common Life in the fourteenth century.[21] The chapter expounds on the value of friendship with Jesus that goes far beyond any other relationship: "Let all be loved for Jesus' sake, but Jesus for His own sake." Although there is no mention of it in the chapter, my mind went to John 15 where Jesus said, "My command is this: Love each other as I have loved you. Greater love has no one than this, that he lay down his life for his friends. You are my friends if you do what I command" (verses 12-14).

It occurred to me that I have a friend who is a king—Jesus, the Son of God—and He gives me permission to use His name to make requests before His Father. God the Father, in turn, has adopted me as His child, and I am now a fellow heir of the kingdom of Jesus (see John 15:16; 14:2-3). Moreover, I have a helper (i.e., a counselor or an advocate) from above, the Holy Spirit (see John 15:26; 14:16-17). Helpers are usually thought of as below the one they help, but this one abides with us and in us while standing above us to help us from above. The whole Trinity (three in one) abides with me (see John 14:23,26). I have been called into a Trinitarian-quality bond with the Trinity and with others who know Jesus as their most intimate friend (see John 17:20-24). This had never "hit home" to me in quite this way before reading this section of *The Imitation of Christ*.

On the one hand, we need to remember that in His high-priestly prayer Jesus asked the Father that all who know Him would "be one. . . . That they may be one as we are one: I in them and you in me. May they be brought to complete unity to let the world know that you sent me and have loved them even as you have loved me" (John 17:21-23). The unity of true believers is no small matter to our Lord. Similarly, the apostle Paul made a great deal of the fact that the wall of partition has been broken down between Jew and Gentile, so there is only one church not two (see Ephesians 2:11-18). We need to take care that we do not build the wall back up again in another way. The church is one holy temple of the Holy Spirit. Its foundation is the apostles and prophets, and Jesus is the cornerstone (see Ephesians 2:19-22). This temple has certain dimensions, and it is filled up to "the fullness of God" because it is filled with the glory of the love of Christ (Ephesians 3:19; see also verses 20-21). We are called to "make every effort to keep the unity of the Spirit through the bond of peace" (Ephesians 4:3) since there is only "one body and one Spirit . . . one hope . . . one Lord, one faith, one baptism; one God and Father of all, who is over all and through all and in all" (Ephesians 4:4-6). The church has long suffered from a serious integrity and credibility gap on account of its lack of unity. This should concern us deeply.

On the other hand, this cannot be a unity at the expense of truth. The Bible contains God's reliable, authoritative, and instructive story from creation to the first-century church, and it even anticipates the consummation still to come. Between the first century and the consummation that is yet to come there is a continuing story that also belongs to God's story. We are living it right now; we are part of it. In fact, all people (and all events) are part of it, whether or not they know it and whether or not they like it. The history of the church since the New Testament days includes the story of Christian spirituality. And here is the problem: Reading this dimension of church history reveals a rather "mixed bag" of principles and practices, some of which fit well under the umbrella of biblical spirituality and spiritual formation but some of which do not.[22] This, too, should concern us.

The best way to recognize a counterfeit spirituality is to become thoroughly familiar with the genuine article. First, the unity that we are looking for stands squarely on full commitment to the gospel of salvation by grace through faith in Jesus Christ alone, without merit of any kind in ourselves (see Ephesians 2:8-9). This eliminates much of what has gone by the name "Christian" through the centuries. There has been far too much confusion about this matter in both official and popular forms of what we might call "works" Christianity, as opposed to "faith" Christianity. But, second, there is also another side to the matter. Yes, salvation is completely by grace through faith, but the kind of grace and faith we are talking about here also creates us anew in Christ Jesus so that we live as followers of Him (see Ephesians 2:10). We are reshaped by God's grace through a genuine faith that works. There is a certain renewed way of life that God has designed us for and assigned us to follow.

Jesus Himself put it this way in Matthew 11:28-30: "Come to me, all you who are weary and burdened, and I will give you *rest*. Take my *yoke* upon you and learn from me, for I am gentle and humble in heart, and you will find *rest for your souls*. For my *yoke is easy* and my burden is *light*" (emphasis added).[23] Rest and yoke do not normally go together; in fact, they seem like opposites. A yoke is the part of a harness that goes around the neck of work animals (i.e., horses or oxen) so they are outfitted to carry or pull some kind of load. Work is the opposite of rest, or so it would seem. But in this passage Jesus put them together in His call to the "weary and burdened" — that is, people who know they need rest because they are tired but have no relief because they are yoked to a heavy load. He was talking about rest for your souls. He was also calling for the restoration of our lives, where we bear a new yoke — one that is easy and light and one that we learn from Jesus Himself. We are identified with Jesus in this and find rest in it. He is with us in the yoke. We know who we are in Jesus because the Bible tells us so, and we live out of the confidence that we are His and He is ours.

We all know that life loads us down. Clearly, Jesus was not talking here about literal physical yokes and loads. But the truth of it is written all over the faces and daily lives of people. Whether or not we suffer under difficult physical conditions due to sickness or labor or relational troubles that bring pain and worry, our souls get tired and life gets hard. We groan (see Romans 8:18-26). The picture that Jesus painted here, and the invitation that He offered, comes from His gentle and humble heart. Anyone who is burdened and weighed down by life can come to Him to get the rest he or she needs and a different yoke, one that is easy because the load is light. Life is just not supposed to be so blasted heavy! God never intended it that way. We cannot escape the mess, but we can truly live lives of rest in our souls.

We can trade our hard yoke and heavy load for His easy yoke and light load. He is gentle and humble toward us, not wanting to overload us but to restore us to a meaningful way of life. As our Lord, He is a master, but a gentle one. The hardest loads to bear are the ones we pile on ourselves through our own personal corruption. As His apprentices, we learn from Him how to do life according to this invitation. This is the restoration.

The gospel is always good news to everyone because there are ways and levels at which we have not worked the rest offered to us in Christ into our lives. As Romans 8 puts it, the whole creation groans—and we groan right in the middle of it all—but the Holy Spirit meets us in that very place to groan with us and for us to the Father, whose plan is to work things out according to His own goodness in our lives, which is to conform us to the image of Jesus Christ (see Romans 8:26-29). In other words, the goal is to work the rest that Jesus offered in Matthew 11 down deep into our hearts and lives, so that we love God and love people well in spite of the mess in which we live. This is to live out Jesus' two great commandments, found in Matthew 22:34-40,[24] which form the best summary we will find of what the yoke looks and feels like. When we walk with Jesus according to His likeness, being transformed into His image, nothing else makes any sense or means anything to us except to go love God and people.

A person well engaged in spiritual formation does not run frantically through life. For many people today, this alone will require a massive lifestyle change in their spiritual formation into the image of Christ.

ιne tragedy is that the lives of many Christians are anything but restful. There is a rest in the soul that brings with it an easier and lighter load in life, and this is what Jesus wants us to have. We cannot be well-formed spiritually without it.

CONCLUSION

When we do life based on the rest we have in Jesus Christ, the spiritual disciplines are not about working harder. They are ways and means of bringing the empowering grace of God into our regular daily walk with God, as we rest in Christ. They are ways of putting up our sails, so to speak, to catch the wind of God's Spirit driving us along toward Christlikeness. This is the yoke that we need to bear as a necessary part of our rest. We need purpose in life in order to have peace in our souls. In various places in the Scriptures our engagement in these practices is commanded, described, explained, illustrated, and shown to be effective. The more regularly, genuinely, and meaningfully we practice these disciplines, the more potential we have for gaining a rhythm in spiritual life and formation that leads to maturity in Christ even through the many setbacks and struggles we continue to experience along the way.

Yes, the realities of life often mess us up, but a life well lived in Christ grows through—sometimes *especially* through—the hard things in life (see Romans 5:3-4; James 1:2-7). As disciples of Jesus, there are some things we will never learn except through applying ourselves to the spiritual disciplines in the midst of difficult circumstances. In a sense, life itself is a school, and what we learn in it depends on how well we apply ourselves in ways that set us free right in the middle of it all. This freedom begins with a deep and abiding knowledge of our identity in Christ: "There is now no condemnation for those who are in Christ Jesus" (Romans 8:1) and nothing "will be able to separate us from the love of God that is in Christ Jesus our Lord" (Romans 8:39).

FOR REFLECTION AND DISCUSSION

1. In this chapter, you read about the spiritual disciplines. What kind of balance do you have between the disciplines that are organized around the Scriptures and those that are not? What is the danger of being out of balance one way or the other?
2. In what ways have you witnessed the Holy Spirit using the Scriptures to make renovations to the hearts of those in your ministry contexts?
3. How does a community interpret and understand the callings of God through the Scriptures together? Because the Bible is both descriptive and prescriptive, what challenges are present for evaluating the formation of each individual and the community according to the Scriptures?
4. What are the biggest challenges for you to move from merely studying the Bible to also including spiritual reading of the Scriptures? How does spiritual reading affect you differently than studying?
5. In a culture dismissive of authority, how would you encourage people to whom you are ministering to take the Scriptures seriously as an authoritative voice in the formation of their character?

FOR FURTHER READING

Johnson, Jan. *Study and Meditation*. Grand Rapids, MI: InterVarsity, 2003.

Masini, Mario. *Lectio Divina: An Ancient Prayer That Is Ever New*. Translated by Edmund C. Lane, S. S. P. New York: Alba House, 1998.

Peace, Richard. *Contemplative Bible Reading: Experiencing God Through Scripture*. Colorado Springs, CO: NavPress, 1998.

Peterson, Eugene H. *Eat This Book: A Conversation in the Art of Spiritual Reading*. Grand Rapids, MI: Eerdmans, 2006.

EPILOGUE

Alan Andrews with Christopher Morton

We anticipate that one of the questions pastors and church leaders will ask after reading this book is, "How do I practically do this in my church?" It is one thing to talk about elements of spiritual formation, but bringing it all down to practical reality in a local church is quite another matter. The praxis of being formed in Christ must work on the soil of a local community of believers or it's not much use.

Three years ago, I spent twelve months traveling with some of my co-workers visiting more than forty churches. In most cases, we spent a half to a full day with the church leadership team discussing many of the elements of spiritual formation. Our purpose was to look at the practical realities of the church situation and determine what could be done to develop churches into "spiritual-formation churches." It was a remarkable learning experience for me!

Being vitally involved in a local church is not a new experience for me. My growing-up years were rooted in intense participation in a local church. I have served as a youth director, as an elder, as chairman of a church board, and as a leader of small-group ministries. I have also taught Sunday school and preached and taught in many pulpits. None of those experiences prepared me for what I would learn as I traveled and met with church leaders and their teams.

I was humbled by how much I did not know. I was reminded again and again that every local church has its own culture and DNA. I also found that virtually all of the pastors were very fine people who longed for their church to be all it could be for God's glory. As I interacted with these leaders, it soon became clear that we were not going to come up with a formula for developing a spiritual-formation church. What was necessary were guiding principles that set the direction and then a process of implementation that would develop by trial and error over a considerable period of time.

Serving a community of believers in their formation in Christ is no small undertaking. The apostle Paul described the pain of the process: "My dear children, for whom I am again in the pains of childbirth until Christ is formed in you" (Galatians 4:19). Spiritual formation is not a program or technique but a careful and painful process that is unique to each community of believers.

In this epilogue we intend only to lay out some guiding principles. A more complete explanation describing what is involved in developing a spiritual-formation church will have to be reserved for another day. However, our TACT group felt it was important to lay out at least a basic direction in hopes that many leaders reading this book will gain some practical benefit.

GUIDING PRINCIPLE 1: Spiritual formation occurs in believers as they engage in intentional personal formation, community formation, and missional formation. These three dimensions of spiritual development must not be compartmentalized or separated but organically connected.

Explanation: The most basic foundation of spiritual formation is belief. Without belief or trust in God's goodness and grace, we are helpless. However, belief issues is what Eugene Peterson, quoting Friedrich Nietzsche, called "a long obedience in the same direction."[1] Our trust in God causes us to pursue spiritual formation.

Our formation in Christ occurs in three dimensions. First, we engage in intentional personal formation. This involves taking personal initiative in our relationship with God through the spiritual disciplines—study, prayer, solitude, worship, fasting, and other disciplines. These disciplines are not an end in themselves; rather they serve us by putting us in a place to learn and hear from God by His grace. The exercise of spiritual disciplines is simply being spiritually wise.

Second, we are formed in Christ as we live in community with other believers. It is in community that we receive teaching, affirmation, and protection and discover who we are in Christ. The most basic principle of community is the ability to "trust God and others with me." Circumstances are a major component in shaping us in Christ. We learn to interpret circumstances well in healthy community.

Third, we are shaped in Christ as we join Jesus in His mission on this earth. So often we think of mission as something we are empowered to do after we have been considerably formed in Christ. This is true to some extent (though we must consider the fact that we all remain needy people), but it is also true that mission forms us. God teaches us powerful lessons about ourselves as we engage in His mission with those around us.

It is essential that these three dimensions of spiritual formation be done organically rather than in a compartmentalized or isolated way. It is the interaction of these three dimensions that increases their effectiveness exponentially.

GUIDING PRINCIPLE 2: The center of the spiritual-formation church is Jesus and His kingdom. The Bible is a Christocentric book. Jesus' primary message was about the immediate nearness and availability of His kingdom to us.

Explanation: We live in a fallen world that desperately needs good news. As Jesus' hands and feet in this world, we are to be His kingdom people. This involves every believer as we seek to demonstrate His love and presence in the world.

As the leadership of the spiritual-formation church, we must also take on the responsibility of teaching and preaching the presence of what Dallas Willard has referred to as God's active care.[2]

Every spiritual-formation church must have leadership that is committed to serving, empowering people, modeling kingdom living (broken as we are), and teaching and preaching the kingdom of God as the centerpiece of all communication. Jesus' call was that the kingdom of God was near and that entrance into God's kingdom would open to us unimaginable vistas of eternal life. Church leaders have a responsibility to continue to echo that same call of Jesus by the power of the Holy Spirit.

When the spiritual-formation church gathers, its intent is to worship and proclaim the King and His kingdom. When the church scatters, its intent is to advance the kingdom of God by driving back the darkness and bringing in the light of God's kingdom in very difficult and resistant places.

We live in a world of two kingdoms in conflict. The kingdom of God is advancing though it often appears that the battle is stiff and hard. The central message of Jesus is that His kingdom is on the move and that God's people are privileged to be involved in the eternal life that is offered. Darkness is being driven back, and the light of God is on the move.

GUIDING PRINCIPLE 3: Every spiritual-formation church must be firmly rooted in the soil of the lost, the vulnerable, and the least.

Explanation: Jesus said, "The Son of Man has come to seek and to save that which was lost" (Luke 19:10, NASB). We are lost coins, lost sheep, and lost sons, as Luke 15 makes so clear. Only a loving God who comes to seek us out is able to save us from our desperate situation. It is God who is constantly the initiator on our behalf.

One of the primary functions of the church is to constantly plant the seed of God's Word in all kinds of soil. We are like hardworking farmers tilling the soil and planting the seed of God's kingdom. The calling is for every believer, including leaders, to be vitally involved with those who have lost their way. But the call is much more profound than just seeking the lost. Jesus' message of the kingdom was also one of offering the kingdom by doing away with the proprieties of society. The little one gets to become a thousand and a small one a mighty nation (see

Isaiah 60:22). The gospel is for the prisoner, the brokenhearted, and the one who mourns. Jesus threw His arms open to those who had not been welcome—the poor, the lame, and the blind.

The simplicity of the kingdom is rooted in repenting, believing, and following Jesus. The call is to anyone who will come. The spiritual-formation church must make sure that seed is sown among the vulnerable and the least of our society. Matthew 25:34-46 makes it clear that judgment will have a lot to do with how we reached out to the hungry, thirsty, and those without clothes.

Yes, the gospel is for everyone, but that means it is for those who are often made to feel unwelcome. The establishment of Jesus' day resisted Him most vigorously. We must be careful to keep the doors of the church open to all who want to enter. In many cases it is those who are most vulnerable among us (the poor, those with special needs) who need to experience eternal life. We must seek them out and welcome them into our communities of spiritual formation.

I often find that church leaders object to this guiding principle most vigorously. They feel that the demands already placed on them are great enough. To suggest that leaders should add intentional involvement among the lost to their responsibilities is the straw that breaks the camel's back. My only response is that it is unimaginable to me that any leader in the New Testament church would find a scriptural basis to object to this guiding principle. Yes, as our churches are structured today, being involved directly with the lost seems difficult. But the problem is more one of structure and expectations than of applying more pressure than is required. Kingdom communities are by their very definition intentionally involved with the lost.

GUIDING PRINCIPLE 4: The spiritual-formation church should seek to create an environment of grace that welcomes everyone who will come to the "rivers of living water" (John 7:38, NASB) that reside in the culture of God's kingdom.

Explanation: Bill Thrall and Bruce McNicol pointed out in chapter 2 that culture often speaks louder than our words. Every church has a culture, for sure. Sometimes that culture says that the poor are not welcome. Often single men and women do not receive the care that is needed. Social proprieties of dress, income, education, and race often determine the culture of our church community. All of these proprieties tell certain people that they are not welcome.

Jesus had one message for everyone: "Repent, believe, and follow Me." Jesus' call was to invite people to become humble learners of Him. Nothing else mattered! In John 7:37-38 Jesus shouted out to people that anyone who was thirsty could come to Him and experience "rivers of living water" flowing from their hearts (NASB). Two things were mentioned as prerequisites to obtaining this flowing water: thirsting for Him and coming to Him. Another way of saying this is "trusting God with me." What an offer of God's grace!

Grace and truth are not exclusive of one another. Jesus came "full of grace and truth" (John 1:14). It is grace that triggers the desire for truth. In a world that demands performance that earns approval, there is nothing like receiving God's grace, which says, "You are safe in Me. You can trust Me to do everything in your best interest. You can come close to Me so that I can develop you into the true destiny that I have for you in My kingdom."

Certainly we cannot bring the fullness Jesus promised to our church families. The best we can do is to seek to substantially offer what Jesus promised. We cannot provide perfect safety, but we can seek to be a safe community—and when we fail, we can humbly admit it. We may not do everything in the best interest of others, but we can certainly move toward that goal—and when our intentions go astray, we can humbly deal with our weaknesses. Just as Jesus made these wonderful promises to us, so our communities must substantially offer the same kind of grace to their people.

GUIDING PRINCIPLE 5: The spiritual-formation church must seek to preach, teach, and practically engage the people in spiritual formation. This means that intentional spiritual formation must be a central passion of the church.

Explanation: Spiritual formation is centrally a divine work of God. No one can cause a person to be humbly broken before God nor can anyone create in someone a desire to know God. These things are brought about by the miracle of God's grace. But if these two gifts of God's grace are present, we can develop the kinds of organic processes in our churches that will provide for the best opportunities to be formed in Christ.

The apostle Paul said, "Oh, my dear children! I feel as if I'm going through labor pains for you again, and they will continue until Christ is fully developed in your lives" (Galatians 4:19, NLT). Our goal must be Christ being fully developed in the lives of those who make up formational communities.

True spiritual formation occurs in an environment where everyone is on the journey of humbly following Jesus. Formation occurs in community, in intentional personal formation, and in mission. In this context, relationships are essential in shaping one another. The church as a whole creates the healthy environment of grace and the overall instruction to set the tone for growth. But it is in the personal times of study, Scripture memory, solitude, prayer, worship, one-on-one times, small-group interaction, and engaging in mission together that it comes alive.

I know that for many pastors and church leaders, just reading this seems virtually impossible. But it can and does happen. Once again, our church structures, expectations, and traditions can be tremendously hindering factors. But organizing churches into small communities that are simultaneously engaged in community, intentional personal formation, and mission (in the context of vocations and callings) will often solve the problem.

I am not suggesting that one solution fits all. All I am pointing out is that I have seen churches organized for spiritual formation function very effectively. However, for now, let me just say that intentional spiritual formation must be a central passion of the spiritual-formation church.

GUIDING PRINCIPLE 6: Equipping people for ministry is critical to the health of the spiritual-formation church.

Explanation: One of the assumptions of this book has been that engaging in mission is critical to our own spiritual formation. Michael Green, in *Evangelism in the Early Church,* said that one of the keys to the expansion of the early church was the ordinary believer "chattering the good news" in his everyday life.[3] We desperately need "chattering churches" in our world today for both our own spiritual formation and the advancement of the gospel.

While Ephesians 4:11-12 is often misinterpreted and misused in this context, it is still important to point out that one of the functions of church leadership is to equip saints for works of service. This is not accomplished by leaders standing behind their congregations encouraging the community of believers to busy themselves in ministry. Leaders in the New Testament were often found right at the point of engagement in ministry. Leaders equip people for ministry by modeling, actively teaching, casting vision, and identifying opportunities. Probably the most powerful form of equipping is example. Jesus said, "Peace be with you! As the Father has sent me, I am sending you" (John 20:21). Just as Jesus modeled active engagement in ministry and equipped His disciples to do as He had done, we must do the same in our churches.

We must never underestimate the value of engagement in ministry in the spiritual formation of our own lives. Equipping people for works of service opens the door for this marvelous formation. In Luke 10, Jesus sent out His disciples two by two to minister as He had taught them. When they returned, they had seen firsthand the power of God operating in their lives. Their experiences had transformed them. However, they could never have been sent out had they not first observed Jesus in action in the ministry of advancing the kingdom of God.

GUIDING PRINCIPLE 7: The spiritual-formation church develops new kingdom leaders for the advancement of the gospel and the spiritual formation of the people of God.

Explanation: Kingdom leaders have a very different identity than leaders who lead like the Gentiles (see Luke 22:24-27). Jesus rebuked His disciples who became embroiled in a discussion about who was going to sit at His right hand in the coming kingdom. His answer went a long way toward defining leadership in the realm of His kingdom:

> But Jesus called them to Himself and said, "You know that the rulers of the Gentiles lord it over them, and their great men exercise authority over them. It is not this way among you, but whoever wishes to become great among you shall be your servant, and whoever wishes to be first among you shall be your slave; just as the Son of Man did not come to be served, but to serve, and to give His life a ransom for many. (Matthew 20:25-28, NASB)

Most leaders in our world exercise authority and power toward personal gain and preservation. Even our very best leaders, who use their power and authority as a means of serving the people they lead, still retain their primary identity from their role as leader. Relinquishing power and authority to lead is a nonnegotiable.

In the kingdom of God leaders do not derive their identity from their leadership role. The fundamental identity of every citizen of the kingdom is that of a servant. This should be even more evident in kingdom leaders. Leaders in the kingdom of God realize that their role as leader may come or go, but their primary identity is that of servant to God and His people. They are not leaders who serve but servants who lead.

Leaders in God's kingdom exist to serve God and the well-being of His people. They focus on empowering, teaching, and leading by example. Yes, they plan, cast vision, and make decisions, but not for personal preservation. Their goal is the health of God's people and the advancement of the gospel. They understand what Jesus meant when He said,

> If I then, the Lord and the Teacher, washed your feet, you also ought to wash one another's feet. For I gave you an example that you also should do as I did to you. Truly, truly, I say to you, a slave is not greater than his master, nor is one who is sent greater than the one who sent him. (John 13:14-16, NASB)

Developing true kingdom leaders is critical to the well-being and growth of the spiritual-formation church. As these kinds of leaders develop and multiply, so does the health and maturity of the church.

GUIDING PRINCIPLE 8: The Bible uses multiple metaphors to describe the people of God, but the primary descriptors are organic — for example, body and family.

Explanation: Throughout this epilogue, I have emphasized the need for organic connection. One of the major problems I have observed in local churches is the lack of connection between specific functions and activities and the church as a whole. It is not unusual to observe stand-alone functions that are an end in themselves but contribute little to the life of the church or to the advancement of the gospel. This breaks down the organic unity and family nature of the church.

The spiritual-formation church thrives on organic unity. Each part of the body feeds on every other part of the body. That is why we have emphasized that community, intentional personal spiritual formation, and mission have to occur as an organic whole. The church is intended to be an interdependent body that receives benefit from the whole as well as its parts.

The church as a whole needs teaching, vision casting, coordinated planning, and a healthy environment of grace; but it also needs small communities that exist to help believers engage in community, personal spiritual formation, and mission. When these two aspects of church are held together in unity and diversity, the potential for a healthy spiritual-formation church is well on its way.

Let us conclude this epilogue by sharing with the reader a sense of what the vision of a spiritual-formation church might look like. Some time ago, I was working through a course on Ephesians by Bruce Milne. He has served as pastor of First Baptist Church in Vancouver, British Columbia, for seventeen years and is now an extensive writer and teacher in the body of Christ at large.

Bruce ended the course with a vision statement for his ideal church. He also ended his book *Dynamic Diversity* with the same vision statement. I believe that his dream reflects much of what is envisioned in the spiritual-formation church. I would add important aspects of spiritual formation, but what I appreciate is the spirit and clarity of the vision.

I have a dream — a dream of a congregation where people of all colors and from every ethnic identity find welcome, warmth, dignity and a sense of belonging; I have a dream of a church where men and women worship the triune God, and serve together as equally valuable in the sight of God, and equal in their capacity to honor him.

I have a dream of a Christian community where children, youth, middle-aged and seniors, boomers, busters, gen-Xers and millennials learn to respect and love and discover their profound need for each other; where people from all wealth and power backgrounds can live and relate and laugh together.

I have a dream of a family where singles and married couples, and married couples with families, and single parents and divorcees are all affirmed in their worth before God and his people; a family where poor and rich, sophisticated and unsophisticated, the physically and mentally strong and the physically and mentally challenged have learned to walk together in love, and to appreciate and affirm each other.

I have a dream of people of God where differences of personality and huge diversities of spiritual stories and spiritual journeys, or the lack of them, are no barrier to acceptance.

I have a dream of all of that many-splendored, multitextured humanity uniting under conscious, blessed rule of the exalter Lord Jesus Christ through his living, liberating, energizing Word, joining in the wondering communion in their worship, along with saints and angels — I have a dream.

And I have a dream of that same exuberant, multicolor family, swept along by the Holy Spirit, streaming forth from their worship place into the community around them — to throw their arms around it, and hug it in their hearts; offering to all who have need the practical ministries of love — to the poor and the homeless, single parents and street kids, HIV/AIDS sufferers and the addicted; and sharing too the joyous good news of Jesus and his great salvation — with the lost and lonely, the affluent and the power-brokers, the cynics and the seekers, the young and the aged, the followers of other faith traditions and the followers of none, local residents and those from every corner of the globe; lifting high the world's only Savior, and doing so in such a way that his holy, all-embracing transforming love is reflected and authenticated in the dynamic diversity of their life together . . . I have a dream.[4]

Will there ever be a church that looks like Bruce's dream? I hope so, but the important thing is never to stop dreaming, hoping, and believing. Dreaming, hoping, and trusting are the stuff of the church. They are the foundation of all spiritual formation!

NOTES

Introduction: The Journey of TACT

1. Donald G. Bloesch, *Spirituality Old and New* (Downers Grove, IL: InterVarsity Academic, 2007).

2. James C. Wilhoit, *Spiritual Formation as if the Church Mattered* (Grand Rapids, MI: Baker Academic, 2008).

3. Jan Johnson, Keith J. Matthews, and Dallas Willard, *Dallas Willard's Study Guide to The Divine Conspiracy* (San Francisco: HarperOne, 2001), 107.

Chapter 1: The Gospel of the Kingdom and Spiritual Formation

1. Thanks to Don Simpson for his encouragement and assistance in writing this chapter.

2. Thomas Gerard Weinandy, *Athanasius: A Theological Introduction* (Farnham, Surrey, U.K.: Ashgate Publishing, 2007), 130–131.

Chapter 2: Communities of Grace

1. Daniel Goleman, Richard E. Boyatzis, and Annie McKee, *Primal Leadership* (Watertown, MA: Harvard Business School Press, 2004), 16.

2. Goleman, Boyatzis, and McKee, 6.

3. See Bill Thrall, Bruce McNicol, John Lynch, *TrueFaced* (Colorado Springs, CO: NavPress, 2004), 68.

4. Marion Skeete, conversation with the authors.

5. Thrall, McNicol, Lynch, 92.

6. For more information on these topics, see *TrueFaced* and Bill Thrall, Bruce McNicol, and John Lynch, *Bo's Café* (Newbury Park, CA: Windblown Media, 2009).

Chapter 3: The Transformational Process

1. Dallas Willard, *The Spirit of the Disciplines* (San Francisco: HarperOne, 1991), 258.

2. Doug Greenwold, *Making Disciples Jesus' Way* (Columbia, MD: Bible-in-Context Ministries, 2007), 36.

3. Jan Johnson, Keith J. Matthews, and Dallas Willard, *Dallas Willard's Study Guide to The Divine Conspiracy* (San Francisco: HarperOne, 2001), 107.

4. Dallas Willard, "The Spirit Is Willing: The Body as a Tool for Spiritual Growth," *The Christian Educator's Handbook on Spiritual Formation*, ed. Kenneth O. Gangel and James Wilhoit (Grand Rapids, MI: Baker, 1994), 225.

5. Eugene H. Peterson, *A Long Obedience in the Same Direction* (Downers Grove, IL: InterVarsity, 1980), 30.

6. Dallas Willard, "Kingdom Living" interview with Andy Pack, *Christianity and Renewal*, May 2002.

7. Numerous authors categorize spiritual disciplines in different ways. There is no unified designation. I have chosen to use Dallas Willard's designations from *The Spirit of the Disciplines* (San Francisco: HarperOne, 1991).

8. Henri Nouwen, *The Way of the Heart* (New York: Ballantine, 1981), 25–27.

9. Watchman Nee, quoted in John Koessler, *True Discipleship* (Chicago: Moody, 2003), 269.

10. Howard Snyder, *The Community of the King* (Downers Grove, IL: InterVarsity, 2004).

Chapter 4: Spiritual Formation from the Inside Out

1. C. S. Lewis, *Mere Christianity* (New York: HarperCollins, 2001), 123.

2. See 2 Timothy 4:10. "Demas, in love with this present world, has deserted me" (NRSV).

3. John Wesley, *The Works of the Reverend John Wesley*, trans. John Emory (New York: T. Mason and G. Lane, 1839), 784.

4. Dallas Willard, notes from Plenary Address at the Spiritual Formation Forum, Los Angeles, 2004.

5. "Complete" in 2 Timothy 3:17 (AMP) is *artios*, meaning "to be fit for all good works." That fitness is more than skill. It also is used in a compound form translated as *equipped* later in the verse, which indicates an emphasis on "skill, fully outfitted, supplied."

6. Galatians 4:19 and Romans 12:2; 8:29 speak of *formed*, *transformed*, and *conformed* respectively with the basic Greek word *morphe*. This is the origin of the English word *form*.

7. James R. Newby, *Elton Trueblood: Believer, Teacher, and Friend* (San Francisco: Harper and Row, 1990), 55.

8. C. S. Lewis, *The Weight of Glory* (New York: HarperCollins, 2001), as quoted in Job and Shawchuck, *A Guide to Prayer for Ministers and Other Servants*, 85.

9. Franz Delitzsch, *A System of Biblical Psychology* (Grand Rapids, MI: Baker, 1977), 292 [originally published in 1855].

10. Delitzsch, 292.

11. Delitzsch, 293–294.

12. William Law, *A Serious Call to a Devout and Holy Life* (Alachua, FL: Bridge-Logos, 2008), 17.

13. Aleksandr Solzhenitsyn, *The Gulag Archipelago* (New York: Basic Books, 1997), 168.

14. Law, 50.

15. Law, 35.

16. Law, 22.

17. Dallas Willard, foreword to *Choose the Life: Exploring a Faith That Embraces Discipleship*, by Bill Hull (Grand Rapids, MI: Baker, 2004), 6.

18. Jan Johnson, Keith J. Matthews, and Dallas Willard, *Dallas Willard's Study Guide to The Divine Conspiracy* (San Francisco: HarperOne, 2001), 107.

19. There is a good deal of variety on who includes what disciplines and how they are categorized. Please see Richard Foster, *Celebration of Discipline* (New York: HarperCollins, 1988) or Dallas Willard, *The Spirit of the Disciplines* (San Francisco: HarperOne, 1991) for additional information.

20. Dallas Willard, *The Spirit of the Disciplines* (San Francisco: HarperOne, 1991), 10.

21. Dietrich Bonhoeffer, *The Cost of Discipleship* (New York: Macmillan, 1979), 69.

Chapter 5: Whole-Life Transformation

1. Dallas Willard, *The Spirit of the Disciplines* (SanFrancisco: HarperOne, 1991), 14.
2. Richard Lovelace, *Dynamics of Spiritual Life: An Evangelical Theology of Renewal* (Downers Grove, IL: InterVarsity Academic, 1979), 229–237.
3. Dallas Willard, *Renovation of the Heart: Putting On the Character of Christ* (Colorado Springs, CO: NavPress, 2002), 30.
4. Dallas Willard, *The Divine Conspiracy* (San Francisco: HarperOne, 1998), 35ff.
5. Greg Hawkins and Cally Parkinson, *Reveal* (Barrington, IL: Willow Creek Resources, 2007), 4.
6. Kent Carlson, conversation with the author.
7. Sandra Wilson, *Counseling Adult Children of Alcoholics* (Dallas: Word, 1989), 268.
8. Wilson, 268.
9. Darrell L. Guder, *Missional Church: A Vision for the Sending of the Church in North America* (Grand Rapids, MI: Eerdmans, 1998), 5.
10. George Barna, *Growing True Disciples* (Colorado Springs, CO: WaterBrook, 2001), 119.

Chapter 6: Formed Through Suffering

1. Mark E. Biddle, *Missing the Mark: Sin and Its Consequences in Biblical Theology* (Nashville: Abingdon, 2005), chapter 1.
2. See C. S. Lewis, *Out of the Silent Planet* (New York: Scribner, 2003).
3. Robert Banks and R. Paul Stevens, eds., *The Complete Book of Everyday Christianity* (Downers Grove, IL: InterVarsity, 1997); see section on "powers."
4. Joel Shuman and Brian Volck, *Reclaiming the Body: Christians and the Faithful Use of Modern Medicine* (Grand Rapids, MI: Brazos, 2006), 32.
5. John Piper and Justin Taylor, eds., *Suffering and the Sovereignty of God* (Wheaton, IL: Crossway, 2006), 98.

6. L. Ann Jervis, *At the Heart of the Gospel* (Grand Rapids, MI: Eerdmans, 2007), 24.

7. Jervis, 18–19.

8. Karl Barth, *The Epistle to the Romans* (Oxford, U.K.: Oxford University Press, 1968), 156.

9. Jürgen Moltmann, *The Crucified God* (Minneapolis: Augsburg Fortress, 1993), 1217.

10. Donald G. Bloesch, *Spirituality Old and New: Recovering Authentic Spiritual Life* (Downers Grove, IL: InterVarsity, 2007), 78–79.

11. Dietrich Bonhoeffer, *Dietrich Bonhoeffer: Conspiracy and Imprisonment, 1940–1945*, Dietrich Bonhoeffer Works, vol. 16 (Minneapolis: Augsburg Fortress, 2006), 284.

12. W. E. Vine, *Vine's Expository Dictionary of Old and New Testament Words* (Nashville: Thomas Nelson, 1996).

13. World PopClock Projection, http://www.census.gov/ipc/www/popclockworld.html (accessed July 17, 2009).

14. Philip Yancey, *Prayer: Does It Make Any Difference?* (Grand Rapids, MI: Zondervan, 2006), 49.

15. Jervis, 99–100.

16. Jervis, 129–130.

17. C. S. Lewis, *The Problem of Pain* (SanFrancisco: HarperOne, 2001), 96.

18. Piper and Taylor, 98.

19. Brennan Manning, *Abba's Child* (Colorado Springs, CO: NavPress, 1994), 37–38.

20. Judith Hougen, *Transformed into Fire* (Grand Rapids, MI: Kregel, 2002), 23.

21. Jervis, 84.

22. Yancey, 100.

Chapter 7: Participating in God's Mission

1. Carl Henry, the patriarch of evangelicalism, pointed this out in his book *The Uneasy Conscience of Modern Fundamentalism* (Grand Rapids, MI: Eerdmans, 2003).

2. Ray Bakke, in lectures to The Navigators on church history, 1989.

3. Darrell L. Bock, "About the Book" in *Luke: InterVarsity Press New Testament Commentary* (Downers Grove, IL: InterVarsity, 1994).

4. "The sinner's prayer" is a prayer in which one acknowledges sinful behavior and receives God's gift of salvation, which was made possible through the life, death, and resurrection of Jesus Christ. This prayer often references Scriptures in the book of Romans that refer to sin and redemption (see Romans 3:23; 6:23; 10:9-10).

5. M. G. Easton, *Illustrated Bible Dictionary*, 3rd ed. (New York: Harper, 1897), s.v. "Samaritans."

6. Bock, "Discipleship: Looking to Our Neighbor, to Jesus and to God," Luke 10 passage.

7. Porter Anderson, "Study: U.S. Employees Put in Most Hours," August 31, 2001, http://archives.cnn.com/2001/CAREER/trends/08/30/ilo.study/.

8. Juliet Schor, *The Overworked American* (New York: Basic Books, 1993), 1.

9. Carl Honore, *In Praise of Slowness* (New York: HarperCollins, 2004), 4.

10. Paraphrase of the preamble of the Declaration of Independence.

11. Michael O. Emerson and Christian Smith, *Divided by Faith: Evangelical Religion and the Problem of Race in America* (Oxford, U.K.: Oxford University Press, 2000), 14.

12. Emerson and Smith, 25.

13. Emerson and Smith, 24.

14. A hereditary bleeding disorder that results in his bleeding longer when a bleed is internal. This is due to a defective clotting protein that, when the correct protein is intravenously infused, allows for normal clotting for a limited period of time. This protein is derived from human plasma through a process called fractionation, in which large pools of plasma produce a concentrate of the specific protein (factor VIII: "FVIII").

15. Eric Stolte, conversation with the author.

16. Greg Paul, *God in the Alley: Being and Seeing Jesus in a Broken World* (Colorado Springs, CO: Shaw Books, 2004), 17–19.

17. *MSN Encarta Encyclopedia Online*, s.v. "Wilberforce, William," http://Encarta.msn.com/encyclopedia_761558751/William_Wilberforce.html.

Chapter 8: The Trinity as Foundation for Spiritual Formation

1. Christopher Morton, conversation with the author.

2. Michael Downey, *Altogether Gift: A Trinitarian Spirituality* (Maryknoll, NY: Orbis, 2000), 54–55.

3. Tertullian, *The Ante-Nicene Fathers*, vol. 3 (Peabody, MA: Hendrickson, 1994), 617; *Against Praxaeus*, 11.

4. See Eugene H. Peterson, *Christ Plays in Ten Thousand Places* (Grand Rapids, MI: Eerdmans, 2005), 44.

5. Clement of Alexandria, "Who Is the Rich Man That Shall Be Saved," *The Ante-Nicene Fathers*, vol. 2 (Peabody, MA: Hendrickson, 1994), 21.

6. Thomas à Kempis, *The Imitation of Christ*, ed. Donald Demaray (Grand Rapids, MI: Baker, 1982), 11.

7. François Fénelon, *Christian Perfection* (New York: Harper, 1947), 43.

8. Augustine, *The Works of Saint Augustine*, vol. 3, pt. 10 (Hyde Park, NY: New City Press, 1994), 110; *Sermon 350A*, 21.

9. Christopher Morton, conversation with the author.

10. Robert E. Webber, *The Divine Embrace* (Grand Rapids, MI: Baker, 2006), 42.

11. Charles Wesley, "Let Earth and Heaven Combine," *Hymns for the Nativity of Our Lord* (London: William Strahan, 1745), number 5, emphasis added.

12. Charles Spurgeon, *The Metropolitan Tabernacle Pulpit*, vol. 58 (London: Passmore & Alabaster, 1912), 184.

13. Eugene H. Peterson, "Evangelical Spirituality," *The Futures of Evangelicalism*, eds. Craig Bartholomew, Robin Parry, and Andrew West (Grand Rapids, MI: Kregel, 2003), 236.

14. Spurgeon, *The Metropolitan Tabernacle Pulpit*, vol. 9 (London: Passmore & Alabaster, 1863), 627.

15. Downey, 38.

16. Augustine, *Nicene and Post-Nicene Fathers*, first series, vol. 7 (Grand Rapids, MI: Eerdmans, 1983), 172; *Homilies on John*, 26.13.

17. Henri Nouwen, *Reaching Out: The Three Movements of the Spiritual Life* (Garden City, NY: Doubleday, 1975), 19.

18. *The March of the Penguins*, directed by Luc Jacquet (Burbank, CA: Warner Independent Pictures, 2005).

19. Webber, 183.

20. Downey, 84.

21. Augustine, *Nicene and Post-Nicene Fathers*, first series, vol. 7 (Grand Rapids, MI: Eerdmans, 1983), 171; *Homilies on the Gospel of John*, 26.11.

22. *The Westminster Confession of Faith*, 29.7, http://www.reformed.org/documents/westminster_conf_of_faith.html.

23. Charles Spurgeon, 54.332, http://trevinwax.com/2007/06/09/spurgeon-on-the-lords-supper (accessed August 7, 2009).

24. Augustine, *The Works of Saint Augustine*, vol. 1, pt. 8 (Hyde Park, NY: New City Press, 2005), 88; *Of True Religion*, 87.

25. Thomas Merton, *The New Man* (New York: Farrar, Straus and Giroux, 1961), 189.

26. Polycarp, *The Ante-Nicene Fathers*, vol. 1 (Grand Rapids, MI: Eerdmans, 1979), 42; *The Martyrdom of Polycarp*, 14.

Chapter 9: The Holy Spirit and Spiritual Transformation

1. Thomas Aquinas, *2 Corinthians*, ed. R. Cai, C.3, lect. 3, no. 112, quoted in Yves Congar, *I Believe in the Holy Spirit*, vol. 2 (San Francisco: HarperSanFrancisco, 1983), 125.

2. Augustine, *The Works of St. Augustine: Essential Sermons*, trans. Edmund Hill, pt. 3 (New York: New City Press, 1990), sermon 22.7, 1.41-48.

3. "It is inconceivable that the incarnation of the Son, Christ's Easter and glorification and the coming of the Spirit Who was promised should have changed nothing and should have brought nothing new. Until that time, something was lacking and the gift of the Spirit was not complete. It is still not complete, of course, since in the present era we only have the first-fruits of the Spirit." From Congar, *I Believe in the Holy Spirit*, 77.

4. Julian of Norwich, *Showings*, trans. Edmund Colledge, O.S.A., and James Walsh, S.J. (Mahwah, NJ: Paulist Press, 1978), chapter 47, 260–262; see also David Hazard, *I Promise You a Crown: A 40-Day Journey in the Company of Julian of Norwich* (Minneapolis: Bethany House, 1995), 98.

5. Julian of Norwich, *Showings*, chapter 48; see also Hazard, *I Promise You a Crown*, 99.

6. This film won the Oscar for best foreign film in 1987.

7. Human sin is rooted in the rejection or turning away from Jesus Christ, God's Word, and the full expression of God's love for creation. This rejection manifests itself in disobedience. Typically acts of disobedience trigger painful consequences in the lives of individuals and communities. It is the important work of the Holy Spirit through the community to admonish, discipline, and comfort. The failure to provide remedial comment is actually an act of anger and expression of hostility to our neighbor. Martin Luther said, "I should certainly rebuke and reprimand my brother, but I should not be hostile to him. If I say to him out of a brotherly heart: You fool, as Christ said to his disciples . . . this is not a sign of anger; it is a sign of friendly love. For if I did not have the welfare of my brother at heart, I would certainly be quiet and let him go. But the fact that I open my mouth and rebuke him is an indication that I love him and seek his welfare. For my failure to instruct and rebuke my brother is actually evidence of anger." From "Sermon on Matthew 5:20-26," *What Luther Says*, vol. 3, ed. E. Plass (St. Louis: Concordia, 1959), 1169.

8. Robert Louis Wilken, *The Spirit of Early Christian Thought* (New Haven: Yale University Press, 2003), 104–105.

9. Brother Yun, with Paul Hattaway, *The Heavenly Man: The Remarkable True Story of Chinese Christian Brother Yun* (London: Monarch Books, 2003), 311.

10. Yun, 312.

11. Yun, 312.

12. David Hazard, *Your Angels Guard My Steps* (Minneapolis: Bethany House, 1998), 126; see also Bernard of Clairvaux, *Sermons for the Summer Season: Liturgical Sermons from Rogationtide and Pentecost* (Kalamazoo, MI: Cistercian Publications, 1991), CF 53.

Chapter 10: The Bible in Spiritual Transformation

1. Literally, "with all your exceedingly"—or better "with all your everything"—perhaps meaning "with all your resources." Targum

Onkelos, one of the ancient Aramaic translations of the Hebrew Bible, has the word *ma'amon* here, which is the term transliterated in Matthew 6:24 as "mammon" (NKJV), meaning "monetary wealth."

2. The Greek word for "gospel," *euangelion*, means literally "good news." Two books that do a good job of making and expanding on the point here are Dallas Willard, *The Great Omission: Reclaiming Jesus's Essential Teachings on Discipleship* (San Francisco: HarperOne, 2006) and Bill Hull, *The Complete Book of Discipleship: On Being and Making Followers of Christ* (Colorado Springs, CO: NavPress, 2006).

3. For a more detailed discussion of the nature and dimensions of spiritual formation from a whole-Bible (Old Testament and New Testament) point of view, see Richard E. Averbeck, "Spirit, Community, and Mission: A Biblical Theology for Spiritual Formation," *Journal of Spiritual Formation and Soul Care* 1:1 (Spring 2008): 27–53.

4. This part of the verse has been the subject of much debate among scholars. Two main interpretations have been proposed: (1) The NIV renders 2 Peter 1:20 as follows: "No prophecy of Scripture came about by the prophet's own interpretation," referring to how the prophet interpreted what he saw and/or heard in the *past*, as recorded in the Scriptures. (2) The NRSV reads instead, "No prophecy of scripture is a matter of one's own interpretation," in the sense that no one in the *present* has the right to interpret the prophetic writings according to his own human will (i.e., according to whatever he wants it to say), since it was not given in the first place according to anyone's human will but under the guidance of the Holy Spirit with divinely intended meaning (see verse 21). The latter view is followed here, but this is not the place to go into all the details.

5. "Spiritual formation" is a synonym of "spiritual growth," "sanctification," and "discipleship" and is sometimes used interchangeably with them. From a biblical point of view, however, the term "spiritual formation" focuses our attention more on the dynamics of how the Holy Spirit works this in us.

6. A number of scholars have been developing this approach to the reading of Scripture over the past thirty years or so. Most recently, Kevin Vanhoozer has developed it from the theological and hermeneutical

perspective in his book *The Drama of Doctrine: A Canonical Linguistic Approach to Christian Theology* (Louisville, KY: Westminster John Knox, 2005). He has drawn from numerous previous works, especially those of Hans Frei in narrative literary theory, Hans Urs von Balthasar in theodramatic theology, and Paul Ricoeur in theoretical hermeneutics.

The detailed work of Meir Sternberg in his magisterial work *The Poetics of Biblical Narrative: Ideological Literature and the Drama of Reading* (Bloomington, IN: Indiana University Press, 1985) brings a great deal to the same approach. In a sense, Sternberg's work develops the agenda anticipated in Frei's seminal book *The Eclipse of Biblical Narrative: A Study in Eighteenth and Nineteenth Century Hermeneutics* (New Haven and London: Yale University Press, 1974). Eugene H. Peterson also makes much of reading the Bible as a script in his very fine book *Eat This Book: A Conversation in the Art of Spiritual Reading* (Grand Rapids, MI: Eerdmans, 2006), especially pages 59–77. We will return to the subject of spiritual reading later in this chapter.

7. See, for example, the brief remarks on these genre issues in Sternberg, *The Poetics of Biblical Narrative*, 41–42, and Vanhoozer, *The Drama of Doctrine*, 282–285.

8. Sternberg (*The Poetics of Biblical Narrative*, 48–57) developed the important point that the Bible is a "foolproof composition," by which he meant that it "is difficult to read, easy to underread and overread and even misread, but virtually impossible to, so to speak, counterread," unless one intentionally reads it in "bad faith," as some are determined to do in the academy or other places where the agenda is brought to the text rather than gained from it. As he put it, "The essentials are made transparent to all comers: the story line, the world order, the value system." The many controversies over the particulars of the text "among exegetes . . . must not blind us (as it usually does them) to the measure of agreement in this regard" (pages 50–51).

9. Jean-François Lyotard, *The Postmodern Condition* (Minneapolis: University of Minnesota Press, 1984), xxiv. A metanarrative is an overarching narrative that explains all of our personal, familial, cultural, and communal local narratives. It explains why life is the way it is for all of us and for each one of us.

10. For a more thorough treatment of this topic, see Richard E. Averbeck, "God, People, and the Bible: A Spiritually Formative Approach to Biblical Scholarship," *Who's Afraid of the Holy Spirit? An Investigation into the Ministry of the Spirit of God Today*, eds. Daniel B. Wallace and M. James Sawyer (Dallas: Biblical Studies Press, 2005), 137–165.

11. The most helpful descriptions I have found are Mario Masini, *Lectio Divina: An Ancient Prayer That Is Ever New*, trans. Edmund C. Lane, S.S.P. (New York: Alba House, 1998); Richard Peace, *Contemplative Bible Reading: Experiencing God Through Scripture* (Colorado Springs, CO: NavPress, 1998); and Eugene H. Peterson, *Eat This Book: A Conversation in the Art of Spiritual Reading* (Grand Rapids, MI: Eerdmans, 2006), especially 1–11, 80–117.

12. Peterson, 4, 10, 90–91.

13. See the remarks in M. Robert Mulholland Jr., *Shaped by the Word: The Power of Scripture in Spiritual Formation*, rev. ed. (Nashville: Upper Room, 2000), 61–63.

14. See Mulholland, *Shaped by the Word*, 20. There are quite a number of unguarded statements in this section of his book. Later he wrote, "I have overstressed the alternative to informational reading in order to highlight the contrast. A fruitful interplay exists between the informational and formational modes" (page 61). He went on to stress the importance of balance between the two, and there is much that is very good in this book. But by the time he said anything positive about informational reading or interpretive exegesis, the damage had already been done and the balance lost in the mind of many readers.

15. See Peace, 17–20; see also Masini, 21–22.

16. Peterson, 57–58.

17. The current biblical and theological debate among evangelicals regarding this matter is illustrated, for example, by the reaction against virtually any form of mystical experience in the Christian life in Donald G. Bloesch, *Spirituality Old and New: Recovering Authentic Spiritual Life* (Downers Grove, IL: InterVarsity, 2007), along with Bruce Demarest's reaction to Bloesch's book in his review in *Journal of Spiritual Formation and Soul Care* 1:1 (Spring 2008): 110–113.

18. Guigo the Second, quoted in Peterson, *Eat This Book*, 91, footnote 1; emphasis and bracketed additions are mine.

19. See Cynthia I. Zirlott, *"Lectio Divina,"* in *The Upper Room Dictionary of Christian Spiritual Formation*, ed. Keith Beasley-Topliffe (Nashville: Upper Room, 2003), 168–169; Masini, *Lectio Divina*, 73–100; the helpful guide and practice of it in Peace, *Contemplative Bible Reading*; and especially Peterson, *Eat This Book*, 79–117.

20. James A. Herrick, *The Making of the New Spirituality: The Eclipse of the Western Religious Tradition* (Downers Grove, IL: InterVarsity, 2003). See especially the fine summaries and evaluations in the introduction (pages 20–35) and conclusion (pages 250–281), from which my brief summary here is taken.

21. Thomas à Kempis, *The Imitation of Christ*, ed. Hal M. Helms (Orleans, MA: The Community of Jesus, 1982), 69–71.

22. See, for example, the very fine survey in Gordon Mursell, ed., *The Story of Christian Spirituality: Two Thousand Years, from East to West* (Minneapolis: Fortress Press, 2001). The most generous but also discerning short summary of the historical streams, resources, and issues that I know of is Bruce Demarest, *Satisfy Your Soul: Renewing the Heart of Christian Spirituality* (Colorado Springs, CO: NavPress, 1999), 255–281.

23. For a helpful discussion of this passage, see Michael J. Wilkins, *Matthew*, NIV Application Commentary (Grand Rapids, MI: Zondervan, 2004), 422–428, 433–434.

24. For a good treatment of the two great commandments, see Scot McKnight, *The Jesus Creed* (Brewster, MA: Paraclete Press, 2004).

Epilogue

1. See Eugene H. Peterson, *A Long Obedience in the Same Direction* (Downers Grove, IL: InterVarsity, 2000).

2. See Dallas Willard, *Renovation of the Heart: Putting On the Character of Christ* (Colorado Springs, CO: NavPress, 2002), 70.

3. Michael Green, *Evangelism in the Early Church* (Grand Rapids, MI: Eerdmans, 2004), 411.

4. Bruce Milne, *Dynamic Diversity* (Downers Grove, IL: InterVarsity,

2007), 173–174. This "dream" is based, of course, on the speech delivered by Martin Luther King Jr. on the steps of the Lincoln Memorial on
August 28, 1963.

ABOUT THE CONTRIBUTORS

Alan Andrews is former U.S. Director of The Navigators and is currently director of the Theological and Cultural Thinkers (TACT) group. For many years, Alan served in various national and international leadership capacities in The Navigators, such as national field leader overseeing the various entities in the U.S. Navigators ministry. He is author of the booklet *Everyone Gets to Play*. Alan and his wife, Becky, have three daughters and ten grandchildren. They now live in Phoenix where they work in urban ministry.

Richard E. Averbeck is professor of Old Testament and Semitic languages at Trinity Evangelical Divinity School. Richard also taught at Dallas Theological Seminary and Grace Theological Seminary. He received a BA in biblical languages from Calvary Bible College, an MDiv from Grace Theological Seminary, a PhD from Dropsie College (Annenberg Research Institute), and an MA in biblical counseling from Grace Theological Seminary. He is author of numerous articles, has served as the main editor of *Life and Culture in the Ancient Near East*, and was the founder and director of the Spiritual Formation Forum. He has a wife and two grown sons.

Bruce Demarest is professor of Christian theology and spiritual formation at Denver Seminary. Bruce has a PhD in biblical and historical theology from the University of Manchester and has written several books, including *Soul Guide: Following Jesus as Spiritual Director* and *Satisfy Your Soul: Renewing the Heart of Christian Spirituality*. Most recently, he published *Seasons of the Soul: Stages of Spiritual Development*.

Paula Fuller serves as a vice president and director of multiethnic ministries for InterVarsity Christian Fellowship. Paula has served in full-time vocational ministry since 1996, and her past roles include responsibilities as the director of outreach and community development and as associate pastor for a large multiethnic congregation in the San Francisco Bay Area. Paula received a BS in finance from UC Berkeley, an MBA from Stanford University, and an MDiv from Fuller Theological Seminary. Paula resides in Fremont, California, with her family.

Michael Glerup received a PhD from Drew University. He serves as the projects director for The Center for Early African Christianity at Eastern University. He is the coeditor of *Ancient Christian Commentary on Scripture: Ezekiel and Daniel* and volume editor and operations manager for the *Ancient Christian Texts* series. He writes a regular column, "Ancient Christian Wisdom for a Post-Modern Age," appearing in *Conversations: A Forum for Authentic Transformation.* Michael and his wife, Kate, a psychotherapist and spiritual director, live in St. Davids, Pennsylvania.

Bill Hull has served as a pastor in the Evangelical Free Church of America and is a popular speaker and author of many books on discipleship, disciple making, and spiritual formation. Bill has a BS degree from Oral Roberts University and an MDiv from Talbot School of Theology. Among his books are *The Complete Book of Discipleship*, *The Disciple-Making Church*, *Choose the Life*, and *Christlike*. Bill and his wife, Jane, are the parents of two grown sons.

Keith J. Matthews is chair of the ministry department and professor of spiritual formation and contemporary culture at Azusa Pacific University's Graduate School of Theology. He is a longtime pastoral practitioner, serving in churches from coast to coast. He is also an adjunct professor at Fuller Theological Seminary. Keith has written several articles and coauthored *Dallas Willard's Study Guide to The Divine Conspiracy.* Keith and his wife, Christa, have three grown children—Cori, Kyle, and Kate.

Bruce McNicol has degrees in finance law, theology, leadership, and organizational development. He speaks widely to international audiences and serves as president of the TrueFaced team, based in Arizona. Bruce coauthored *The Ascent of a Leader, TrueFaced, Behind the Mask, The High-Trust Culture,* and *Bo's Café.* He lives in Phoenix with his wife, Janet, and their three children, Nicole, Chad, and Ryan.

Keith Meyer is a graduate of Wheaton College and Trinity Evangelical Divinity School. He has served three churches as senior pastor and most recently as executive pastor at Church of the Open Door in Maple Grove, Minnesota. He has been married to Cheri for twenty-nine years, and they have two grown children, Kyle and Cara.

Christopher Morton serves with The Navigators as the chief theological and cultural researcher and as special research assistant on economics and finance to the chief financial officer of The Navigators. Chris has a BSBA in accounting, an MBA from the University of Colorado, an MA in theology from Fuller Theological Seminary, and a PhD in theology from the Nazarene Theological College of the University of Manchester (UK). He and his wife, Tanya, have three children.

Peggy Reynoso and her husband, Paul, work with The Navigators in Hispanic-focused ministry in San Antonio, Texas, and served as missionaries in Mexico for twenty years. Peggy is a member of The Navigators' National Women's Network leadership team. The Reynosos have five children—Daniel, Nathanael, David, daughter-in-law Jennifer, and daughter Paula, who died tragically at the age of nineteen.

Bill Thrall is coauthor of the best-selling books *The Ascent of a Leader* and *TrueFaced.* Bill speaks internationally and is cofounder of Leadership Catalyst. Bill founded and for twenty years pastored the influential Phoenix church Open Door Fellowship. While there, he developed an effective character development training program and continues to mentor men and women around the world. Bill lives in Phoenix with his wife, Grace. They have three grown children—Wende, Bill, and Joy—and nine grandchildren.

Dallas Willard is professor of philosophy at the University of Southern California in Los Angeles. Dallas is an ordained Southern Baptist minister and has written numerous articles and books, including *Hearing God*, *The Spirit of the Disciplines*, *The Divine Conspiracy*, and *Renovation of the Heart*. Dallas and his wife, Jane, have two grown children, John and Rebecca, and one granddaughter, Larissa.

※ ※ ※

Gary Bradley, whose painting appears on the front cover and end papers, has a BS in economics from Old Dominion University. Gary has launched several businesses as well as the arts movement known as Via Affirmativa. Gary has been an executive for several nonprofit organizations and is currently a vice president of the U.S. Navigators. Gary and his wife, Julia, have three adult children and six grandchildren.

Read more on discipleship, culture, and theory.

Dictionary of Everyday Theology and Culture
Bruce Demarest and Keith J. Matthews, general editors
978-1-60006-192-9

This resource provides everyday people a guide to understanding Christian theology and key social and cultural issues in the contemporary world. With a practical focus, it helps readers understand core Christian truths that provide the framework of the Christian worldview and apply these truths to life and service as followers of Jesus.

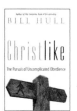

Christlike
Bill Hull
978-1-60006-694-8

Bill Hull says that to make a difference in the world, you need to become different yourself. The final determination of whether or not you are becoming Christlike is not attendance at a church training program; it's how you act in daily life. *Christlike* aims to change outward actions by inner transformation through uncomplicated obedience.

The Complete Book of Discipleship
Bill Hull
978-1-57683-897-6

The Complete Book of Discipleship is the definitive A-to-Z resource on discipleship for every Christian. This well-organized, indexed guide pulls together such topics as spiritual growth, transformation, spiritual disciplines, and discipleship in the local church and beyond.

To order copies, call NavPress at 1-800-366-7788 or
log on to www.navpress.com.